# FAMILY SECRETS

## Love and Hate

### BY
### DIANA ROJAS

HEMINGWAY PUBLISHERS

# TABLE OF CONTENT

# *PART I*

*Secrets, secrets… Everybody has secrets. But the other question is how well you can hide your secrets from curious eyes. "Family Secrets" is a new story about families with ambition and power in a small world. Two great families with their dynasties hide their skeletons in the closet. Only a twin girl who lost her parents in a terrible murder i going to discover too many secrets behind her back; no doubt she finds her only true love. Despite hate and revenge in her heart, she is going to find new hope in a mean world of men.*

*An adventure through France, Morocco, and the US will bring joy and fun to all who love abroad culture and traveling.*

# CHAPTER 1

*France is the center of the spiritual and refined culture of Europe and the high school of taste, but we must be able to find this "France of taste." Those who belong to it are hiding well. Few may be those in which she lives and works. In addition, it may be people who are not very firmly on their feet, partly fatalistic, dark, sick, partly pampered, and mangled, so ambition is what makes them hide. But that's life - a rapid waterfall and a strong current, which carries human years, forever, and people like little ants in the world, running a vast and bustling divine sky. God created the universe, as some would like to see it, on the seventh day after creation. He gave people the friendliest feelings: hope, faith, and love. Unfortunately, some did not appreciate this gift and have defiled it. I wonder if they can re-make from a black sheet into a white page.*

Gloomy clouds reached Marseille, preventing the sun's bright rays from lighting the city. A cool evening breeze refreshed people's faces with its breath. If you listened carefully, you could hear the melodious sounds of the sea. It was a wonderful summer time, and the best way to enjoy it was outside. The most memorable time for relaxation and enjoyment of nature and scents is at night when the sky is cloudless and studded with many bright stars. Lovers have always spent this time outside on the amazing beaches, studying the constellations and making wishes at the sight of falling stars.

The story I'll tell you was happening here, among the picturesque corners of nature on one of the sides of Marseille. A lot of foreigners come every year to visit sunny beaches. We call them tourists.

A dusty yellow road leads through the fields and gardens directly to a small, close-knit family mansion of Sauvage Roux. The magnificent mansion hangs on a cliff, its wide French-style windows facing the sea. The beautiful creamy two-story house seemed as ordinary as its landlords - a typical French family.

The owner of this beautiful nest is Raphael Sauvage Roux. He's a very handsome man of thirty-six years. Of course, he knows his merits, but he never used them. Women who knew him just raved about him, wanting to get his attention or even a small fraction of interest. Raphael, surprisingly, doesn't take them seriously because there is one he will love until the end of his life.

Francine is an ordinary woman and does not have anything outstanding, except that she is the chief editor of the local city's popular newspaper "Le Monde." Every morning, she and her husband drive downtown to work. Francine is proud of her beloved Raphael because he has accomplished much more in his life than she ever did. His job is really responsible and takes too much effort. He travels a lot and makes people's lives unchangeable. He is a diplomat. Raphael has always tried to be an objective and committed representative of state interests. He has been in his job for almost eleven years. In his fair hair, he already has noticeable silver shininess. Besides his main responsibilities as a good worker, he also has responsibilities in front of his kids as a good father. Their unconditional love has blessed them with two daughters and a son.

Philippe was the oldest and smartest of the children. His mother often watched him while she cooked lunch. With every birthday of his, she noticed how he became handsome and more like her first love. But mostly, this young man had inherited more of her facial features, but her husband was not upset by this because the other two daughters – Emilie and Caroline, as two drops of water look like their father.

Not far from their property is a ranch, where their grandfather lives, Mohammed Hassam. He is a direct mom's father, a faraway immigrant from Moroccan lands. His story has never been spoken, and Francine preferred not to talk about it. She loved her dad, and he always helped her with anything she needed. Mohammed owns the private sector and is keen to cultivate thoroughbred horses; usually, he sells them to wealthy people. His ranch occupies a fertile area for horses and for his children and grandchildren. Around the ranch stretches a huge body of water where the fishermen have a good catch and where Caroline and Philippe love to swim and ride the best horses at Mohammed's stable.

It is the most memorable day of their summer vacation when she is free from school with Emilie. The best time for Caroline is when her sister and her brother go hiking and spend time around unknown places. Each of them is in their own unique and spiritually rich. But the most shameless child of Sauvage Roux is Caroline. She seemed to deliberately force her beloved parents to worry and punish her for her actions, but they still loved her. Raphael adores his twins, no matter if they do something wrong and then point fingers at each other.

Blonde twins are at the age of seventeen, both very gentle, affectionate natures with eyes the color of young leaves; their innocent, pat black eyelashes have already broken the hearts of the neighbor boys. Caroline always dreamed of dolphins and really wanted to work there; Emilie is more sought for mathematical and chemical sciences, hoping to become a professor at some university one day. That evening, Caroline realized that her dream wouldn't come true.

Francine called her daughter into the living room to tell her the news about her future. "Sweetheart," started her mother, "we decided that in three days, you'll go to Meknes to stay with our uncle Ali."

Emilie was behind the door and overheard the conversation. She is very pleased by the fact that her parents are going to send her sister overseas to study. She will have more opportunities to win Philippe's heart. She doesn't like his great affection for her sister Caroline; she tries her best to be his favorite, but his love is too strong for her twin sister. This is manifested every time when they are together. The news about her sister's departure gave her more confidence and boldness. "Mama, am I going to Morocco with Caroline, too?" Emilie came around the corner.

"No," said Francine shortly, "You'll stay and continue your studies in college, and your father and I have decided."

Emilie showed all her disordered personality, but in the eyes of her sister Caroline, she saw jubilation and inexplicable brilliance. What that meant, no one guessed.

Philippe was very upset. He quickly left the room and went upstairs to his bedroom. Caroline proudly turned her face away from her parents' decision, put her hands on her hips, and quickly headed out of the house. Emilie looked after her insidiously, hugging her shoulders. The parents looked at each other in amazement and shrugged their shoulders, surprised by her behavior.

Caroline came into the yard, where her friends were playing, and immediately disappeared from their sight. Like a bird in the sky, she walked confidently on the dusty road. Her stunning pose was similar to a swan floating on the lake. Little bells rang on her right ankle, an ankle bracelet given by her grandfather, Mohammed. She was proud of it because none of the girls had any jewelry decorations like she had. Her long, colorful skirt flowed, and a gentle wind played with her slightly wavy hair. The sun was already sinking behind the horizon, and the last rays of light fell on the girl's hair, leaving behind a golden gleam.

Suddenly, she stopped when she saw dust rising on the road. She saw a horseback rider, unfamiliar to her. A young fellow of nearly twenty years old suddenly stopped his horse, guiding it into a light circling trot. Caroline folded her arms and looked at him majestically as if waiting for something unusual. He mumbled something to her, carefully assessing the appearance of a stranger. Caroline pursed her lips and looked at him anxiously. She had never seen him before. His look was quite different from those of these lands, maybe German or British.

"In my opinion, you're not worthy of a true gentleman."

The guy grinned at her back, raised his right eyebrow, and said, "Are you a fine lady, huh?"

"Yes," she said firmly, nodding her head positively.

"Then why don't you drive a car without a companion?" He laughed out loud in a teasing manner.

Caroline turned away from him and casually continued her way. The young fellow blocked her road once again with a great desire to get acquainted with her.

"Where are you hurrying? Do you live here?" calmly asked the stranger, with obvious eagerness to get to know her closer as much as possible at this moment.

The girl looked at him incredulously and said, "Yes, I'm going to my grandfather, Mohammed."

He released the reins, got off his horse, and looked into her face closer than society norms allowed, breaking all the space rules. "If you want, I'll bring you to your granddad," he gently suggested, cocking up his right eyebrow.

"I have no time for you," she answered rudely, hissing through her perfectly white teeth.

"Stubborn Angel!" The guy very politely took her hand in his and kissed it, promising her a very close friendship. Caroline drew her attention to his sky-blue eyes and light brown hair, which flirtatiously moved with the wind. She agreed with the feeling that there was no choice but to let him do so as he proposed. And they walked slowly on the road to her grandfather. This handsome stranger took the reins of his horse, firmly holding them.

Caroline liked his smile and his eyes; she couldn't take her eyes away from the pink and clean face of this young man. He awakened in her something sleeping at the bottom of her soul, and these were unfamiliar feelings to her. They told each other a story, and they laughed. But Caroline couldn't even imagine with whom she got friended and what the consequences of this interaction could be. But the fact that they felt sympathy for each other was true. Finally, the guys came to the ranch. They spotted Mohammed in the barn inside, preparing a black horse for Mr. Fury. The young man came close to Caroline's grandpa.

"Uncle, I want you to meet my new friend," he said.

Grandpa smiled and admitted, "Oh... so you've met?"

Caroline turned angrily to her grandfather and said, "No, I do not know him. We are not acquainted, and I haven't seen this man before."

As soon as Mohammed opened his mouth, a dark figure appeared behind him. It was a man with an unpleasant look; he was riding a beautiful black Friesian horse for pleasure. A gloomy man rode up close to Caroline and looked at her with an appraising gaze, standing next to his son.

The tall man turned pale when he met Caroline's green eyes. His horse reared up, sensing the tension of emotions in his rider. John looked at his son strictly and roughly ordered him, "So, get into the saddle, now! I'm not going to wait for your ass," John worried, with sparks of anger in his eyes.

The guy threw up his hands in confusion, "But I want you to introduce..."

Father severely interrupted his speech. "Are you deaf or something? I think I told you clearly to go home."

Caroline was very surprised by his actions, and she didn't like this man at first sight. He seemed arrogant and rude to her. His rage knew no bounds; it was immediately clear that there was nothing good coming from this.

John gripped the reins bridle and gnashed his teeth with the thought, "I'm pretty sure this is Rafael's daughter: same eyes, same innocent look! Now, this stupid idiot is in my hands. Too long I have searched for him and Francine with their offspring. And now fate has decided to make me a gift and handle them into my hands. I can easily make a plan of bloody revenge. Rafael knowingly touched his hands through someone else's property and wanted to hide me in jail. Everybody has to pay their price, and now the time has come."

The poor fellow even had no time to say goodbye to the girl as his father forced him to follow and disappear just as he had appeared.

Caroline sadly lowered her head, watching as the dust climbed behind them and how they gradually spread out from the field of the picturesque view.

She turned her head towards Mohammed with thoughtful words, "Grandpa, why did this man behave like this? What does it mean, and who is this guy? They look so arrogant and self-confident."

Mohammed took a deep breath, slowly pulled tobacco out, and filled his mouthpiece. "Oh, sweetie..." Her grandfather lit the pipe, "this is a dangerous family, and they have dirty deeds. They shall be punished by Allah, for Allah is all-seeing and all-knowing," he sadly said.

Caroline looked down, adding, "What a shame! And this young man was so kind and cheerful to me."

Mohammed moved his gaze to his granddaughter and told her, "Girl, yes, this fellow is nice, but I know that you will never be happy with him, so it's best for you to stay away from him."

Caroline protested, "But why?"

Mohammed pursed his lips and said loudly, "Because they are gangsters. They don't know what virtue is."

Her frail body trembled, and her eyes became barely wet, "Then why did the young man call you uncle and not sir?"

Grandfather looked into her eyes and said, "Because I am. He is my godson, so I'm his uncle."

Caroline looked at him and added, "What's his name?"

"Brian Fury," calmly replied the grandfather.

# CHAPTER 2

*The sea of feelings and the ocean of love envelop human hearts and souls, sometimes forcing us to act contrary to reason. It is because of the wealth of feelings that we make irreparable acts that entail positive or negative effects. What to choose and which path to walk is always a decision upon us.*

Into Martin's room entered his father, John, in no mood at all. Martin was sitting in an armchair, listening to his favorite music, shaking his head, and looking at half-nude young models in a popular men's magazine. He ignored the presence of his dad, enjoying his free time.

"Martin," barked his father, "I found a family of a former cop. Do you know that the Sauvage Roux family is again in our hands? We shouldn't miss the opportunity to make a good punishment. We must act strictly according to the plan. Do you hear?"

Martin lazily raised an eyebrow and looked at his father, who was ready to tear his hair out. Then the guy slowly, as in a slow-motion movie scene, stretched to the table for a cigarette and lighter and then smoked.

"So what?" He said.

"The fact is that Rafael looked at someone else's wealth, but I will not stand it. I can't let this go. Is it clear to you or not?" angrily shouted John.

"Yeah... Yeah..." hissed Martin, shaking his head.

Father sharply moved towards the door, realizing that his son was not going to support him, but he waited and then decided to hook him up.

"And stop smoking this shit. Your room stinks and smoking is bad for your health," John stepped out of the doorway and slammed the door so hard that a pot with a flower on the top shelf shook and fell on the wooden floor. Of course, debris scattered on the nice rug from the broken vase. Martin only cocked up his eyebrows gently, smoking the cigarette and staying in his armchair as if nothing had happened.

John Fury hurried to his office room to make a call to his wife. He was going to ask her to come and take Brian home back to the US.

"But beloved, since you just arrived, why do you want to do that?" Adeline asked in excitement.

John's face turned red with rage. "He needs to focus on his education and not hang out here with the local children roaming the dirt yards," he lowered his tone. "After all, I want my son to be a smart, educated man."

"And what about Martin?" bothered his wife.

"Don't worry about him; we have stuff to do," John sweetly murmured into the phone.

"I beg you, darling. Don't drag Martin into your dirty business because he-"

His tone cut her off, "Enough, Adeline, I know what to do, and you did not decree," and he abruptly hung up and began pacing the room back and forth, thinking about his evil plan. John wearily collapsed into a black chair, which groaned under his weight like a crying puppy and called his old servant. When he appeared at the door, John ordered him to call for Martin.

"But excuse me, boss," like a mosquito, squeaked the servant. "Your son, Martin, left twenty minutes ago."

"What?" John slammed his palm against his table. Furiously grinding his teeth, he said, "How dare you let him go, you fool?!" And he jumped from his heavy chair and waved his fist angrily above the bald, reddened servant's head. "Get out of my sight, or I'll chop you."

The frightened servant quickly ran away scared.

But John shouted out loud again, "Where the hell did he go? Come back and tell me which car my son took?"

The scared Frenchman appeared around the corner of the door exit and, in a trembling voice, said, "The one that was in the yard."

John collapsed back into his boss chair, "Damn it! This pup went out to see girls," rubbing his chin, he said. "Oh, fine... you're free for now."

Men are completely unable to control their passions. Unfortunately, some pathetic bunch will spoil the whole picture, allowing their animal instincts to take over the mind. Martin was a hopeless womanizer. Around him was always a bunch of girls. Each of them tried to get his attention and affection.

"Oh, Mr. Fury, you are so attractive and seductive," huskily said one girl.

"Oh, Martin, you're so smart and just my hunk," whispered the other.

"Oh dear Fury," said another, "with your mind and wonderful sense of humor, no one beats even my brother. You know what attracts us, and you use it. You go all just perfect," a serious case and funny jokes.

Martin, lazily but with interest, looked at her, took her hand, and brought her closer. He gently smiled at her seductive chin and placed her round butt on his lap. His lips leaned against her neck, and the tip of his small nose touched her skin as if to collect the most precious scent in the garden of flowers.

Martin Fury is only twenty-two, older than his brother by two years, and his indomitable character could not suppress even his father. All of his 'lectures' about morality are futile. Martin loves to drink, smoke, have fun with girls, and win or lose every last dollar in the casino at poker. He had never been in love, and all because he believed that love is a mass of short-term tomfoolery. His passion is the annual horse races, in which he was always a winner, and on the winnings, he lived. He absolutely adores boating and yachting, golfing with friends, and recently started to admire race cars. The warlike character and good presence of mind never left him and did not let him down. Despite his brutal recklessness, he likes to escape into the mountains to hike and seek new adventures.

The peace of nature outdoors brings more calmness into his busy-like world. He enjoys publicity and suits and ties, especially in the company of a fine woman, but this time, he desired a change. He isn't sure yet what exactly it is, but definitely something that heats the blood in his veins and shakes his heart and mind. Craving for adrenaline and spicy feelings is heating up his heart. Wild and free, he knows his benefits, and for sure, he'll do it no matter what it takes, just because he is Martin – the captain of Adventures Hearts.

# CHAPTER 3

*There is no peace without a war. Always and at all times, good fought against evil, creating a stereotype that light always defeats darkness. But can we name at least one case where evil won?*

The evening was late when Caroline returned home, impressed by the meeting with a pleasant young man. Naturally, she could not resist the temptation to tell her sister.

"You know," started Caroline, "tonight I met an interesting guy about my age." She boasted about her adventure story, raising her head proudly.

"What do you mean? Do I know him?" Emilie asked, lying on the bed.

"No, you have no idea who he is," grimaced her sister.

Emilie, biting her lower lip in curiosity, said, "And who is he?"

"His name is Brian Fury," Caroline said with a gleam in her eyes.

"But that is not a local name," Emilie was surprised. "Doesn't sound French."

"You guessed it, sister!" Caroline showed her tongue at Emilie. "He is American."

Emilie rolled her eyes toward the ceiling as if fallen into a trance and began to think. Caroline sat on a table, legs dangling, and made faces at her sister.

Suddenly, somebody knocked at the door. In unison, the girls asked, "Who?"

The door opened, and there stood Philippe. He filled the entire doorway as if inserted into the frame of a portrait. He raised his left eyebrow and asked, "Can I come in?"

"You already came in," they said in one voice again.

He walked up to Caroline and said, as if chewing cereal, "Emilie, Mom wants you to come to the kitchen. She needs you there."

Emilie grinned, looking at her sister's face, and put her hand to her mouth.

"Philippe, I'm Caroline," she said sternly. "When will you learn to distinguish us?"

He lowered his head and closed his eyes with embarrassment, feeling uneasy. "I'm sorry. How could I have been confused between you two again? But you look so much alike," he said apologetically.

"Yes... and our personalities are the same," Caroline said with reproach in her voice.

Emilie got out of bed, almost silently passed Philippe, and headed out of the bedroom. She closed the door behind him and went to the kitchen, from which came a pleasant aroma. Francine was busy preparing dinner. Less than five minutes later, the door flew open with all the force behind Emilie, and from there, Philippe and Caroline took off like crazy. Her sister was running, laughing, and calling her brother all sorts of names. She screamed down the stairs, trying to run away from him. Philippe threw a pillow at Caroline's back. She screamed, stumbled, and almost fell on the stairs. Philippe caught her, grabbed her leg, and began pulling her down the stairs. Caroline laughed and scratched. He picked her up off the floor and twisted her arm behind her back. The girl struggled and tapped her foot on the wooden floor.

"Let me go, stupid. It hurts."

"And you'll never tease me again like you did?" Philippe hissed, looking at her face.

"No," she answered calmly.

He removed his hands from her elbows and let his sister go. She picked up a pillow and quietly went to her room, but sharply, with the speed of the wind, Caroline turned around and gave a big slap to

Philippe. When he turned to fight back, his face slammed into her bedroom door. He grabbed the door handle, trying to open it.

Emilie went to the kitchen. As soon as she saw her mother, she decided to report her sister's secret.

"Mom, Caroline fell in love."

Francine looked at her daughter with a worried expression. "Fell in love? With who?"

"Some Brian Fury," Emilie said, with a hint of jealousy in her voice.

Mother shook her head and narrowed her eyes. She swiftly shifted her gaze away from Emilie's eyes in fear and utter confusion. Once again, she faced turmoil within her family. The woman closed her eyes, and memories of John trailed one after another when they were still young. In their veins, hot blood steamed. She recalled the last moment they saw each other, and intimate memories surfaced.

"We were young and loved each other like crazy, but my pride ruined our relationship. John, back then, was very handsome and witty. I wouldn't let his feelings get the better of my mind. He was very angry when I rejected him. At that moment, he grabbed my waist and kissed me violently. To say he was very rude, I can't. He was an intelligent man, a gentleman, and never raised a hand on a woman. I clearly remember his brown eyes full of light and beautiful pink lips. I blame myself for leaving him and going to Marseille to forget it. That's where I met Raphael and married him. But I don't regret it. I stayed here and gave birth to my beloved children. Since then, I haven't seen him because we were constantly on the run and hiding from the mighty Fury. Now, they've shown up in our lives again." She breathed heavily, placing her hand on her left chest, and bent slightly from weakness in her knees. She felt as if the ground was slipping away beneath her feet. Emilie, chewing on her mother's pastries, gazed at her in surprise.

"Mom, what's wrong? Are you okay?"

"I'll go upstairs. When your dad comes home from work, ask him to come to me," said Francine softly.

Emilie looked fascinated at her mother and thought, "I wonder what I could have told her that affected her so much?"

The hour was late when Rafael returned from work. His bright eyes wearily looked at the pale face of his wife. At this point, she resembled a freshly painted white wall; her lips trembled convulsively, and her eyes expressed nothing.

"My God, my dear, you look terrible. What happened?" he asked, concerned.

"Rafael, the Fury family is here, somewhere in the area, and they probably already know that we nested here. Don't you think there is a threat to our lives?"

"What do you mean?" Raphael gasped. "That sounds not good..." he drawled uneasily.

"I think we should go somewhere for a while. We can wait until the storm calms down," advised his wife. "So tomorrow, after dinner, Philippe will leave for Paris."

"Let him go," sighed Raphael heavily. "We will inform him about us later, and Caroline will be in Morocco by that time. Today, I will write an explanatory letter to Uncle Ali and send money for her to live there. Emilie will go with us."

Francine agreed with his decision. He hugged his wife and kissed her. The night passed in love.

As dawn broke, the crimson sky slowly gave way to the rising sun, casting its first rays on the tops of trees and roofs of houses. Marseille was still immersed in a sweet dream. However, birds began to wash down their songs. The day promised to be rainy as clouds gathered in the south, ready to moisten the soil.

Caroline was an early bird who flew without permission to an empty beach. The sea was inviting and attractive, probably because of the cool breeze. But this did not prevent her from choosing a convenient place to lay the light rug on the yellow sand, spread out towels, take off her cap and glasses, and get ready for swimming and sunbathing. With a bright and happy gleam in her eyes, she looked at the sea, with large waves rolling on top of each other. She threw off her clothes and ran on tiptoe to the sea. The first wave was refreshing; it cooled her body, covering it with small goosebumps. Caroline immediately hugged her shoulders, trying to keep herself warm. The pleasant water gently caressed her body like a shawl. She enjoyed the feeling and wallowed with pleasure and enthusiasm.

Caroline stopped swimming for a while, her attention captured by a horseman galloping playfully on a black horse. He was magnificent and fast, graceful and powerful like a Greek god riding his Pegasus. He seemed to barely touch the water surface and the drops and splashes created a blue-white image of innocence on a painted canvas. They were together—the rider and his black four-legged beast—seeming a single being of incredible power and grace. The stranger rode his horse straight and skillfully; it was a delightful spectacle for Caroline. His friend was flying like the wind over the water, enjoying the good weather and playing with water spray. The owner of the horse stopped abruptly, and the beautiful horse reared up on the background of yellow sand, picking its hooves in the air.

The eyes of the attractive stranger drew attention to her. At that moment, Caroline felt embarrassed and awkward. Her cheeks blushed, her heart caught on fire, and she no longer felt the cool water. She was hot, as if fiery tongues whipped her inside and out. The bottoms of her palms burned warm, and she caught herself thinking of a hot tub with bubbles. She pressed her palms to her cheeks but continued to gaze at the rider and his dancing horse.

The wind blew at her back, and a big wave knocked her down and dragged her into the depths. Despite being a good swimmer, she couldn't resist the power of the water. It got harder and harder to fight the strong waves. The horseman didn't delay a moment. He jumped from his horse's back straight into the water and, slid under the surface of the upcoming rolling wave, quickly swam to the girl. She felt the salty water of the sea intruding into her mouth and nose.

A sudden sharp pain in her chest, as if pierced by a sword, prevented her from coughing. Her consciousness betrayed her, and with heavy thoughts, she realized she was slowly sinking beneath the water. Small bubbles rose one after the other to the surface. The man who rushed to rescue Caroline swam to her, and under the water, his strong hands caught her weak and helpless body. He took her arm, placed it around his neck, and swiftly moved toward the shore.

The next wave caught up with them again but assisted in his effort. Having reached the shore safely, the guy carried her, holding her in his arms. He put Caroline on a cover and felt for a pulse. Luckily, it was there. The hope for her salvation was alive. The guy gave her a heart massage, but to no avail. Then he leaned toward her, his mouth touching hers gently, almost imperceptibly, as if to feel the taste, fearing she might crack if pushed harder. Three times, he gave her artificial respiration and looked at her, his head bent over her cold, pale face. His short-cut forelock was so wet that drops trailed each other fast, dripping on her chest and slowly strolling down into her swim bra. He was gasping.

Caroline coughed, and the water came out of her lungs, running down her chin, neck, and shoulder. She felt weak and frightened, a sharp pain in her throat from the salty water. Her eyes met his, as black as coal. The guy sighed with relief and smiled at her, barely audibly saying, "From now on, be careful." He placed a towel on her chest.

Her hand rested on his arm, and panting, she said, "Thank you, Monsieur, you saved my life." Caroline tried to get up but fell back onto the blanket, still weak.

"You'd better stay calm for a while," he said soothingly, stroking her hand gently, grimacing as he still panted, trying to catch his breath.

Caroline looked at the sea and saw his graceful black horse playing briskly near the water. "Is that your horse?" she asked, coughing.

"Yes," he smiled at her. "His name is Ivanhoe." The guy got up from his knees and held out his hand.

Caroline, with growing trust, placed her arm in his, and he helped her stand. Though her knees were still weak, she tried to manage a confident posture. Their eyes locked again, but this time closer. She felt a unique warmth in his touch, almost burning to the point of wanting to scream, "Ouch," but she didn't. She couldn't explain what was so attractive about this stranger; gazing into his eyes felt like she knew him from a past life. Is it possible to feel such a strange connection?

"You have eyes as bright as emeralds," he finally broke the magnetic silence between them. His voice sounded like the most lyrical music in the world. Only now did she notice his voice was soft and gentle like velvet rose petals. "I have never seen such beautiful eyes." He winked at her mysteriously and let go of her hand.

Caroline looked at his funny, snub, wet forelock. He looked at her enticing lips and pulled away, feeling the desire. "So young, I can't take her seriously," he thought. Then he turned around and started walking to his horse. Caroline looked at his manly, tanned body and slowly closed her eyes, letting the breeze dispel the mirage. He was like a dream come true.

But when she blinked and opened her eyes wide to make sure it wasn't just her imagination, she saw him still walking to the horse. She could not help but shout out loud to him, "Hey! Can I get to know the name of my savior?"

He gracefully turned his face back to her, and a gorgeous smile spread across his lips, showing off his straight, perfectly white teeth. "You can call me Martin, just Martin."

Brian looked at his yellow-packed luggage and waited for his father and brother to arrive. He walked out to their beautiful veranda covered in flowers and pots and turned his attention to the road. Dust started to rise; Martin was returning home. Riding Ivanhoe as fast as possible, Martin's approach brought a little smile to Brian's face, his eyes sparkling with joy. He hastened to the door and walked out onto the porch to meet his brother and welcome him in.

Martin dismounted and, in a state of excited joy, ran to Brian, hugging him in a manly way. "I met her!" he exclaimed, his eyes wide with excitement and his cheeks blushing.

"Who?" Brian was surprised, raising his eyebrows. He knew how hard it was for Martin to get into such a mood—catastrophic excitement!

"She is like the sky, so clear, like the air, light and pleasant as joy!" Martin said, shaking his brother's shoulders with a strong grip.

"Since when did you become a poet? What miracle did you meet?" Brian asked, intrigued.

Like a madman, Martin ran up the stairs to the second floor of his room. Brian raised his eyebrows, puzzled by his brother's behavior, and folded his hands on his chest, plunging into speculation. At that moment, John approached him from behind and said, "Your mother is waiting for you in the car. Go, it's time to go."

"And what about Martin? Will he go?"

"No," John said abruptly. "He'll stay. We have not finished yet." He patted his son on the shoulder.

John made sure Brian was comfortably placed in the car and waved at him as he was leaving. He cherished Brian so much that he couldn't fail to follow the written plan.

As the car moved from its place and disappeared from sight behind an oak tree, his father climbed up the stairs straight to Martin's room and told him to get dressed accordingly, get armed, and be ready to leave on their business at ten p.m.

The day, as expected, was rainy and overcast, with occasional drizzling rain. The stars in the sky couldn't be seen as clouds shrouded the sky, disappearing from human sight.

That night, Caroline decided to spend it at her grandfather's ranch with her beloved friend, whom her father had given her on her sixteenth birthday. Philippe was preparing for a trip. He packed his things in the luggage, taking a photo of the family and of Caroline. He kept her picture in his hand, looking at it with thoughts of how much he loved her. His concentration was interrupted by a knock at the door. Turning around, he saw Emilie at the threshold.

"Oh... it's you, Caroline," Philippe said with bitterness in his voice.

Emilie came closer, looked into his eyes, and said sadly, "Why do you think about her more than me? It's impossible that you can't distinguish us."

Philippe put his hand on his forehead and said apologetically, "Oh! Is that you, Emilie? I'm sorry. What is wrong with me?"

"You love her more than me, huh? Even though we are twins. Why, Philippe? She is brave, and I am not!" Emilie said, her eyes filling with tears.

"Don't say nonsense. You are her sister," Philippe fumed. "I'm leaving. It's better to say goodbye, and we will not argue as usual."

She stood in silence, waiting for hugs and goodbyes. He approached her, kissed her forehead, and then, sweetly smiling, shook her hand. Philippe took some of his things and left the room.

Emilie looked at his bedside and saw that he had taken a photo of the family and Caroline. She quietly left his room and watched as he said goodbye to their parents in the living room. Not seeing Caroline, Emilie decided to put on her sister's dress and, through a secret passage, went into the yard to play with Caroline.

Philippe, carrying his bags, walked to his green Peugeot and saw his beloved sister. Emilie picked up her skirt, teasingly waving it as Caroline would.

"Caroline, I am so glad to see you, honey. I thought you were not going to say goodbye to your lovely brother," Philippe said softly, walking closer to Emilie.

At that moment, Caroline was returning to the house to say farewell to her brother but stopped near the bushes at the sight of Emilie, dressed in her outfit, talking to Philippe. She listened in on their conversation.

"Philippe, how could you think I'm not going to say goodbye to you?" Emilie said, raising her head proudly, portraying her sister.

"What?" Philippe was happy. "So you thought about me," he murmured softly, hope in his voice.

"Yes," Emilie nodded convincingly.

"Caroline, I love you," he said softly, holding her hand.

Emilie knew this was her only chance to feel Philippe's body heat and enjoy his embrace. She ran to him, throwing herself into his arms. He embraced her, pressing Emilie closer in a tight hug.

Caroline, surprised, opened her mouth and viciously put her hands on her belt, thinking, 'What is this? How dare my sister pretend to be me? Doesn't she love him like a brother? She is completely out of her mind.' She continued to sternly observe them, burning with curiosity to see how it would all finish.

Philippe gazed into Emilie's eyes, unaware he was being deceived. Emilie read tenderness, warmth, and affection in his expression.

"I love you too, my Philippe," Emilie said, biting her lower lip with a gasp.

He lowered his eyelids and turned his attention to her flaming lips, which were invitingly parted, waiting for a kiss. Emilie could not bear the tension and, with dramatic passion, eagerly clung to his lips. He responded with equal passion and love.

Caroline watched them in a trance, shocked by their behavior and unable to understand their actions. How could a brother and sister do this? What a scene!

The kiss between them was not too long or too passionate. It was spontaneous, driven by a simple desire, characteristic of all love. Emilie pulled back from his lips, gave him a sharp slap, looked at him with offended eyes, picked up her maxi skirt, and ran into the house. Philippe laughed loudly, got into the car, and drove off, speeding past Caroline, who had hidden behind a bush.

She got up and walked briskly into the house. With a pounding heart, she climbed the stairs and entered Emilie's room. Opening the door, Caroline saw Emilie lying on the bed, sobbing. She quickly approached her sister, grabbed her sharply by the elbow, and forced her to look her in the eye.

"What the hell did you do? Why are you wearing my clothes?"

"Leave me alone. I don't want to talk to you," Emilie sniffled.

"Oh really!" Caroline was outraged. "Then be a good girl and tell me what happened."

With fear in her eyes, Emilie looked back at her sister. "What?"

"Why did you kiss Philippe?" Caroline demanded.

She was so angry that she was ready to strangle her with her own hands. Rage reflected in her clouded green eyes.

"You saw it all?" Emilie asked, amused and shaking.

Caroline put her hands on her hips and stood in a pose. "Do you really think I'm blind?"

Emilie turned away, but Caroline's demanding glare bore into her. Emilie, feeling overwhelmed, turned and fled the room like a bullet.

Quickly descending the stairs, Caroline heard the creaking of car tires in the yard. She jumped to the window and, with a troubled look, gazed outside. She saw a black car and people in masks with arms. There were four of them, clearly eager to enter the mansion. Three of them broke the front door while the fourth one stood guard, armed to the teeth.

With fear and confusion, Caroline bit her finger. She returned to the room and hid under the day bed, gathering up her maxi skirt. Emilie, confused by her sister's behavior, sat on the bed, blinking in surprise at Caroline, who was frantically waving for her to come and join her. Shots rang out, followed by screams and strange noises. Their parents resisted but were quickly subdued. An intruder burst into the girls' room. From under the bed, Caroline saw only his feet. She clamped her lips shut and made no sound.

The stranger grabbed Emilie by the arms and struck her across the face. Emilie screamed and begged him not to hurt her, but her pleas were ignored. Caroline peeked out and saw the back of the stranger's head as he tormented her sister. His strong hands tore at her clothes. Caroline heard the crack of fabric and noticed buttons rolling around the room. Emilie screamed and covered her shoulders with her arms, trying to shield herself. Her cries for help were met with another slap. Caroline wanted to help but felt weak and helpless. She realized their parents could not come to their aid, as they were likely already dead. With a pain in her heart, she squeezed her eyes shut and put a hand to her lips. The intruder's rough, hoarse voice sounded familiar:

"French bitch, oh baby, now you'll be mine! I've waited for this moment to enjoy you, honey."

Emilie struggled and protested. The intruder pushed her onto the bed and threw himself on top of Emilie. The hungry beast finally tore off her underwear, and she screamed in her wild voice as he pinned her down. Caroline's heart froze in fear; it was too much for her young mind, this terrible thing that she was going through. She bit her finger to stifle her own cries. The intense fear made her feel the hot blood rush to her head and heart. Caroline sobbed softly under the bed, her hands on her sweaty forehead. Tears streamed down her cheeks, leaving a wet trail. She could not hide her eyes, which were fixed on the moving figure of this inhuman beast. When he finished his dirty work, he grabbed Emilie by the hair, completely nude, and dragged her now unconscious and naked body out of the room. Caroline saw her sister in this state for the first time and cried even harder, clutching her long, wavy hair in pain.

The intruder dragged Emilie into the living room, where her parents were bound with ropes. Emilie was handcuffed to a radiator, unconscious, bruised, and bleeding. Three other intruders were rummaging through the house. Caroline crawled out from under the bed and gently pulled a sheet rope from the closet, which she had once played with. She fastened it to the radiator under the windowsill and, without hesitation, used it to escape through the window.

The house—her home—meant everything to her. Its wooden walls held the pulse of life, everything that made them the Sauvage Roux, their essence. It was the home for people who could overcome any challenge.

Running away in terror and despair, Caroline's weak voice tried to call for help, but a lump in her throat muffled her cries. An armed man in a black suit at the door saw her but did nothing, giving her the chance to escape and survive. She turned to look at the mansion, now in ruins. In the living room, two men were on their knees, rifling through a brown suitcase. Another man in a black leather jacket stood smoking a cigarette, staring disdainfully at her mother, Francine. Finishing his cigarette, he waved to his accomplices, signaling their departure.

All four men got into a black Chevy Tahoe. As they drove away, the mansion, which Caroline had loved so much, exploded and shattered like a house of cards. Caroline stretched her hand toward her only home and cried out, collapsing onto the grass. She got on her knees, weeping, and bowed her head, clutching her hair. It was a tragic end to her once happy and joyful life.

The night in Marseille was quiet and tearful for Caroline. The moon hid behind a large, dense cloud, casting a cool, quiet radiance over the gleaming expanse of water. Suddenly, the sea seemed to come alive with flickering flashes, as if filled with thousands of fireflies. These brilliant, scattered lights twinkled wherever she looked.

A tear rolled down Caroline's pink, hot cheek, leaving a wet trail. Her eyes, deeper than the sea, faced the sky, taking in its greatness and power. The clouds parted like a theater curtain, revealing the yellow sparks of stars scattered across the night. Among them, Caroline saw the white expanse of the Milky Way calling to her, beckoning and dissolving in her eyes. Lying on the grass, she pinched a weed with her hand and sang a sad song about love and family. She felt delirious and mad, unwilling to return to the harsh reality that she was now an orphan. Quietly, barely audibly, she whispered to the sky:

"Life broke all of my dreams against the sharp rocks of reality; my soul is broken together with sweet dreams of a wealthy future."

# CHAPTER 4

*And it came to one of them; it is going with modesty, it said:*

*"My father is calling you to give you a reward for what you did for us."*

*And when he came to him and told him the story, he said:*

*"Do not worry, you escaped from unjust people!"*

Mohammed Hasaan rode through the former estate of the modest Sauvage Roux family. The house was reduced to nothing but bricks and fragments of a once happy time. Mohammed sat with his head down on a dun horse, uttering a prayer in Arabic: "*In the Name of Allah, calling for you…*"

The old man raised his head with sorrow. With a sad expression on his face, he gripped the reins of the horse and rode toward the sandy shore. He rode a small segment of the path and saw a person lying in the grass. Mohammed quickly jumped off his horse and ran to the helpless victim. It was a girl, and in her, he recognized his granddaughter.

"Caroline, oh my Lord, oh God! Wake up." The old man took her by the shoulders, raised and began to lead to feelings. She was lifeless, but her pulse and heartbeat could be felt. Then Mohammed dropped the girl on the grass and raised his hands toward heaven, "Praise - God, the Lord of gracious, merciful, and the king of a judgment day! My daughter is still alive! Alive!"

Caroline could hardly open her eyes. She heard a prayer in Arabic spoken by her grandfather. He never told her about his life. His story about his arrival to Marseille was very foggy. He explained that he was an immigrant forced to leave Meknes due to a quarrel with his uncle, Ali. Although they did not share power, one of them had to go.

Caroline, gasping in pain, said, "Grandpa, I'm an orphan."

Mohammed looked at her sadly and replied, "I saw the ruins of your house, but I didn't even realize that all are dead." He said in a muffled word, "But you're still alive, and it is a sign."

The girl raised her eyebrows in disbelief and bewilderment, shaking her head, and asked, "What? What sign?"

The old man looked into the eyes of his granddaughter, took her face in his palms, and, on a hypnotic note, gave her the instruction, "Caroline, you're alive, and it means a lot. You have to avenge the death of your family. God chose you, and only you have to do justice. You have to do it."

The girl nodded positively and continued her speech, "Yes, and for the rape of my sister too." Blinked off and finished, "The enemy, I will chasten him with a strong penalty or kill him if it falls to me with apparent authority."

Mohammed smiled slightly and stroked his thin, long, white beard. This girl, who looked such a delicate flower, seemed dangerous now. This beautiful flower grows with thorns. What will happen in the future? Well, nobody knows except Allah.

Her grandfather helped Caroline to get up and sat her down, weakened, on his horse's back in the padded saddle. He took the reins in his hands, and his companion, meekly, slowly followed him back to the ranch. Caroline sat with her head down, barely moving a horse and its feet. Now more than ever, she needed a rest and recreation. At home, Mohammed had prepared a room for her, and she settled in with the items stored in the farm's attic. She made her bed, and she collapsed with great fatigue. Her soul was more exhausted than her body, yet despite her illness, she felt tremors in her hands, legs, and back. Caroline closed her eyes and sank deeply into a long, all-consuming dream. The windows of her new bedroom were open and chiffon, light curtains gently stirred. The weather deteriorated sharply in the distance. Above the sea shone bright lightning, the clouds thickened, and the street darkened. Wind tore the tops and crowns of trees, screaming and threatening. Rain suddenly whipped on the roof and was heard more than usual.

Caroline's room got dark, and the shadows of the tree branches appeared on the walls. In the stables, the horses whinnied nervously, and hooves beat the ground. Dark, like a ghost fog, enveloped a small part of Marseilles. People hid in their homes, waiting for something unusual and unpredictable. With the alarming rate of dark blue clouds approached the city and seriously hung over. The sea roared and moaned restlessly. Waves crashed against the rocks, leaving the foam balls. All flights were canceled at the airport. In the street were no people. The weather report predicted severe thunderstorms with possible hail. From the sea, the cool breeze blew. The curtains in Caroline's room rose high, inviting the unknown.

A mysterious shadow slid across the ceiling and walls of the room. It loomed over the bed and slowly descended towards Caroline's face as if studying it. The girl lay quietly, her pale face expressionless. The sleeves of her gown trembled anxiously, and cold breath ruffled her golden hair. Caroline was in a deep sleep already. High above the sea and the hills rock, she saw herself in a delicate blue robe in large female hands. She is like Thumbelina in the Giant Palms. The female soft voice spoke to her: 'You stole from me everything... In Caroline's face blew the cold, almost icy air. She straightened her arms, and the sleeves of her gown fluttered her, but the voice behind her back continued, "But you lost ... the man that is dear to me, now he will be mine," in this voice, the girl felt a note of irony "Look..."

And the palm of her hand, where Caroline was, turned her toward the rocks, where she saw the branch of one of the roads that led to the main freeway. The voice fell silent, allowing Caroline to see everything for herself. Through the mist, which was moving balls of gray, she saw a green Peugeot. It was very similar to her brother's car. Behind it were two black BMW cars that drove like sharks overtaking its prey, they chased after him, Peugeot wound on the road, trying to come off. A black devil slipped past its production and blocked the passage further. On the rain-sodden road, the car lost its control and turned sharply, slipping on the wet pavement, leaving behind it yellow sparks like a bullet from a pistol. It began to dive down a cliff to the beach, and the auto fell instantly and exploded.

Caroline tearfully cried out, "Philippe! No! Just not you!"

Two black cars were parked on the road, and the criminals saw the burning of their victims.

Caroline turned her face to the person holding her and recognized Emilie. At this moment, her sister seemed different. Emilie's hair was still light, but her green eyes blazed with fire. Her lips were dark red, and around her hair was dull and dark fog, indicating the black soul. Her lips stretched into an ironic smile. "My poor sister ... now he belongs to me."

Caroline felt exhausted but calmly asked, "Who are they? Who are the murderers?"

Emilie lifted her chin haughtily without shifting her eyes from the sight of Caroline, and the flow of air rushed in the face of her sister, "Fury ... Fury are the killers." And a nasty laugh, with echoes, accompanied Caroline more and more deeply into the darkness.

The door to the room swung open with a bang, "Father, I don't like in what kind of business you drew me, it's cruel, I didn't want to..."

"Come on you!"

Pats on the shoulder of his son, John said, "Tell me, you also enjoyed the event and what you got up..."

"I feel like a villain," distressed Martin, hardly paying attention to the words that his father said.

"And come on, you're just well done for Papa," John said cheerily, "You helped me to destroy the enemy family, and I'm more than sure you got pleasure from this business, too."

"I'm sorry, father, but I want to relax." Martin sighed, heading to the exit.

"Do not be a coward in actions!" Strictly said John. "You never stop at only one intention! Remorse doesn't matter much," with his finger in the air conducting, shouted upset John Fury.

Martin listened to his father's lecture until the end, standing with his back to him, and then immediately left the room. He headed down to the courtyard, seeking fresh air after the storm. The image of the running girl with golden hair still lingered in his mind. He recognized her. He saved her in the sea for what, to destroy her family in the evening? God! He's a scoundrel! He felt to himself so bad and dirty. His conscience tormented him, and is it still there? Martin sat on the grass, opened a bottle of whiskey, and took a sip, then another sip. He threw the hands back on his head and lay on grass already wet from the dew, and exhaustion overtook him.

# CHAPTER 5

*You got me with a new libel wounded.*

*Well! To the grave I can see more clearly my way...*

*The monument from anger washed by you,*

*Soon it crushed my quivering breast.*

*You sigh... How long?*

*With sweet revenge the eyes*

*Light up again for an enemy;*

*Will you languish all night long?*

*"To live without taking mean revenge, - you say - I can't!"*

*And now I know from the crude grave*

*Have sorry for your age,*

*Not yours, cunning broken power*

*And that, why are you, my enemy – a man*!

*F. Nicshe*

Jain Mozhardin finally raised his hands to the top of the old man Mohammed.

"What is the emergency call?" asked the countrywoman from Morocco.

"I'm scared. God decided to play a cruel joke with me." The old man's face wrinkled, and his eyes grew dim, "My granddaughter hadn't come to life has been like two days."

Jain Mozhardin looked at Mohammed and asked again, "And what happened?"

Mohammed told the girl's life story and her tragedy, "After a terrible storm two days ago, Caroline had not regained consciousness. She sank into a deep sleep and probably..."

Jain Mozhardin interrupted Mohammed, "Don't even think about it. Maybe there is hope. Lead me to her," the woman said mysteriously.

The old man rose from his wooden armchair and, barely moving his feet, showed the way into her room. Before Jain Mozhardin walked in, he took her hand and said, "I beg you, help her..."

Jain Mozhardin smiled sweetly, went into the light room, and closed the door behind. She sat on the edge of the bed and looked at Caroline. 'What a beautiful creature, like an angel in the halo of sanctity resting on the clouds,' Jain Mozhardin thought. Caroline's long eyelashes laid a shadow on her cheek. Lips like pinkish roses were slightly opened. Jain marked the true appearance of Caroline, "For our hakim, it would be a great wife,"

The lady smiled sweetly, "Even the beautiful Reina is not a worthy opponent." Jain Mozhardin's hand rose above the girl's head but quickly removed it and pressed it to her chest, "Oh, God! You're like a block of ice, but fortunately still alive."

Jain Mozhardin got out of bed and sat down on her knees in front of the window. Clasped hands before her breast and pleaded, "Our Lord! Accept from us, for You, indeed - hearing, who knows everything…"

After the prayer, she went to Caroline and pulled a small bottle of aromatic oil from her hidden pocket. She brought it close to Caroline's nose, and a faint blush appeared on Caroline's face as she inhaled the scent.

'Yes … dear, terrible shadow willing to carry you into the abyss'- Jain Mozhardin thought. The woman whispered some prayers over Caroline, and at the end, she left her in the room by herself.

Mohammed was sitting like a dog at the door, waiting for them. When he saw her, he asked, "How's she? How's Caroline?"

"Don't worry too much. Tomorrow, she will speak, and again, life will be hitting her. She's temporarily in a lethargic sleep," said Jain Mozhardin.

"Oh, to Allah! - With the ease," he sighed.

"Did you come by yourself?"

"No, I am accompanied by Moulay Ali."

Mohammed smiled broadly with delight, "Where is he?"

"In the yard or in the stables, inspecting your horses," gently and calmly replied a seer.

"Today, in your honor, I'll make a nice dinner. You were fed and delighted," the old man, as a child, ran to his best friend in the yard.

"Martin, I beg you, don't persuade me to be your company to this brutal place called the casino, you know," Victoria outraged, "That I can't stand by these institutions.

"Sister, dear, dear," he begged her, running around the room. "Why don't you pay attention to me? I'm for you with all my heart," Martin grinned.

Victoria looked at her brother angrily and seriously, "Back off, ha... You have a lot of girls who indulge you, so they're not enough for you?" She asked rudely. "You added on money. Chasing them will drag you into the grave, and your best friends will kill you," she screamed with bitterness in her voice.

Martin looked at Victoria insidiously; he went on one knee and held out his hands to her, "I know the hatred and envy of your heart. You are not big enough not to know hatred and envy. So be as large enough to not be ashamed."

Victoria grabbed the one glove and slapped Martin on his back with it.

He laughed, telling her several times, "However, the truth hurts..."

Their father came in and looked at the children, assessing the situation; he put his hands on his hips, wrinkled his brow, and asked, "So... What's going on here? What a showdown?"

Victoria looked at her father and said innocently, "My brother is a villain; he wants me to go with him to the casino, and I want Brian to go to the movies."

"You lie, you lie, it's not true," yelled Martin. "It's all of her..."

John smiled, looking into the eyes of his son, "Martin, I know your adventures, and I do believe her than you. Martin, it's not good to cheat on a father..." waving his finger like to a child, said John.

Martin turned and went into his room. On the phone, he called his butler and ordered him to prepare the red Cadillac.

The evening promised to be calm and pleasant, filled with a romantic aroma. The sun had set behind the towering buildings, and the lights of Chicago began to glow, brightening the city. John stepped onto the balcony and saw Martin's butler. 'Interesting,' he thought. 'Where is this pup going now?' Martin prepared a small bag, put on his sports shoes, and went down to the car with a grace, easy gait. The father watched his son. 'And I thought he would wear a tuxedo to entertain the girls. Hmm ... where did he decide to rush?'

Martin jumped into the car and, with creaking tires, went to the bridge. He wanted to lose, relieve stress, put heavy stones on a soul, and just unwind at the back of his champion. As soon as he arrived at the ranch Coyote, he was met by Dawson, a young Canadian who helped him in training. Martin left his car and effectively removed the sunglasses and asked the friend to ride Ivanhoe.

"Yes, sir, in a minute, your horse will be ready," and he ran into the stall.

Martin Fury took the bag and went into the locker room to change clothes.

He put on a suit for riding; he sighed and went to the site. A pleasant breeze greeted him kindly. Martin was in anticipation of an evening walk. The guy looked around the area, and his gaze settled on the well-shaped figure of a brunette with curly hair. She was talking with John Bly, his rival in the race. Martin put on his gloves, clenched his fists, and bit his lower lip as he watched his adversary. Bly broke off his conversation with a dear lady, shook her hand, and walked away.

She gently held her gaze on him, and Martin, seeing it, didn't miss the opportunity to exercise his flirt, "You have a lovely filly," with a bright smile, walked over to her Martin.

The girl noticed the attractive dimples at the corners of Martin's mouth. He seemed like such a nice young man, and his beautiful chocolate eyes sparkled like bright stars.

She modestly lowered her eyes, wondering, "You think so?"

"No, I'm sure of it," calmly said Martin, looking at the girl's legs and licking his lips.

"And where is your horse?" the lady asked gently.

He liked her shyness and mystery. His raven friend was summed up to Martin. He took the horse by the bridle and looked at her appreciatively mare, "Your horse seems a thoroughbred?"

The girl raised an eyebrow and smiled slightly, and she said, " Do you want to see her?"

"And who would refuse such a temptation?" Smartly, he smiled.

The beautiful creature turned its back to him and put her foot in the stirrup. He looked at the girl's legs, then slyly looked down and jumped on his horse.

"Young man, you want to compete?" she asked.

"Yes. Let's start with the white line and up to over there, that tree," Martin showed her the place of finish.

On the count of three, they raced on horseback as the demons. Martin's Ivanhoe was running and was in front. For the lady, it was hard to catch up with his stallion, but Martin decided to play to flatter the pride of a stranger. She came first, though aware that there was something fishy. After she left the field, Martin rode for a while and then decided to follow a lady. As the villain, he found and watched her. When she decided to take a shower, he emerged from the clothing wardrobe in the women's locker room and ambushed his victim in a bathroom stall. Martin held her against the glass and clung to her wet lips hungrily and passionately.

She resisted and struggled, but after the sweet and hot kisses of his, she gave in - put her arms around his waist and then slid her hand on his wet back. Kisses were long, assertive, fiercely wanting her flesh, but he yelled as she scratched his back with nails like a wild cat. Passion has swept them both. He wanted to demonstrate his power and authority. He was one of those men who wanted two things: danger and play, so he wanted a woman as the most dangerous toy. He didn't want to understand that his father had taught that a man should be brought up for war and women for the recreation of the war and everything else is stupidity, but Martin wanted passion and madness. And now, in the hands of passion, he felt defenseless.

The pretty lady followed Martin's lead as he invited her to straddle him. She was eager and thrilled, her body craving his touch. They kissed, embraced, and moaned in unison, lost in a fast, passionate encounter. Afterward, he returned home exhausted and weary. On the threshold of the stairs, he met a sister who was saying something, accompanying gestures and words of her story. Martin didn't pay any attention to her yelling. He calmly walked up the stairs, barely entered his room, and slammed the door right behind him. With great reluctance, he took off his shirt and looked at his back in the mirror. When he saw red stripes, Martin wilted. The bed and freshly smelled sheets accepted him eagerly. He closed his eyes, and the dream carried him away.

In honor the meal was ready for guests. All three gathered at one table and discussed things of the past days. Moulay Ali is an old man like Mohammed. He cheerfully told to his brother about his adventures and the glorious son named Raymond Moulay Ali, the hakim of Rabat, "Raymond, my son, is a true warrior who never sits still," Moulay Ali said with pride.

Mohammed raised his eyebrows in surprise and looked at Jain Mozhardin, whose dark brown eyes glimmered slyly, and then he asked, "I wonder if the bride was found for this fine fellow."

Moulay Ali twirled his thin white beard in his fingers and said, "Reina wants to become his wife, but their marriage still is out of the question because of the endless strike that my son loves."

Jain Mozhardin lowered her eyes and put her words in a conversation, "However, Reina is a beautiful girl and respected in our area. She is famous for her ingenuity and a flexible mind, but she is very proud and capricious."

Mohammed became absorbed in thoughts of Caroline. He began to think about whether he should let her go off to such distant lands and what was expected there for her.

Mohammed, from the guest's conversations, didn't like Reina. She seemed a mysterious person to him, a woman who wanted to get not only a hakim but his land too, where he acted only to his laws and money into the bargain. Moulay Ali looked at his friend, deep in thought.

He became very interested in what Hasaan thought, "Mohammed?" asked Moulay Ali, "What do you think?"

The old man smiled slightly, "Oh, about my granddaughter and her future. Interesting, what is it happening now to her?"

Jain Mozhardin turned her attention to Mohammed, realizing that the old man was completely confused. She decided to resolve the situation, "Mohammed, with your granddaughter, everything is fine. Just now, she is resting and recruited new forces."

"And you think that this is normal? You're kidding me!" The old man protested.

"You called me in time. Her heavy condition could be timeless soon, but she recovers and wakes up from her lethargy," brown, like chocolate eyes, looked at Mohammed, "I know you love her. She's a nice girl and..."

"Where did you get that? You don't know her..." he looked incredulously at her dark face.

She humbly bowed her black, thick eyelashes and put her bun in a mouth. Mohammed waited for an answer. Jain Mozhardin continued, " Her face is wide open, and her plump lips are sensual and sexy," she paused, watching nervously stirring cheekbones face of Mohammed.

"You are well aware that the East says that this is a woman of love; you can rest assured that your granddaughter will be a heartbreaker," Jain Mozhardin stopped at her phrase and slowly continued her dinner.

Mohammed never thought about it, reflecting on the Jains words, he lowered his head sadly and looked at his plate.

Moulay Ali kindled a desire to see her by himself to evaluate her and see if she was as beautiful as Jain Mozhardin says. Many women passed before his eyes, each with her own virtues, yet a good or bad woman still demands the whip, a truth Reina sought through all known methods. In the flashes of her love, injustice, and blindness to all she dislikes, even when aware of her love, she remains a surprise, a lightning bolt in the night near the light. She is like cats and birds. Moulay Ali knew that too long had been hidden in a woman, a slave, and a tyrant. That is why the woman is not capable of friendship because she knows only love. Moulay Ali smiled in his soul with the thoughts: 'Ha, and look at these men: their eyes saying that they know nothing better on earth as it lay near the woman, and all because at the bottom of their souls - filth, but those, however, the soul of man is deep, its flux noise in the underground caves, a woman realizes his strength, but does not comprehend it, and the soul of a woman is a surface, mobile, stormy film on shallow water - these are the women of the East.'

# CHAPTER 6

*Will – is a force which is due to existence.*

**A. Schopenhauer**

The sun rose, casting its morning rays on Marseille on a Saturday morning, which is at the mercy of sleep. The unusually attractive and alluring blue sky promised a beautiful, clear day, inviting people to the beach. The wind was barely noticeable. A sunbeam struggled to slip into Caroline's room through the window, eventually succeeding. The light fell on her eyes, causing them to screw up in discomfort. The bright ray awakened Caroline; she instinctively placed a hand over her eyes and wrinkled her nose, emitting a soft moan. Her body, like a metal, stuck to the surface. She felt muscle weakness and a failure of some sort. The girl opened her eyes and looked out the window. The curtains moved slightly.

She gained a deep breath of air in her lungs, lazily got up from bed, and felt a pain in the neck; she touched her pain muscle with her fingers and slightly massaged it. Her calm eyes examined the room, searching for something new and unfamiliar. Wandering eyes fell on a little table and soft ottoman beside it. On the windowsill, singing a song from the branch, jumped a little bird as if welcoming a girl. The corner of Caroline's lips involuntarily stirred, wanting to smile. Something nice lifted her sad heart. In silence, the girl sat on the bed and patted her eyes slowly, watching the bird. She was such a quick creature with its twisted tail swiftly.

She shifted her eyes from the little bed on the floor at the foot of her bed. On the floor were little slippers trimmed with gold and silver. The tip of the nose was slightly elevated and concave. Caroline was very surprised with this shoe. She swung her legs off the bed and tried them on. Finally, she forced herself to stand. Her legs felt as if they were filled with cotton wool, making them difficult to move. However, through sheer willpower, she managed to reach the dressing table and sat down on the ottoman.

Slowly, she looked at herself in the mirror and was horrified: 'I have never been so neglected: disheveled hair matted from sleep, dark circles under the eyes.' The girl opened her drawer and took out the cotton swabs, then she soaked some liquid and rubbed her eyes. She took a comb and brushed it through the hair several times. 'Now I look like a normal girl.' She scratched her back with a brush and did a little massage on her hands and feet.

With her thoughts in disarray, she approached the large closet, unsure of what to wear. The selection was limited to just three dresses. After some deliberation, she settled on the light pink dress, which effortlessly slipped over her body. Without bothering with styling, Caroline opened the door, left the room, and found herself in the parlor, where her grandfather and two unfamiliar individuals were seated.

Her sudden appearance caught the attention of all present. Jain Mozhardin could not even think that Mohammed's granddaughter was so beautiful and nice, 'blond with emerald eyes and graceful figure will be a real treasure in our area' - thought Jain Mozhardin – 'Reina would be furious, meeting this girl.' Mohammed sprang from the couch and instantly found himself near the granddaughter, hugging her.

"Oh! Caroline, you couldn't even imagine how I thank God for what he brought you to life, my girl," with tears in his eyes, an old man explained, "I'm so afraid to lose you forever," Mohammed shook with joy, pulling her hands.

Caroline is staring with wonder at her grandfather, not knowing what he is talking about.

Jain Mozhardin came up to Caroline quietly, and the gentle voice said, "Honey, you slept four days, and your dream could drag on indefinitely, but your grandfather called me from Meknes, and I brought you out of this condition," explained the situation Jain Mozhardin.

Caroline looked at a woman of thirty. She slowly came up to her close and touched with her palm the woman's cheek, treating the dark skin and black of her eyelashes. Carefully, with a deep interest the girl was evaluating her clothes that hung in many tiers on the body of this stranger. Mohammed is watching his granddaughter and decides to introduce guests.

"Caroline, these guests of mine came from Morocco by my invitation," Grandfather explained, "This woman named Jain Mozhardin is a local seer and healer, and this man…" he pointed to the Moulay Ali, "Is my best friend and comrade, Moulay Ali, he accompanies Jain Mozhardin." Caroline inspected the people suspiciously and, without saying a word, walked past them, wanting to see her only friend at the stables. She slowly, like a ghost, came to the door and retreated into the yard. Moulay Ali was stunned by the beauty of the girl. She is awesome and submissive. In general, it will be easy to persuade her to Islam and marry Raymond. Now, Moulay Ali was considering how it would be better to communicate with her. Jain Mozhardin caught the train of Moulay Ali's thoughts slightly, smiled, and looked back at Mohammed.

"When can we take her with us?" Without departing from the subject, the woman demanded Raphael's promise; "Ali wants to see his niece."

Mohammed lowered his eyes and reluctantly answered, "Tomorrow, you can go to Meknes with Caroline. You need to tell her everything and prepare her for a trip."

Jain Mozhardin decided to do it.

On this cool evening, Brian sat in his stately mansion apartment, surrounded by wandering Rottweilers and Dobermans, seeking out any intruders. In his hand, he held a cup of coffee, engrossed in technical literature. While he appreciated the work of law enforcement agencies, his true passions lay in computers and medicine.

He has few friends, but the most faithful and loyal. His friends worried that he had no idol, no lover, and that all the time he devotes to college and reading books. He believes that the book - is the best friend in which you can find so much wisdom and most usefulness for his witty mind. Brian has always been prudent and cool, and he never showed his emotions. He was cold as ice, and ice can burn just like the fire itself. That's why he seems to some ardent and attractive.

Every weekend, he drives with his friends to the tennis court to unwind a little bit.

One day, Martin, looking at his brother, desired to learn how to play tennis too, so they could enjoy each other's company, but he failed. That kind of sport was just not for him at all. Then, he decided to plant his bad habits but was again defeated. Brian is practically unapproachable and very correct, and this greatly irritated Martin, especially 'no drinks, no smokes, no flirt, no sex and a lot of such NO... But why, then we live for? In addition to all that mentioned above, this blue-eyed hunk draws most of the brother's girlfriends with its bright, almost angelic look. Women are interested in the mystery of his views, tranquility, and even more - inaccessibility. The desire of these young ladies is to conquer this "iceberg," but no one has never been able to succeed in luring him into their female trap. He simply didn't meet her, that unique and inimitable. Colleagues, friends, and acquaintances think he is out of this world.

And they all seemed the same to him. Women for Brian, a mess, weakness, confusion in thoughts, and finally - the source of the worst follies committed by a man who does not pull it to the women, it would be all it takes to win. He more and more came to this conclusion by looking at his brother.

Brian was deeply troubled by the realization that his family, particularly his father, had become deeply involved in criminal activities. He was aware that they were all part of a gang, and he felt powerless to change the situation. Brian knew he had to accept things as they were, as he was under the influence and guidance of John. Nevertheless, he was very pleased with the fact that the disposal had a team of military, necessary machines, which the father brought from the Japanese, three estates, two powerful corporations, and two banks. The only thing which they did not have was a military aircraft. John failed to establish friendly diplomatic relations with Russian heads.

They didn't want to recognize him as one of the major leaders in the United States and, therefore, ignored John's Fury calls. His best friend, Trey Parker is a very fruitful help in international business. Recently, they together made a good deal on weapons sales to the Japanese, and on the earned money, they opened a new company for developing projects to improve technology. The grand opening day door ceremony was attended by all members of the

Fury family, Parker, and other large shareholders, for this evening arrived ambassadors, consuls, interpreters, reporters, and other major shots of the state. In the exceptional room were a lot of people, who learned about and discussed their interests.

Brian and Martin couldn't leave the shared spot from the buffet, where they relished the food. Everything was so delicious that you couldn't drag them out. Martin was standing with a saucer in the hands sideways, watching the girls. Brian pretended not to notice it:

"Pretty ladies here, aren't they?" said Brian, with his gaze following an eye-catching brunette in a navy elegant dress.

Martin raised an eyebrow and said with a sneer, "Bro.., I don't understand how you can always be so calm, cold, and indifferent to women. Are you..."

"If you say it, you'll get on the forehead, got it?" He blasted into a rage, scratching the bottom of his palm.

"Oh, oh, oh, I'm scared," Martin said, drinking a glass of champagne. After enjoying its taste, he turned to his guests, and his eyes froze at the sight of a shapely lady's legs and a graceful waist. A girl in a black evening dress was very attractive. In Martin's mind, the idea to seduce her revived quickly. Brian grabbed his brother by the arm and said softly, "And don't do it. You will regret it later."

"Oh, what do you know about women?" Sighed Martin.

The girl turned her face to the brothers and drew her attention to them. Martin stood still at a meeting with her gaze, heavily swallowing his drink. This was the same brunette with golden brown, almost like a falcon's eyes. Winking, she waved at Martin and smiled sweetly at him. Brian caught her enigmatic smile and pushed his brother's shoulder."Go ahead. Say hello to the lady if you're familiar with her. She likes you. Just please don't do anything stupid."

Martin, clutching to his chest a glass-like his own, came over to her and her boyfriend.

"Good evening, good day today, isn't it?" Martin said hesitantly.

"Oh, well, Mr. Fury," the lady said with courtesy. "Dad, do you know this young gentleman? The lady smoothly turned to the man standing next to her with a glass of red wine."

"Ha-ha, and how! Mr. Fury is known by everyone." Her daddy smiled with satisfaction and some kind of slightly uncatchable pride; "Sweetheart, we know him as the luckiest risk-taker, a good player at our poker table, and the finest rider."

"Yes, a good rider," she agreed with her father in a husky voice. She appraisingly glanced from toe to head at Mr. Fury and continued drinking her champagne, still gazing at him with promising new adventures smile.

Martin grinned, and his magnetically dark brown eyes sparkled like two hard black diamonds, "You should be a proud dad, by the way; your daughter introduced me to a great thoroughbred filly she hides here in stables."

The girl's father looked at both of them, feeling perplexed. They were speaking in a coded language that only they understood. Feeling bored, he decided to greet his old friends instead. He excused himself and hurriedly left the young people alone.

"Mr. Fury, do you really think that I have a great thoroughbred..."

"Yes," quickly interrupted her, Martin, "I have not seen such a marvelous and fast thoroughbred."

"Really? And how many of them you have seen so far?" In a sexy and seductive way, biting her lower lip, she asked.

Martin felt the weakness in his knees being around her. The heat from his body made him move his tie and grasp for some air. His thoughts became confused, and his speech faltered. His eyes slowly wandered in search of another object to focus.

"Mr. Fury, are you all right?" She winked virtuously, showing off her mystic smile.

"Mmm.., I guess yes." His voice sounded deep and horsy. "It seems to me I... I think I should get away for a while."

At this point, it was hard for Martin to control himself; he smoothly shifted his eyes to Brian and noticed his side smile and approving nod.

Martin mumbled to himself, 'Here's a rascal.'

"What did you say?" Asked the girl still gazing at Mr. Fury with great pleasure to continue their perspective friendship with benefits.

"It's not for you, sweetie. Better tell me your name ..." he gently whispered to her.

"I'm waiting for you tonight here in the garden with roses, and you love to admire stars, don't you, darling? See you at exactly ten p.m., honey," the girl whispered in his ear and slowly walked away to the noisy guests joining them.

Martin hopelessly closed his eyes and laid his hand on his forehead. 'Christ!'

"I can see that you know each other pretty much," said Brian, approaching his brother from behind. "I can see she intruded into your heart."

Martin didn't answer; he didn't have the strength to say anything. Brian emptied the martini glass, patted his brother on the shoulder, and walked into the conference room.

# CHAPTER 7

*Suffering is the most rapid way to comprehend the truth.*

***Zarathustra***

The sound of the sea is moaning, harboring a melody of melancholy. Caroline's packed things were placed in the trunk of the taxi, and Mohammed made out certain formalities with the documents.

Jain Mozhardin draped Caroline in light silk, covering her golden hair with a brocade shawl. Caroline obediently followed the instructions of this mysterious woman. Her mind filled with thoughts of her upcoming life in this unfamiliar land. Alongside a sense of anticipation, she also felt a hint of anxiety, her thoughts becoming entangled in inexplicable confusion. However, the presence of Jain Mozhardin calmed her, and Caroline relaxed, feeling cared for her. She confided herself in the hands of this woman and was not afraid of the unknown.

"Well, look at this. Do you like it?" Jain Mozhardin asked the girl, turning her to the mirror.

The new image delighted Caroline. She looked at her reflection and realized that this new image she liked very much, and her smile lit up her face. Her eyes sparkled, and her hands wandered all over her body, feeling the clothes' smoothness. Jain Mozhardin was happy that she could charge the girl's mood and recharge her with her positive energy. In return, Caroline felt grateful towards this woman, along with an inexplicable sense of sympathy. She turned slowly in front of the mirror, admiring her new appearance, before finally turning to face Jain Mozhardin, who returned her gaze with an appraising and kind smile. Caroline approached the woman and took both her hands in her palms.

A gentle, mellifluous voice finally escaped from her lips, "Thank you very much for your attention. I really like the way I look now," gazing into her eyes, said Caroline. "I'm like a princess from the eastern fairytales, never thought that I would be here as it is now," she smiled.

"I didn't even guess that I was meeting such a sweet girl as you. I don't know why, but I immediately liked you, and I am very glad that you remain happy with my gift."

After this frank recognition of each other, they went outside where they had been expected by Mohammed and Moulay Ali.

Raymond's Father set a goal for himself – no matter what but immediately united his beloved son with Caroline. Her beauty subdued Moulay Ali so much that he forgot all about her future main rival – Reina.

Everything was ready to leave for the airport. Caroline wanted to say goodbye to her grandfather and at the same time to ask him a main question.

"Tell me, did the police find the killers?"

Mohammed lowered his head sadly and shook it negative response, "No. Unfortunately, the police found nothing. Decided to close the case with the assertion that it was an accident because there was a gas leak, and the house exploded."

"Well, of course, the police was corrupted," said Caroline bitterly, "and I know who did it."

"Do you know?" Mohammed was surprised.

"Yes, I know. And I promise that I will take revenge."

"But who is it?"

"You will find out," said Caroline. "I will miss you so much and often remember you." She threw herself on his neck and hugged him tightly.

Mohammed was overwhelmed by her sincere goodbye gesture.

"Come back, I'll wait for you always, my granddaughter," and he kissed her cheek and gave her hand into the Moulay Ali's arm and Jain Mozhardin.

All three of them got inside a yellow cab, and the vehicle's engine started. Caroline pressed her hands against the glass, looking at Mohammed; his silhouette started disappearing from the rolling-up tears stuck in her eyes. Her heart was pounding, and she could hear her beating pulse in her ears. The taxi moved fast to its destination.

Jain Mozhardin saw the girl's suffering and decided to support her, "Honey, come here and put your head on my shoulder."

Caroline looked up at the woman with a trust and moved closer to her. Jain Mozhardin stroked her face and told her soothing words, and then she clasped her hands in Caroline's hands.

Caroline watched through the window, observing as the native place of her rush past, where most recently she played and frolicked, riding horses with Philippe, bathing in the sea, took dancing classes, and now it is all in the distant past. This car was carrying her away to where her new life was waiting. The girl, feeling a pain in her chest, closed her eyes and tried to relax, pushing the thoughts away. The wounds from losing her parents had not yet healed and still ached within her. But Caroline knew as soon as she arrived in Meknes, she would educate and gather all of her power into a fist and would be the one who would see herself in the massacre with the enemies.

Remembering the brutal scene of her sister's rape and cruel reprisals with her father and mother, Caroline didn't even suspect that men could be so cruel. She knew them under the name of Fury, exactly these murderers she would search for when the time was right. Her eyes were dimmed by a terrible desire to grab with a death grip one of them in the throat to silicate forever.

The passionate desire for rage coursed through her veins, but every passion has its moment when it turns fatal, drawing its prey into the abyss. There, she fell and flew, hardened by her own foolishness. But Caroline's passion was completely different. It was more like a baby dragon, which had just been born, pulling its still unable to fly wings. But the time will come when the wounds heal and tighten, and the passion of the desire will unite with her spirit and "inspire," and the dragon of her heart will be ready to have a terrible battle. But now Caroline doesn't know any reason to be with a male except hatred, contempt, and desire for revenge.

Three of them arrived at the airport in Marseille. The runway was clean, and everything was ready for flight. Passengers climbed up the ladder to board the plane. Caroline, accompanied by Moulay Ali and Jain Mozhardin, was approaching to land the aircraft. After checking the tickets and documents, all of them were placed in soft and very comfortable chairs in the salon. Jain Mozhardin sat next to a girl so she wouldn't feel lonely.

Caroline comforted herself in a chair and drew her attention to the hatch.

The opening of the Fury and Parker new company was successful. On a competitive basis, the company's employees "Lex" gained a working structure for future cooperation based in Chicago.

John's face shone with self-satisfaction and pride, and he was as happy as a little boy who bought a new toy gun. Brian and Martin were now settled down in one of the offices in the company, they solved the issue of employment as a start. Their community welcomed a father who guided his sons in determining their duties and recognizing each one's abilities. John entrusted Brian with the role of manager in the technical department and the head of the enhanced weapons storage. Martin was appointed with the job easier – the Head of shareholders and managers.

John observed the situation with his shrill eye and knitted his brows.

"So," he snarled, "Where is Victoria?"

Martin shrugged.

Brian said, "It seems that she rushed to Paris with her new love boy."

John gritted his teeth and made a pout with his thoughts, 'What the hell? Damn this France'.

Victoria Fury is the most agile and most fortunate child in this family. Gently steps and goes far. Will always find a way out of any situation, even if thousands of roads lead to confusion. She relied on her feminine intuition to find only one that leads to a truth.

Headstrong and proud, smooth and soft, John adored his daughter and all she did wrong has always been forgiven. She is the one true woman as John considered her; this woman is capable of confusing any man's mind, even the most obstinate and legible.

With open, innocently treacherous eyes, she captivated the hearts of wealthy men in Chicago. Yet, she grew bored, weary of them, and thus, she ventured out in search of something new.

Martin was afraid of her for some reason he could feel his equal rival here in the field of life. Brian, on the other hand, was a friend of hers and trusted his dreams and got good advice from her. For him, she is like a mother, sister, and maybe one more. Her only desire is to find happiness and to be loved and never be a slave to her man, only to preserve her freedom because freedom - is the force that is in her hands. She held on to its tail tightly as if she did not want to escape from it.

Today, everyone was busy, and nobody was bored, even lazy Martin, who had decided to introduce his brother to his friends, about which Brian didn't even guess. He was busy planning his workplace while sitting at the computer; he modeled the possible setting of his office.

Floating, barely touching the ground under his feet, Martin gracefully walked into Brian's office, and he wasn't alone. At his side, he was accompanied by his best friends. Brian left his tall chair to greet his brother. Martin's comrades are all basically guys in their mid-twenties, mostly dressed in dark suits. They were tall, graceful, athletic, and well-built young men, bearing a striking resemblance to each other. Collectively, they made an impressive sight. Martin took the lead in introducing him to his friends, harboring a great hope that one day Brian would join their gang.

"Brother, meet with my friends, Jack Duke, William James, Henry Douglas, Chris Wren, and my best friend Jayson Parker." Brian shook hands with each of them, showing off an affable smile.

"I didn't know that you have so many friends."

Martin grinned and winked, whispering so only Brian could hear, "You don't know anything about me."

Brian looked suspiciously at Jayson and said, "And aren't you accidentally Trey Parker's son?"

"Incidentally, yes..."

It wasn't long after meeting with the new guys, Brian had already chosen a friend for himself – like-minded and complimenting his interests among all Martin's friends. The new friend turned out to be Jason Parker. This young stud, barely turning legally twenty, with a very open heart and incredibly tender soul, which can be easily hurt by careless words for a long time to forgive and forget.

Only in Jason's presence did Brian's cold heart melt, and he was becoming an interesting conversationalist and an excellent companion. Their friendship grew, and they were mostly all the time spotted together. Local magazines and the pages of freshly printed newspapers were portraying them together all around at the most significant events.

Martin noticed this and was glad that his brother was finally accepted into his circle of friends. Thus, he learned how to conduct free and lead a permitted way of life. Brian attended all the educational institutions where were his new friends. Jason, on the weekends, was always evaporated in the gym or sports club. Brian gave up the tennis lessons and became more and more sucked into his office duties as work must be done first than pleasure and leisure. And he has paid less attention to Jason and more talking to Chris Wren. Surprisingly, Jason was not offended; he was a free-roaming cat, just like Victoria walked herself, being engaged with what his soul desired.

But Victoria has disappeared from the field of view in her friend's circle and paparazzi spots for some time. There was no answer of greeting or cheering from her, and this mysterious trick began to disturb the Fury family.

# CHAPTER 8

*If we treat the power with conscience, it will be kissing us.*

The human soul and its limits have been made so far some amount of internal human experience, height, depth, and distance of this experience, all of which lasted until now the story of the soul, and it has endless possibilities - this is designed for a born psychologist and lover of the "great hunt" in a hunting area. But how often he has to say in despair: "Oh, I am alone! Oh! I'm so lonely in this great forest!" And he wants to have a hundred assistants for hunting and some well trained dogs, which he could send into the history of the human soul that they all drove there with his whole game.

In vain: he is bitterly convinced each time that it is difficult to find assistants and dogs in the area that excites his curiosity. The disadvantage of sending scholars into new and dangerous areas that require courage, wisdom, the subtlety in every sense is that they are not suitable where there begins a 'big hunt,' as well as great danger just there. They lose their flair and acuity of vision.

Being in the East, Caroline was more convinced that unusual people were Muslims. Islam is based on ancient Arabic and Jewish traditions and sought to deform the mystical, emotional, and aesthetic relationship of man to the world at all levels: at the level of ideas, concepts, theology, and ceremonies and at the level of sentiment. He strove to ensure that the structure of the Muslim faith was absolute, devoid of any reminders of the beauty of the mortal world, including his own beauty and perfection.

The women here were like prisoners with limited abilities and no right of choice. They don't know what freedom is and are burning their life days in front of the mirror, like dolls, dressing up and waiting for their men. Their conversations were repetitive, discussing the same topics day after day—clothes, jewelry, and rivals. It all seemed like a complete waste of time.

Caroline is irritated by the monotony and stillness. She knew by hearsay that there was a bride for Hakim, but she had probably never seen her for some reason, and she was not interested in her either. Though Reina was interested in Caroline, Jain Mozhardin disliked Reina so much. Once upon a time, there was an unpleasant conversation between them in the garden. Jain Mozhardin had overtaken Reina near the fountain and started it, "My dear Reina, I think that the moment came when we have to talk and to agree here."

"What do you mean?" wondered the young woman.

"You are well aware that you are a reluctant person for me here..."

"What comes over you?" protested Reina.

"All this time, I have endured your presence, but now it's time for you, and when you have to leave, the sooner the better," Jain Mozhardin said softly. Reina Parker was stunned by her words, but Jain Mozhardin didn't calm down and continued to demand, "Go away, Reina, it's the best you can do in this case."

"You repulse me because of this girl..."

Jain Mozhardin interrupted her speech and dramatically, with some tension, replied, "This girl, as you say, will become a new member of our family, and she belongs to this palace. Our Hakim deserves to marry her."

"Why are you so confident? Look at her, and she's a child. She isn't ready to be a wife yet. She is green as that fruit before the August crop," proudly raised her head, Reina.

"A strong woman is hidden in this child who will satisfy all the needs of our people and her husband, too."

Reina was angry and hissed through her teeth, "I'll never give up."

Jain Mozhardin slyly smiled and replied to this statement, "Do you want to see how Raymond will ignore your presence and devote all of his attention to her and not to you? I think it is demeaning for a girl like you."

Reina, in silence, looked down and thought about her words. Indeed, in some ways, Jain was right.

"Reina, the sooner you leave our lands, the better for you," calmly and in a convincing tone, stated Jain Mozhardin.

"Well, I will leave," strictly answered the young lady. "But be aware, I'll be back, and everything will be mine," with these words, Reina retired from the garden.

Jain Mozhardin looked at her leaving way with a smile, proudly raising her head, feeling her victory.

Morning arrived. The sun rose above the horizon, and its rays pleased the sad faces of citizens. Caroline was lying on the couch and listening to popular music when Jain Mozhardin sat beside her.

The girl looked at the seer and asked her, "Tell me, have you ever been married?"

Jain Mozhardin looked down sadly and replied, "Yes, just once, but my husband was killed in the army of Moulay Ali when they were fighting for our land in the desert."

"I'm sorry, Jain Mozhardin, I didn't want to disappoint you. I just thought that such a beautiful woman like you can't be lonely."

"I loved him very much; we stayed in the marriage for six years."

"Why don't you have children?" Wondered Caroline.

"Probably because Allah has punished me for disobeying our parents. They were against our marriage with Cyrus, and so Allah hasn't blessed us."

Jain Mozhardin paused after these words. There was a silence. It took a little when she spoke again, "I guess you noticed that I relate to you more than to a friend or sister..."

"Yeah, more like to a daughter," slightly smirked Caroline.

"For this reason, I decided to give you my dearest treasure, and I'm sure it will be safe while you have it."

"What do you, Jain Mozhardin? You don't need to do it!"

The woman got up and went to a tiny room, where she took a small casket and brought it to the girl. Jain Mozhardin opened it and showed it to her friend.

"Oh, God!" Exclaimed fascinated Caroline, "It's a gold ring with a diamond!"

"Exactly. This stone gives virtue, courage, and victory, it's the symbol of innocence, strength, and courage, and it for sure will give you confidence and strength," Jain smiled at her.

"I cannot accept it," Caroline was hesitant.

"The stone has a favorable effect in the event if it is inherited, I'll give it to you, and I want you to be its lord," the woman passed it over to Caroline and smiled.

Caroline took the casket in her hands and brought it closer to her face to view the ring. It is made from white gold in the form of a marquis-cut diamond, is large and extended along the whole ring; the stone shimmered like a rainbow.

The girl looked at Jain Mozhardin and said, "Thank you very much. It is beautiful, and I really like this ring."

"You're welcome, sweetheart. Though it will bring luck to you," Jain smiled.

Caroline took it out of the box and tried to put on her index finger. The ring fit her perfectly, sliding smoothly along her finger and shimmering in the light. Jain Mozhardin observed Caroline's fascination with the ring's beauty and decided to leave her alone with her gift. The girl regarded it attentively.

Her focus was interrupted by loud noises outside near the main entrance to the palace. Caroline whirled and ran out to a white balcony, from which was seen the main courtyard. Jain Mozhardin immediately followed the girl.

At the Courtyard, Caroline saw the great major of this city, legendary – Raymond Moulay Ali Hassam.

Everyone around is talking about this man, his expeditions, and his wanderings. Caroline, for a long time, wanted to meet him; however, the long absence of the hakim fueled her curiosity on low heat every day. In spite of her hate for men, she wanted to see a real man and a warrior in spirit and in body. And finally, the day came when he returned from his wanderings, which lasted three months.

Now he was sitting on his white as snow horse, dressed in royal splendor, and very similar to the one of three wise men from the picture in the Gospels.

Caroline drew attention to his face when he took off his white bandage. He is so uncommon - a typical, eastern face, somewhat dark, soft eyes open, full of deep wisdom and kindness and even more, the girl was surprised by his sky-blue eyes, which were rare in these areas, but this man exuded a real, true to an Arab man will and strong character. Caroline proudly lifted her head despite allowing herself to be influenced by him. As she watched him, she chose not to argue with the man and instead decided to become his closest friend. Jain Mozhardin watched the girl with deep interest, wanting to know her thoughts.

Caroline turned to her woman, taking her hand, "Soon, the dinner will be ready, and we have to be there."

The young woman looked at Jain Mozhardin and nodded back at her approvingly.

A woman rang the bell, and three dark women entered the room. In the hands they were holding towels and some boxes. Jain Mozhardin clapped her hands twice, and the servants of one another quietly retired to the bathroom. Caroline held a fascination in their eyes while Jain Mozhardin went to Caroline, helped to lift her dress, and dissolved her hair. Two maids had Caroline in the bathroom where the water was covered with red roses; it smelled of green tea and mint, which gave her courage.

Caroline, with pleasure plunged into the water and relaxed, considering in detail the room as if she had never seen it before. It was very nice; all charged to the blue-blue tiles on the ceiling, which rose above her head, flowers, elaborate moldings made of white clay. Two chocolate women quickly washed Caroline's head and moisturized creams, gels, and mousse to pamper her tender young body, which was fragrant, and screamed that it was fine. Caroline was wrapped in a terry-long veil after bathing; she was carried into the room where Jain Mozhardin sat her in front of the huge mirror.

"I will make from you a queen," Jain Mozhardin smiled, "Ready?"

"Yes."

Jain Mozhardin loosened her wet hair and started to dry. The girl obeyed without question to this woman, confided to her hands. Caroline liked how she was taking care of her, looking after her beauty, clothes, and even jewelry. She learned a lot while staying here: how to put on makeup, choose the oil for your body and skin when it's better to take a bath in the morning or evening and dress according to the situation in the house. Jain Mozhardin, for Caroline, is more than a girlfriend or sister; she completely replaced her mother, and Caroline fell in love with Jain by letting her reside in her heart, which was so lonely. And now she realized that the power of the East owned her entirely.

The last decoration, spangled with pearls and diamonds, fell on Caroline's head, making her a real queen, a lady of beauty and grace. The girl got up from the padded stool and went to the big mirror to see herself in full view. Looking at her reflection, Caroline didn't believe that this was her because today, she was extremely beautiful and attractive.

On her feet, she saw open shoes covered with small stones and sequins, which sparkled like a rainbow. And her new clothes were too beautiful for words. Caroline liked most of all a muslin shirt with long sleeves and a short, free, decorated embroidered vest. Caroline was fully prepared for dinner. Jain Mozhardin took her arm, and together, they descended to the family table.

Suddenly, Caroline stopped at the entrance and breathed out heavily. She felt suffocating. Jain Mozhardin glanced at the girl with a concerned look, "What happened?"

Caroline did not answer. She gasped for air and bit her lower lip, trying to figure out what had affected her so much. The strange tingling in her chest was certainly uncomfortable.

"Are you sick?"

"No," replied heavily Caroline.

"What's wrong with you?" Jain's worried tone was insisting and surprising. "Come on, they're waiting for us." She encouraged her.

The doors opened, and Caroline walked in carefully. She was looking calmly around in a slow search of her uncle's eyes. She appeared in front of the guests and the family in all her glory.

Uncle Ali, at the sight of his niece, stood up and greeted Caroline and Jain Mozhardin, "Here, my beloved!" He exclaimed.

Caroline was standing in her site like a frozen pale statue; her eyes were turned to the guests, Uncle and Hakim.

Raymond was very cheerful and was talking with his retinue. However, he stopped and was still having fun when the views of his friends were turned towards two young ladies. Raymond stood, stunned by the appearance of a beautiful girl he had ever seen. The girl with long hair was there in front of his blue eyes, shining in the rays of light like a veil of gold brocade.

Caroline sat in a little shallow curtsy, as it was before the court of the king, to deliver this outstanding person an evident pleasure. Raymond gazed with a watchful eye at Caroline from head to toe, especially appraising her graceful figure in the open Eastern dress. She firmly stood his mind, moving to the table and placing herself near Ali, who presented her to his guests and admired her. Next by her took her place Jain Mozhardin, her eyes were fixed on Hakim.

Ali got up with the cup of wine and talked to the guests with a speech, "Oh, people! Worship your Allah who created you and those who came before you," he looked at everybody, "Maybe you'll be God-fearing!" He paused.

Caroline leaned toward Jain Mozhardin and asked quietly, "What is it?"

"It is the prayer from the holy book."

And the guests repeated for Ali, "Amen."

Caroline was sitting in silence and only occasionally looked at the hakim, who so delicately dealt with a number of seated guests around him.

After dinner, Raymond caught Jain Mozhardin by herself near the kitchen and grabbed her by the elbow with a question, "Where is Reina? Why she was not with us?"

"How? Don't you know she went back to Chicago to her father and brother?" Asked Jain Mozhardin. Her eyes widened in surprise.

Raymond seriously knitted his brows.

"No, I don't know. But why has she left?"

Jain Mozhardin sighed heavily and answered, "She decided that you don't need her and left. I'm sorry, I don't know anything."

And Jain Mozhardin quietly walked away across the hall to the kitchen. Raymond stood still with a frustrated expression, just hearing the sad news. He probably had some feelings for Reina but didn't know how to express them to her. He was always uncomfortable in her presence. He looked at the porch and saw her – his Uncle Ali's niece.

The moon went behind to a large and dense cloud, but a large expanse of water in the fountain shone, molding a cool and quiet radiance. Suddenly, the water flashed, flickering and flashing, as if the water covered many fireflies. There were hundreds, maybe thousands - of flickering flashes scattered everywhere, brilliant flashing everywhere the eye could see. Caroline heard the crack of branches and turned sharply to see who was there.

She saw Raymond approaching her. He was over twenty-two years old, life in the wilderness, and his constant battles had tempered him, and he was a tall, handsome young man with an iron muscle. Dark face from cruel wind and weather has been spiritualized by thought. On this beautiful face shone like two stars, pure as crystal, with blue eyes. He was dressed in a home way, in a crimson satin vest and trousers, strapped at the waist with a silver belt. His gait is like a confident man. A moment later, he stood beside her. Caroline, leaning on the railing, turned the face to him and defiantly spoke, "Ah. Well, a legendary major, Raymond."

Across his face, there was a barely perceptible smile of light, "Mademoiselle Sauvage Roux, I see that you are well aware," said Raymond in French with a strong Arabic accent.

Only now, Caroline noticed that he was born in the north, as his dark skin color was due only to tan, which is reminded of toasted wheat bread. In general, it seemed to Caroline pretty sympathetic. Raymond decided to get acquainted with this amazingly attractive girl.

"I have always enjoyed the conversations with the French. They are nice people and not proud."

Caroline smiled pleasantly at his words.

"But they have one major flaw..."

Caroline was surprised, "What?"

"They are Christians."

Caroline responded to this that Christians, by contrast, believe that the biggest weakness of pagans, Jews, and Muslims is that they are not Christians, but she herself, being a conscious girl, said that the religious arguments are not her strong side. Raymond has approved a manifestation of humility; a weak woman's mind should not be rash to intrude into the depths of theology.

Caroline asked about his sea voyages and wished to know more about his campaigns. Raymond was very surprised by her pure interest in this sphere of his life because no females would ask him about his personality and his interests in the battles. Finding a proper companion in her, he told her about his life. Caroline enjoyed her conversation with him so much that she didn't notice how quickly time passed. Raymond escorted her to her bedroom door and bid her goodbye, kissing her hand as gallant gentlemen in France often do.

Being in a good mood so far, Caroline undressed herself and, with great fatigue, collapsed into her wide bed. She closed her eyes and smelled a slight sweetness of men's cologne. Her nose wrinkled in obvious surprise, and the tip of her tongue felt a drop of sleekness in her mouth. She tested it, trying to define its origins, and failed.

The day was very bright and hot. Martin was driving the car with an open top, and Jason sat beside him. The red Jaguar of the last model was turning smoothly. They were listening to music, having fun and singing performers. The sun blinded their eyes, and the guys put on dark sunglasses. The breeze was blowing in their face and ruffled their hair.

Jason was telling a friend about the fact that today he finally met his sister who came back from Meknes; he is willing to dance at her wedding, "She was going to get married there..."

"So...?"

Jason's face was a bit serious. After a short silence, he replied, "I don't know, you know something happened there. She was prevented by someone, so I want to go home and talk to her about it. I wonder who is offended my sister," with displeasure bit his lower lip, Jason Parker.

Martin watched the road, carefully turning the steering wheel; he quickly glanced at his friend and asked, "Do you have any assumptions?"

"God forbid her fiancé Moulay Ali Hassan, I will kill a scoundrel..."

Martin slowed down and looked anxiously at Jason Parker.

"Who? Say again. Is that Raymond?"

Parker shook his head, trying to remember. After a prolonged silence, he said, in the air, snapping his finger to Martin, "Listen, exactly, it's him."

"Asshole..." with displeasure, Martin hissed between his clenched teeth.

"But why? What is it? I don't understand..."

"My father had a problem with this guy," started his explanation to Martin, with a deeply serious expression on his face. "This

Raymond intercepted the big ship with a large commodity on it. It was sent to Spain."

Jason brushed his hair with a pocket comb and leaned against the car seat. He pressed his lips hard together and quickly glanced at Martin, "So? Did John roll his neck?"

"This is an open question and still a problem. Because this guy is a big fish, and you can't take him with just bare hands," Martin said anxiously, rubbing his lips with a hand.

Jason shook his head and said, "Jesus Christ."

The two friends sat in a long silence while driving and thought about the situation. Martin was nervously biting his lower lip, thinking about the idea of how to tell his father about Raymond's location, but he had a big desire to show his dad that he could do it by himself; he decided to hook up with Brian to this business, with his cold-blooded mind. Well, they could make a good plan to capture the enemy without their father's assistance.

Martin shared his thoughts with Jason, and he replied that he was naive and that he should act very carefully. To catch the enemy, they needed to first befriend him, gain his trust, and strike when he least expected it. Martin agreed with this strategy, and they planned to approach Brian after Jason had visited his sister.

A car ride has done well for Martin and Jayson. They drove up to the Parker's mansion and parked right in front of the main entry. Jayson entered the hallway first and was met by his father's butler.

"Oh, Mr. Parker, you are back already?"

"Where is my sister? Where is she?" Looking around, demanded Jason, placing hands on his hips.

Martin stood still behind his friend with folded arms on his chest. He expressed a serious, concentrated look.

The butler pointed to the office of his father. With rapid steps, Jayson and Martin went to the library. He opened the door and met with his sister's questioning facial expression. The gleam in her eyes flashed instantly, like lightning.

She got up from the chair and ran up to her brother, stretching her arms to him, "Jayson, brother."

They embraced warmly. She rested her head on his strong shoulder and his warm palm covered her silky hair in a gentle rub.

Martin humbly looked down and crossed his arms in front of him, gazing at his perfectly manicured fingers. Jayson slightly turned sideways to him and said, "Take it easy, you are not this kind of person," he winked, "Meet my sister. This is Reina."

"Hey, I'm Martin Fury. Nice to meet you!"

Reina looked at him as if he were a cartoon character or comedian.

"I thought you were different."

"Don't take my indiscretion, really?"

"More serious guy," the tips of her fingers touched the wrist, and the corners of his lips turned down, expressing a lack of interest in the interlocutor.

Martin found himself in no ease, and he turned to Jayson, "Don't you mind if I wait for you in the car?"

"Yep… Go."

After Martin's departure, her brother looked into Reina's eyes and asked impatiently, "What happened? Why do you look so sour?"

Reina fell into the chair with a deep sigh, "Jayson, it's over," she lowered her eyes. "I am not getting married."

"Did you break up with your fiancé?"

She looked into Jayson's hazel eyes with obvious sadness, "No, I abandoned him. He is not aware of my departure."

He squeezed her hands in his palms with a sorrowful expression on his face, "But why did you do that? I'm sure there's a reason."

Jayson wanted to know the 'root of evil' in his sister's heart.

"When I saw her – my competitor, I realized that the way to Hakim's heart… and," she paused her speech in a long silence, and then she finished, "to Raymond's heart is closed she was too strikingly beautiful, even though still so green."

Jayson looked understanding at Reina.

"In comparison to her, I'm just a gray mouse."

"Don't say that, sweetie." Jayson bent down on one knee in front of her, "You're the best and the most beautiful girl. Look at those black curls and those deep, awesome eyes, full of feelings," he caressed his sister.

"Really? Do you think so?" A spark of hope flared in her eyes.

"Of course," he smiled at her.

Martin was sitting in the car and in the rhythm of the song, was bumping his hand on the car door. After a while, he was joined by Jason, breathing hard from his quick walk.

"Friend," he turned, "you were right. Raymond is her fiancé."

Martin pressed his lips nervously, thinking well, he invited Jayson, "Let's go to 'Lex' and tell everything to Brian, and there we'll decide what to do."

Jay nodded.

"OK, let's go."

# CHAPTER 9

*Knowledge is power.*

***Monticello***

'If you have the knowledge, let others light their candles in. A bird doesn't sing because it has an answer. It sings because it has a song. We are not what we know but what we are willing to learn. Good people are good because they've come to wisdom through failure.' Day after day, month after month, Caroline learned the East better and better from Raymond's stories. He interrupted his military expeditions for her sake. He valued every minute that was held with her. Hakim performed all her wishes, even breaking the traditions and rights of the local women. He did everything in his power to please her and satisfy her needs. At the request of Caroline, Raymond's former teacher taught her to ride Arabian horses. Caroline's and Hakim's friendship grew stronger day by day, though Jain Mozhardin claimed that the friendship between a man and a woman is impossible because the woman knows only love, but in their case, everything was possible.

Raymond perceived Caroline in his own way. In her pure sight was not even the slightest hint of something more than friendship, and it surprised him because the local women loved him as a man, the lord of their hearts. Caroline was the opposite. She was interested in military skills, weapons, and all that had the slightest relation to the hostilities; she even hired teachers so they taught her self-defense.

Raymond, with pride, watched her, fostering in her a strong spirit and a power of will. Almost every evening, Raymond makes a fire in the courtyard and plays the guitar, singing different songs in Arabic. Caroline comforts herself in one of the big soft cushions, drinking tea and listening to Raymond, enjoying his playing and singing. The girl noticed that the spiritual force that inspires poetry and music of the people professing Islam comes from the chanting and the retelling of the Quran. She understood the essence of the Arabic language. It turns out that this language is the language of revelation, the language of God, as he spoke through the mouth of Gabriel to the prophet of Islam. The idea of God is the spiritual substance, which was the final result of critical thinking. When Raymond finished singing, Caroline asked him, "Ray, what art means to you?"

He put down the guitar aside, legged in Turkish, and looked into the girl's eyes.

"Art, for me, is the profound interest in the internal world of feelings ... This quest for spicy, elegant, sensual pleasure."

Caroline looked away from him and looked at the fire again, which was still dancing to the music of the guitar that temporarily stopped. The girl pulled a silk scarf on her shoulders, feeling the cool breeze of the night.

Raymond took out his hookah and smoked, blowing the smoke figure skater in the air. Caroline turned to a friend "Ray?"

He has one eye glanced at her, and responded, proudly raising his head, "Uh ..."

"Why do you study the Quran? What does it represent?"

Raymond collected his thoughts, licked his dry lips, threw a smoke ring in the air again, and said, "The Quran is the first monument prose parables, comparisons of the story. It is the basis of the religion of Islam; this scripture contains regulations of worship, moral precepts, and legal establishment. It defines the customs and traditions of the most important moments in the lifestyle and behavior patterns of millions of people," Raymond leaned toward Caroline and explained in detail the texts of the Quran recited at public and private prayers, in the state and family celebrations, for a variety of occasions, everyday life - he finished the story.

Caroline was leaning on her arm, her chin resting on her hand, thinking about what he had just told her. He raised his left eyebrow, going on, "In addition, a Muslim does not want to be fooled by art, as for him, the world by itself is immeasurably more beautiful than any work of art," he grinned and added, "no more than a mechanism that God set in motion, pulling the strings.

Caroline stared at him, surprised by his words.

Raymond smiled.

"Hmm ... m, yes, yes, and you didn't know, did you?"

The girl swallowed hard in confusion and thought tangling, and her eyes lowered to the ground. To defuse the situation, the hakim said, "I've heard that you have a birthday soon, isn't it?"

"Yes," positively nodded Caroline.

After a moment, Raymond said, "I have a surprise for you, so to say, a gift on this occasion..." he smiled at her, continuing his speech. "Tomorrow afternoon, I'll show you."

Caroline's charming pink lips stretched into a smile, and green eyes sparkled like two big emeralds in anticipation of something interesting.

"Come on," he took her by the hand gently. "I'll walk you to the room, and I'll also have to rest. Today was a busy day."

Dunes, dunes, and again dunes; they're so broad and severe, powerful and ruthless under the hot sun. You can easily lose your way and die, especially when you travel alone. You can die from the sting of a small scorpion or die from hunger and heat, or you will be stabbed by local bandits. Do you want to die? Choose any type of death. Here is such a mysterious and unpredictable desert. The sun rose above the sand, and the hot desert wind circled grains of small pebbles. The night was cold and windy.

Caroline dressed for riding, put her boots on and a thick broad-brimmed hat, and walked down the hall, hoping to meet Jain Mozhardin to prevent her from leaving. By the stairs, she faced her uncle Ali.

"Uncle, have you seen Jain Mozhardin today?"

Ali rubbed his thin white beard and said, "It seems to me that she left an hour ago with servants to the market to buy some food."

"I see." She nodded.

Being in a good mood Caroline went to the kitchen for something delicious. In the cupboards, she found sweets and began to take them over. Halvah and peanuts are her favorite sweets; licking her fingers, Caroline was planning her day. Orange juice was also good, and slowly, the girl sipped it with pleasure.

"Bon Appetite," said Raymond, entering the kitchen.

Being surprised, Caroline shivered and a blush appeared on her cheeks.

"You decided not to wait for breakfast with everybody and to eat everything alone, right?" smiled Raymond, showing off one of his amazing broad smiles.

"I... I just ... just ..." Caroline cringed in shame.

He put his hand on her shoulder and sat down on a chair next to her, "Eat for Health. I want to savor the fruits too," going through the contents of the dish, he chose bananas, two oranges, an apple, and a kiwi. Caroline raised her eyebrows in surprise; she was watching him. He winked at her and, in ten minutes, ate everything that was put on his plate. She blinked off, eyes wide, watching him. Hakim finished his breakfast and said to her, "Well, do you want me to show your gift?"

Caroline briskly nodded when he stood up and instantly followed him. He led her into the fold toward the stables, where the horses were whining and knocking with hooves. Raymond, in Arabic, called his people and told them something. Caroline was intrigued by him and stood beside her friend in the hope of something supernatural. A gentle, caressing breeze blew in her face, softly touching her skin and developing a golden aura around her image. Impatience and curiosity grew with each passing minute; Raymond was long in his silence. He was perfectly calm and immovable, like a leaden statue, drawing his attention to where he should appear, Caroline's surprise.

She nervously rolled over from foot to foot, wringing her hands and biting her lower lip. The heart in her chest was beating fast. She threw back her head and closed her eyes, languishing in thirst for knowledge about this enigmatic surprise. Raymond watched her with the corner of his eye, and it took pleasure to see her so full of interest and excitement. He enjoyed her behavior. Caroline abruptly stopped, frozen in place, not moving and not breathing, when she heard a roar and a noise and a lot of people screaming at Raymond. She grabbed his hand with fear in her eyes and looked at him.

"What is that noise?"

He smiled, shaking his head:

"Watch and enjoy..."

Caroline saw with a worried, wandering look how from the corner, four Negroes with all of their forces tried to pull on the reins amazingly beautiful horse, rising on its hind legs. It was neighing and resisting these Moors, threatening with its strong, black legs, furiously hitting its hooves on the ground. The horse's mane and tail gracefully flowed down. Its red body shimmered in the sun, indicating its health and strength. Black, raven hair was flying in the wind when the animal rose and grew on its hind legs; it sorts out the front legs in the air as if demonstrating its power. The horse's muscular legs pointed out that it's hardy and, moreover, is capable of racing long distances and for a long time. It took a lot of effort to keep the animal in place because the horse was very strong and hot. Warm air is ejected from its flared nostrils as it sniffs and sighs.

Full of admiration and pleasure, Caroline turned to Raymond and rapidly twittered, "I saw a lot of horses at my grandfather's stable and Uncle Ali, but they were such a treasure I had never seen."

Raymond smiled and replied, "And you will never see it again..."

"Why not?" She was pop-eyed.

"Because he is the rampant horse of the Wild West, purebred Mustang," proudly said Raymond.

Caroline looked away from Ray and again glanced at the animal, thinking about how lucky her life was that she could see this beauty, but she was disturbed, and she asked the hakim, "How did you get this Mustang?"

And he told her the story, looking at the horse.

"He was caught in Texas by roping cowboys; the Americans transferred it by ship to Spain for sale on one of the auctioned luxury markets. He was bought by a wealthy gentleman, but he couldn't curb his horse, so he decided to shoot it. He said, 'If it's not mine, then it is no one's.' When he took aim at the Mustang, I saw him, called, and asked him how much he wanted for the horse," Raymond was biting his lip and stopped to talk, remembering that day.

Caroline looked at him worriedly and asked, "How much he asked for the Mustang?"

Raymond looked down and said sadly, "Forty thousand euros, but I gave him more because I loved the stallion."

The girl shook her head.

"I will not accept this gift..."

Caroline turned sharply and went in a confident free walk towards the tack room, where she loved to throw knives at a target. Raymond carefully watched her walk and gestured to his servants, that they led away the mustang. Hakim followed Caroline with a lot of questions trailering in his mind. The girl was in a quick stride, holding the throwing knives. Ray caught her from behind and grabbed her arm, forcing Caroline to look him in the eye.

"You refuse my gift to you?"

She smoothed her hand and said sternly, "Yes, I despise..." – her piercing stare was heavy and confident. Raymond gritted his teeth, and he also looked at her back, reflecting her moodiness.

"Why not? What is in it?"

"It's very expensive," she said, looking at him straight in his blue eyes.

Young, hot hakim came to anger and, of all the words spoken by him, let slip about his feelings, "For the special person to my heart isn't important, even the precious gift. I would be very happy if my beloved took it." He abruptly broke off, noticing that Caroline's facial features had changed. He realized that he had blabbed something under a stream of anger.

Caroline desperately looked at him, realizing what he had just said. His words seemed to her like a dagger that slashed her heart. She dodged his gaze after his speech; Caroline didn't want to spend even a minute or more around Ray and, with the speed of a butterfly, took off and ran towards the palace.

Chicago is an October sort of city, even in spring. It was so easy to disappear, deny knowledge, and mask that something dark had taken root in the smoke and din. This was Chicago on the eve of the greatest fair in history.

Fury and the Parker Company developed its work in Lex very well. The life in it was in full swing. Everyone was a conscientious worker and an excellent staff to have on board.

John and Adeline were often out of state, traveling abroad hand in hand, so all the duties were brought to Brian Fury and the Parker family. Victoria has finally returned from her long vacation in France, alive and well, a bit tamed and calm, though. She also had work to do, as her father quickly found her things to be responsible for. She was very pleased with it and had no word of complaint.

During these few months, the company has achieved significant results. They won prestige in the leading market finally and gained an excellent reputation among competitive corporations. Relationships with foreign delegations strengthened more and more. Brian, his brother Martin, and their friend Jason became reliable young leaders among prospective candidates of their rank. The white stripe in their lives brought them success and luck. The company was finally containing the full house of the family clan Fury. They were responsible for all computer operators: skinny Chris Wren, a curly head Henry Douglas, and green-eyed William James. He, actually always dug something new in the Internet for their comrades. Guys respected him very much, and his wife was finally accepted with a cheering smile. For Martin, it was hard to live with the thought of Raymond. Day after day, he tried to urge Jayson to tell the truth to Brian until he achieved his desire.

That last October day, Brian was sitting in his office. He was typing an urgent report document on his computer when Jason and Martin entered without a knock.

"Hey, brother!" Slowly merged forward to him, Martin and trailering behind Jason.

Brian put the work away and quickly settled back in the chair with a concentrated facial expression.

"Martin, Jason, what's up?" he said indifferently.

"Yes," he sighed. "We're here to consult with you..." Martin started with hesitation but an obvious decisive tone in his voice.

Brian crossed his legs, "Hmm ... I'm listening..." with confidence, he said.

Jason decided to pursue another idea.

"Brian, tell us if your father had any problems with the ship, which two years ago was sent to Spain?"

Brian frowned and thought for a bit, recalling a case. He ran his hand over his forehead and sat nervously on a chair. After thinking for a while, he said, "Yes, I remember something. A ship with first-class weapons was sent to Spain. However, it was intercepted by some terrorists, leaving many victims, and our people were killed," sadly, he said these words "I remember that John was very angry, so furious; he shot his beloved dog and then sat over him, bowing his head."

Martin looked down sadly, remembering this period of his life. Jason continued to ask questions, "Do you have any idea who was that?"

"Of course, this is a man equal to us by force because no one can do it. Or it can be Russians, or whatever it is," remembering the name of this person, he smacked his lips "and ... but remember, Moulay Ali. However, the Russians were too far away from our affairs, and Father had concluded with them business cooperation."

"What kind of cooperation?" Asked Jason.

"Father kept friendly relations with the captain of the Air Force; I think his name was Sergey Sokolov." Silence hangs in the air.

"But if it is not Russians, then this Ali put his hand on." Brian gazed down thoughtfully. Jason's and Martin's eyes met instantly and locked. Brian noticed tension and concerned facial expressions on both of them and wanted to know more:

"You know something? Come on, guys, tell me about it..."

Jason paused, and Martin decided to tell everything he knew, "We know where to find Raymond Moulay Ali Hassan..."

Brian jumped up from the chair, "So what are we waiting for? Let's tell Dad," and he grabbed the phone. Martin pulled the phone out of his brother's hands, saying, "Calm down, Brian. Actually, we'll not tell John anything about it; do you know why? Because the time came when we have to prove to John that we are not suckers, and we're real men, and we can handle decisions independently, without involving our father," Martin said confidently.

Brian folded his arms and put his leg forward.

"Are you sure that we are ready for this?"

"Of course! What are the problems?" Martin opened his arms.

Brother, shaking his head, asked, "And what do you want? What do you suggest?"

"Expand the fighting; karma is calling this Raymond rat," fascinating this picture in his mind, bit his lower lip Martin.

Brian jumped up on the spot in surprise, wondering about his brother's ideas.

"Listen," he protested, "You're really crazy, and you don't have enough thoughts in your head, but how could you come up with this?" Brian was sweating from the slightest thought of acting behind his father's back in such a way.

"No... no way, guys. I'll call Dad. I'll tell him everything."

Martin and Jason exchanged glances, and one of them asked him, "Huh, it's better to be a freckling chicken. So, Brian, you're with us or in the bushes?"

Brian hesitated and soon asked back without any desire to argue further, "Who else is involved in our team?"

Martin smirked.

"All our friends in this picture."

Brian smiled back with an intrigued look, "What the hell! And that skinny Chris is also included in the plans? The wind will blow him out there in the East!!!"

Jason supported the conversation, "Why not? He's also useful. He will be our sniper. Everybody has a job."

"Oh, yeah, right. He has the worst vision. And you want him to be a sniper? So, he shoots all our guys by accident!"

Brian already felt the taste of the military action and asked his friends about the plans.

Jason proposed to become friends with Raymond first, enter into his confidence and win his trust, and then capture him unarmed and confiscate everything that he stole. But Martin had another theory. He wanted to raise his father's army and all attached to it and suddenly attack the Moroccan Hakim, defeat his forces, and capture him in prison. The brother's idea Brian liked more than Jayson's. Brian took over the responsibility for the war plan and for its implementation. Martin decided to be responsible for weapons and vehicles. Jason assumed the obligation to answer for the number of people in the army and its regime. The three of them sat at a round table and drew on paper the strategy and tactics of the battle. They worked on it with enthusiasm, full of energy and great ideas. Savoring every detail of the plan, they have come to a conclusion - to collect a large number of armed men in the early days and, in a month, attack Meknes, where Raymond lived and reigned.

The night silence reigned around. From the window bars on the moonlit floor dropped a black lacy shadow. Caroline relaxed and lay down on her silky bed. She smelled green tea and mint. Jain Mozhardin entered silently in her chamber, carrying a tray with a glass of pineapple juice and marshmallows for Caroline.

A young woman sat quietly on the bed and glanced into the girl's eyes, which were very sad and unfortunate. Jain Mozhardin asked the girl, "What happened to my dove? You didn't appear tonight at the Palace. And you didn't come for dinner. And why again do I see the sad face?"

Caroline is lying quietly on the bed and just looking through the window, but collecting her thoughts, she replies, "Raymond was lying to me all of this time. Just today, I discovered his true feelings..."

Jain Mozhardin understandingly looked into Caroline's eyes, "There is innocence in a lie, serving as a sign of a strong belief in something. Here was his love for you."

Caroline looked in a dark face against which her black eyes sparkled.

"So, you did know and were silent all this time!"

Jain Mozhardin laid her hand on the girl's arm, comforting her with a soft, insinuating voice, "Dear, love reveals the sublime and hidden properties of a loving one, everything in it is rare and exceptional, so - and it is misleading with respect to the fact that it is the rule. Do not judge Ray; he loved you the way you are..."

"It's not true," interrupted Caroline. "He loved my outer shell, face, body, and hair. Everything about me attracts him. I am a golden honey for a bear."

Jain Mozhardin shook her head and her golden earrings hefty rattled.

"And why are you surprised about it then? Haven't you noticed that men need women a faith in the body, with hot blood, elastic muscles, and insatiable temperament, never get tired of loving labor? The 'local stallions' are very susceptible to white-skinned and blond women. However, they are not too white-skinned and too blond."

Caroline corresponds exactly to their ideal. The nervous smile was barely perceptible on her face. An unpleasant lump suffocated her throat; she swallowed hard and expressed her disappointment,

"The thing is that he didn't lie to me, but I can't trust him anymore. I was shocked by this."

Jain Mozhardin lowered her long lashes and offered to Caroline, "My dear, do you want me to tell you something about men and women? What is their relationship?"

Caroline knew that Jain Mozhardin could say many wise things, and it was useful to learn the experience from her life, so she didn't reject her offer. And she leaned back, allowing her to start her speech.

"First of all, he wants to know if a woman gives herself to him, or whether she is ready to give up everything for him, that is, or the more she treasures around" - Jain Mozhardin stopped, thinking about the following idea.

"Is it true?" She asked.

"Yes," Jain sighed, remembering what she was going to say, "the third, finally, does not stop, and that was in his possession and the thirst of incredulity. If a woman sacrifices everything for him, he asks himself whether she's doing it for him, as he is, or for a mirage, which she created herself instead of him to feel loved. He wanted her to know the depths of it until the last of his soul, and he had the courage to unravel himself. Only if she is mistaken in him, if she loves him for the secret corners of his soul, for his gluttony hidden as much as for his kindness, patience, and mind, only then he feels her owner fully," finished her story Jain Mozhardin, stroking Caroline's hand.

The girl, with her open face, looked at Jain Mozhardin and added, "You know, being here in the East, I came to this conclusion..." She paused.

"Which one?"

"Men still treat women like birds who get lost and arrive to them with some tops: they think of something delicate, fragile, wild, whimsical, sweet, full of soul, but also for something they need to lock up so that they wouldn't fly away."

Jain Mozhardin looked at Caroline approvingly and said with her cute smile, "I like your reasoning. I agree with it" - a woman was going to leave Caroline, giving her a chance to rest, but the gentle voice of a girl called Jain Mozhardin stopped at the door.

"I heard you can see the future. Tell me what my destiny will be."

Jain Mozhardin agreed with pleasure to fulfill Caroline's request because she wanted more than ever to know the girl's future. They sat at a small table and Jain Mozhardin looked into her eyes and then in the mirror. Caroline smiled and watched the actions of the seer. Jain Mozhardin wrinkled her face and said quietly, "What is it?"

Caroline, with a worried face, looked at the seer and asked, "What is it?"

"I see death, blood..."

"My death?!" exclaimed the girl.

"No, our people's death. Enemies... they'll come to us with battle."

"Who are they? What enemies?"

"These are not native people..." Jain Mozhardin thought, staring into the mirror, "this is a battle... a fight... with foreigners who will come to get even with our Hakim," - quietly moving her lips, she said, "We need to share this with Raymond, otherwise it will be too late, and the death will take him," closing her eyes, said Jain Mozhardin.

Caroline was worrying and began questioning her friend, "Maybe we can prevent all of this?"

"No!"

"Why not? Well, there should be a way out," yelled the girl.

"What is meant to be will be called FATE."

# CHAPTER 10

*If you are one of those who want a war, and this turn needlessly called your need, this is the source of your virtue. Truly, this is the new good and evil! Truly, this is a new deep murmuring and the voice of a new spring.*

There are thousands of trails, that had never been walked and thousands of healthy and hidden islands of life. They are still inexhaustible and still undiscovered for human mysteries. In the future are carried developments with the help of a secret flap and reach the small hearing good news.

Blue, blue sky dissolved in Caroline's eyes. She was looking at the racing clouds, where through the fog of her imagination, she could see the sea, waves hitting the rocks. She could hear a running herd of sheep and a powerful motley herd of horses. Longing for her native edges corroded her heart, she closed her eyes hard with a huge pain in her soul, remembering the best times of her life. In those memories, she saw Philippe's smile, heard his laugh, and felt his gentle touch, pampering her ear with gentle words. All that popped into her mind so suddenly that its tides again slashed its healing wound after that terrible night.

The girl shifted her eyes from the sky to a wild Mustang, which brought Ray. The stallion was grazing on sparse less green growing. Caroline was sitting on the top of the little haystack, tucked her feet under her and hugging her knees. She watched him with a sad expression on her face, then lowering and raising her wet-with-tears eyelashes. The cheeks of her face glowed, and she felt unbearably lonely and unhappy, and no one understood her. Jain Mozhardin wanted her to marry Raymond. Moulay Ali and Uncle Ali were busy with their own problems, and Raymond looked at her as the object of his adoration and a potential woman to tame somehow.

Caroline sniffed, looking at the Mustang, "And you, my beauty, too, in the same position as I am? They want to subject you to their will and their manners and curb your insatiable thirst for freedom."

The stallion turned his attention to the girl, scrutinizing her. The wind ruffled his black mane. He was standing quietly, with a proud fit strictly slapping with a tail. The stud had the courage to approach a girl and sniff her. He did it carelessly and in disbelief. Caroline didn't move so as not to scare the animal; she left to sit in the same position as she had before.

A golden coat of Caroline's hair was covering her shoulders. The horse approached her and sniffed her hair easily and her light jacket tied under the breasts. Caroline slowly lay down on the straw, and her eyes met with the stallion's eyes. The girl threw her arms back and put them over her head. The animal with its muzzle tickled her belly and pulled the hem. She grinned and pulled the solid cubes of sugar out of her skirt pocket, giving them to the Mustang to sniff. Apparently, he loved them, and he asked for more treats. Caroline opened her hand, allowing him to eat one cube of sugar at a time. She smiled when she heard how they crunched in the horse's mouth. The animal approached her even closer, begging for the next bit. She stood up and walked toward the pen, without turning, in the desire to see him follow her. Noticing that she had left him and moved away, he followed behind her. Caroline went to the colonies, where she could pour some water, take a large bowl, and filled it with fresh water.

The wild, amazing Mustang jumped up on his hind legs in a playful way, neighing loudly, nodding his muzzle, and jumping close to the water. From thirst, he dipped his lips into the bowl and blissfully delayed in the drinkers. Sated, he snapped up his muzzle and lightly doused Caroline. The girl laughed, covering her face with her hands. Once again, looking at her, he strained the front legs, head down to the ground, and jumped up on his hind legs like a bright flame in the chaos. His fox-red skin shined in dazzling bright rays of the sun, and the wind played with his long mane. As if in front of him was his chosen one, he was drawn, showing all its beauty and grace.

Caroline, in fascinating moved her lips and whispered, "I know how I'll name you."

He ran in trot to her and leaned to her hands. She took him by the mane and gently held her hand to his brilliant body.

"Your name is Flash Magnifico."

Handsome confidently glanced into her eyes and put his front foot, offering his friendship. Biting her lower lip, Caroline wanted to ride him so bad that she rubbed his flexible back and gently tickled his belly. For him, it was a mild form of the game. The girl moved away from him by three meters and turning in his direction, making flips, jumped on his back. Mustang jumped slightly, and Caroline grabbed his mane, stooping a little; she squeezed her knees at the feet of his stomach in case she would fall. And Flash galloped headlong, competing with the wind.

Raymond walked out of the palace, holding a lasso. After looking around, he called Jain Mozhardin and asked about Caroline.

"I don't know; she was in the courtyard today, and where she evaporated, I have no idea," Jain Mozhardin explained to the hakim.

He opened his jaw when he saw Caroline riding the wild, rebellious horse. Pointing a finger at her, he asked, "What is this?"

"Where?" Jain Mozhardin wrinkled her forehead in surprise, looking in his pointed direction.

The awesome horse raced like a swirl along a deserted road, kicking up the dust behind. Caroline seemed like she was in one union with this powerful, wild, untamed animal and majestically galloped on top of him, moving her posture forward. His and her hair ruffled wind blowing in their faces. She was comparable to the heavenly goddess, descended from the Greek heavens on fiery Pegasus. They flew over the surface of the sandy road, regardless of one's views and words. Caroline let his mane and spread her arms wide to the side like bird's wings, screaming out loud, "Freedom! Fly, my friend, fly!"

Raymond, with pride, looked at the girl, realizing that this creature would never be his; it was born to be free and independent. And if you put it in the golden cage - it will die, so let's find the one for whom Allah has ordained it. Ray sadly lowered his eyes and looked at Jain Mozhardin, who was totally unaware of what was happening in his heart.

"A false idea of free will," he thought, "We now treat completely indifferent to this concept. We know too well that this," the hakim bowed his head. "This is not ours, freedom-loving Christian, a lover to break our laws and customs. We hate Christians because of freedom, self-confidence, for a straight mind, and at the same time, we salute us into slavery, misery, and self-imprisonment."

The sun had set over the horizon and the last rays of it still cast its light on the towers of the palace. Raymond was sitting in a yoga pose on his bed with his head down and reading a prayer, "My Lord, will cause me to be grateful for your grace which you revealed to me and my parents, and that I was doing good that you want, and bring me your grace in the number of your servants the righteous!"

At the end of the prayer, he stood up and put his feet in shoes that were embroidered with silver. His concentration was interrupted by Jain Mozhardin's steps. She came to him with the talk about something important because she had never bothered him for anything, and moreover, in the evening.

"What is it, Jain?" asked Raymond, expressing a worried look on his face.

A woman, in hesitation, said, "Hakim, I want to warn you..."

Raymond raised his right eyebrow in confusion, not understanding her point.

"Last night, I prophesied to Caroline," she started, "what I saw, I really didn't like."

Hakim put his hands on his hips and nodded to her, "Ok. Tell me, what did you tell her?" With a tense and trembling voice, he ordered.

Jain Mozhardin was hesitating, swaying from foot to foot, and she didn't know how to tell him what she had seen, but she collected with thoughts and decided to warn, "I saw a war with foreigners. They want to kill you."

"So, everybody wants me to be dead. Those are not news to me." He said quietly, without giving much attention to it.

Jain Mozhardin took his hand and turned his gaze back at hers. Their eyes locked.

"Raymond, these rivals are equal to you," she bitterly explained.

He shifted his eyes from her and slowly walked over to the open window, leaning his hands on the window sill:

"Is this Osman, my second cousin? Only he can be equal to me."

"Are you sure it's him?"

"I know some people can be."

Jain Mozhardin was shaking her head without believing in the hakim's words, "Do you know who? Who are they?"

"Americans," he said in a dull voice, sensing a disaster. "I captured a ship "Chaos" too close to Spain, and now they want revenge." Clicking his tongue, said Ray, "but why so long they did not respond and just now decided to look into my tent?" He protested, waving his arms in the air in confusion.

Jain Mozhardin came to the door, ringing with her dangling jewelry, and was about to leave him alone with thoughts, she just said, "I don't know the leader. War is your craft here, so think about it, but we have to be safe". And she left him alone with her narrated news.

Raymond sat on the couch and leaned his head on his hand. In his chambers granted his father, he was admiring of Caroline, whose name was all over around in everybody's rumors. No one believed that this fragile girl tamed that copper, shiny, wild stud. Moulay Ali has decided that she will be able to reign with his son by the state.

"I found a woman who will rule them, and everything is given to her, and she will have a great place!" Happily, exclaimed Moulay Ali, raising his hands to the top.

Raymond looked at him as a naive boy and, in a sad voice, said, "No, Father, I will not marry her, she is not our blood, and the thirst of her spirit is stronger than my will."

Moulay Ali frowned and didn't believe what he had just heard from his son. He was indignant, "What do you mean, Ray? What kind of talk is that?"

"I'm not her idol," gestured toward his father, Raymond.

"She hates men and their nature. She will never love me the way I feel about her. Her heart is cold."

"And do you believe in this tinsel? Often, they want to just skip over hatred, envy, and love. Often, they attack and create an enemy so they can hide the fact that you can pour on the love, attacking..." Moulay Ali explained to his son the wisdom of life. He grabbed him by the arm, firmly saying, "Be a conqueror-man, go and take what you have in your tent, make a force, if you need; force it to submit you, do not lose the possibility of losing your queen, because another will come and take her on his white horse," waving his index finger in the son's face, taught him Moulay Ali.

Raymond agreed with his father's words and decided tonight to take Caroline with her will or without it. The decision was made. Looking forward to this event, Raymond's eyes sparkled like stars in the sky. He won't share her with anyone else. He thinks that destiny brought her from France for him. And there's no way around it.

The Chicago sky was shrouded in clouds with a pink and red shine, predicting the evening. Trails were packed with cars, buses, and motorcycles; everyone returned home from work to their families. The company "Lex" ended the working day, and employees were leaving. Victoria entered Brian's office and found him not alone. He sat with Chris Wren, Jason Parker, Martin, and Henry Douglas.

"Ups, Brian you are not alone?"

"Victoria stopped at the threshold of the door." Brian, spinning in his chair, shook his head negatively, "As you see… nope. Well, come in. Everyone here is our family."

The young men laughed in one voice. The atmosphere seemed very relaxing in the room, and Victoria cheerfully smiled at them back and felt a little uncomfortable. Jason narrated in the nature of their conversation, "We're here trying to decide where to go to have some fun, but we don't want to leave without a company. You see a young, pretty lady like you. Maybe you will join us?" He offered, reaching out her a hand.

Victoria is smiling sweetly, waving her hands, denying Jason's offer, "No, you can go, and I will go home. I love my way of life. No offense, though."

Martin quickly jumped off the edge of the table, where he was sitting, dangling his legs, and ran to his sister, grabbing her arm.

"It's time to change your sedentary lifestyle into active," he confidently said, with a hint of fun in his voice.

"Guys! Let's go to the disco," he called friends.

"But Martin," Victoria is trying to be stubborn; her heels were creaking on the granite floor.

Jason shouted to Martin, "Grab her... Don't let her go!"

Everyone was laughing, from the stubborn sister to the funny, warmed-up brother. Martin smacked his lips and turned to Victoria, who was clattering her little female fists on him. He bent down and lifted her, threw on his shoulder. The girl's feet were dangling in the air, she was indignant at his back, "What are you doing? Let me go now."

Jason was walking beside his friend Martin and was smiling at him, 'I love it.' Brian grabbed the keys to his car and opened his navy blue Bentley Continental Convertible.

Martin loaded his sister into the back seat of the car and slammed the door. Jason jumped into the open window of a vehicle and comfortably arranged next to Victoria, winking at her. Brian got behind the wheel, and Martin joined up beside his brother. The rest friends of the Fury family got in nearby cars.

Brian looked out the window and yelled to the guys, "So, we're going now to West Illinois Street. There's a nice place called "Underground," nice rest over there."

The car engine started, and everyone followed Brian's vehicle.

Victoria pouted, resenting the brothers that they tried to interfere with her normal life, especially today when she was in a hurry. She really needed to be home in time. Being an independent woman and an adult, she was living apart from her parents in a large apartment, which was among the famous skyscrapers of American life. She doesn't need such a big house as her father has, that you are always lost, where and whose room. She sat and looked out the window, thinking about her problems and affairs. Brian pulled out from his jacket a cell phone and phoned home.

His butler answered, "Fury's Mansion. How can I help you?"

"Hello, Goofy! My greeting."

"Yes, Sir. What are your orders?"

"I'll be with my brother very late tonight. If my dad asks about us, you don't know anything?"

"Yes, Sir. I got it." Brian's butler replied immediately.

Martin looked in disbelief at the smiling brother and asked him, "Is that Goofy answered?"

Grinning, Brian said, "Yes, he is."

"I don't understand you. Why do you keep in the service this camel?" Martin spread his arms."

"I like him. I'm always in a good mood after talking to him," explained Brian, putting his fist to his chin. Martin made a disgruntled face, and after a moment of silence, he turned to Jason, "Do you like Goofy?"

Jason didn't hear what he had just said; he was listening to music in the headphones and shaking his head, looking out the window. Martin turned and waved a hand across the seat in front of Jason's eyes.

"Hey, there!"

Jason took off his headphones and asked, "What is it?"

Martin made a pout, "I'm asking you, Do you like Goofy Brian's butler?"

Jason wrinkled forehead, surprised by this question, "Well," he shrugged his shoulders, "He's normal, I think. Sometimes, he's ridiculous."

Martin made a sorry look and stretched his slightly puffy lips in a tube; he turned away from Jayson and was completely disappointed with his answer. Brian quickly glanced at his brother, grinned, and nodded his head.

# CHAPTER 11

*A great man shows his greatness by the way he treats little men.*

**Thomas Carlyle**

The night was peaceful and quiet, and only in the far distance, the wind whistled miserably over the sand hills. Caroline was on the second floor of a small balcony that overlooked the thick garden, where colorful peacocks screamed during the day. While combing her golden hair to shine, she recalled some moments of her past life. Over time, she had taught herself not to pay attention to everything that came from her imagination: dreams, hopes, and all that fantasy. They were no more than the ghosts hiding in the dark, and they never existed. Life seemed to her so dull despite the beauty that Morocco offered with its descriptive history wrapped up in a unique shell. To live did not mean to reflect on the fact that whatever was or might happen, or maybe there really was. 'To live' meant to be the way everyone wants you to be for others. To live – would constantly mean, every day, to be someone that you have never been. After all, deep down, Caroline was very afraid! What would happen if they suddenly discover that she is not as strong as she seems? Caroline, at an early age, learned to be how they wanted to see her. She learned to hide her fears for outward calm and composure. And now she was getting stronger and fighting fiercely, holding from the last effort. Like in that day when she resisted the sea waves, she struggled for life. The girl was brushing her hair for a long time, until they were shiny, and then she just put them on the side as usual.

Raymond quietly opened the door to Caroline's room and slipped inside, barely making a sound. His eyes scanned the room, searching for her. A light breeze blew into the room, causing the chiffon curtains to flutter, through which he caught the beautiful sight of his girlfriend. Caroline watched the stars and, with curiosity, watched a firefly plucked from the sky. Raymond drew his attention to the fact that the look of this young woman was somehow lost - she seemed so lonely, helpless, like a little fragile bird that had fallen out of the nest. 'It's interesting - he thought - how she can have such an unusual character: almost masculine firmness and fascinating femininity, charm. A burning heart always ready to conquer and charm, and absolutely too many cold faces.' Just a minute ago, he came to take her by force, and now his thoughts were confused. He wanted to enjoy it, here in this silence, standing and admiring the beauty of this rare jewel of this country.

Caroline took a deep breath, feeling fatigue in her legs. She turned toward the door, which was part of the balcony, and her green eyes met with unusually blue eyes of his. The girl froze in Hakim's unexpected presence. Breaking the almost captivating silence between them, she asked incredulously, "Ray?"

He is so calm with his hands down, dressed in free, hanging clothes home-like robe. In his white dress, he reminded her of Casper from the cartoon about the ghost. His eyes sparkled, and a calm expression on his face was hidden by an intriguing smile. Raymond looked at her greedily as if eating her piece by piece. Caroline stepped over the threshold and found herself face-to-face with him. Her gentle looked examined him from head to toe. The girl's look stopped on his half-open lips, and they were slightly trembling. He looked at her bare shoulders, the neck, where he found a pulse, an erogenous point, so excited him. He swallowed heavily.

Caroline bit her lips, suspecting the purpose of his coming, considering the somewhat dark face of the guy and his manly cheekbones. She crossed her arms, staring at him with a demanding look, wanting to get an explanation right now and no later. Raymond held his hand to her shoulder and gently touched it, gently stroking his fingertips. Caroline's face became very serious, and her lips closed to the influx of rudeness and cruelty. Gently, he looked into her eyes, raising his hand higher and higher to her neck. Unbearably rapid hurricane rose in her spirit, pouring cold shudder all over her body.

Her delicate nostrils trembled as she raised her head to look into his face. His ocean-blue eyes narrowed, revealing his intentions with a steely glint like sparkling stars. Caroline pulled away, her eyes flashing with fury in response.

"What's wrong with you, Ray?" Angrily, she said through her teeth, wanting to get an answer immediately.

"I came to get what was in my tent," with a note of confidence in his voice, he explained.

Caroline's eyes slowly widened, and then she quickly shook her head in horror: "No! It can't be, and you, too? I thought we were friends."

Raymond frowned in displeasure as if he woke up from a sweet dream and asked, "What? Are you hiding someone else except me?"

That was it for him. He got enraged. His eyes darkened with anger, and his facial features became sharp and slightly coarser. The cheeks of his jaw were clearly on his face. He was physically heated up. He got mad and turned sharply to her with his massive body, strongly held her frail shoulders in his arms, and demanded in his deep, enraged voice, "Who else wants you? Who?"

He shook her so strongly that she saw stars above. She turned her head, forcing the words out, "I hate, I hate all of you..."

Raymond set his teeth with violence and again asked her, "Why? Answer me..."

Caroline lowered eyelids, and her face expressed sorrow and grief. Barely moving her lips, she began her story, which she so didn't want to remember, "I lost my parents, brother, and sister; they were killed in a particularly brutal form..."

Raymond released the girl slowly down on the sofa. With great interest, he looked at her.

"That night..." continued Caroline with pain in her voice, "The world collapsed for me forever. All my dreams were defeated I became an orphan, alone in this vast universe. My only wish was to die. I was saved from a terrible death because I was hidden under the bed."

Caroline stopped, wiping tears from her hot cheeks. She took a few deep breaths and then continued, "In front of my eyes, my sister was raped, she screamed and struggled, and he slapped her on the face, slapping her left and right. Her legs were hanging off the bed, and after a while, I saw the flowing blood. Closing my eyes with my hands, I was crying under the bed, giving myself a promise that I would take revenge and no man would dare to touch me. They killed Emilie, thinking that she was me." Caroline sniffed her wet nose and rubbed rolling tears off her blushing cheeks.

Ray looked at her and slowly approached his girlfriend. Her tiny hands were in his large hands.

"What? Was your sister a twin?"

"Yes, but in some ways, we did not look alike..." She gazed back into his eyes.

Raymond gently placed his fingers on her bare shoulders, and they flinched from his touch. Quietly approaching her ear, he whispered tenderly, "I'm sorry I offended you, desecrated our friendship... I didn't know that your feelings were so hurt. I went crazy about your body, beauty, personality, and especially your rough character. To me, you're perfect, and I want you to be mine, only mine, forever."

Caroline felt pale after his words but quickly took herself in her hands; she walked away from his piercing gaze and rang the bell twice. A chocolate brown maid of hers appeared on the verge. She told her to prepare a bath, and with a casual flick of the wrist, she gave her to understand that she needed to leave. Ray looked at Caroline.

"Go, Ray, leave me alone," Caroline turned away from his curious gaze.

"Will you forgive me?" He asked, gently approaching her closer, still looking softly at her perfectly round chin.

Caroline quickly lifted up her head in a proud gesture, pursing her lips, and said sharply, "What? Are you still here?"

The hakim was about to leave her alone when he suddenly stopped in a doorway, "Tomorrow morning, we have our last lesson in archery, and in the evening, we will be horse riding, so I want you to be prepared."

He immediately left the room with a cold expression on his face.

Caroline was entering the big swimming pool holding her servant's hands. The steps going down deep were colored with different mosaics. The colons of the tower's ceiling were decorated with green-blue and gold arabesques. They say that all of this beauty was copied from Constantinople's baths. The Christian architect who built this entire miracle was after Moulay Ali's ex-wife's order.

The most amazing thing was while you're taking the bath, you can feel like you're one of the eastern fairytale's heroes. After Caroline's bath, the brown servant woman made a girl lie down on a massage bed, took some body oil, applied it on her skin, and made a rapid rub along her whole body, legs, and arms. While the servant was making her beautiful, Caroline was shocked at the mess of what Raymond could do with her if she didn't stop him.

The weather was getting clear and promised a peaceful morning. Like the bright mosaic, the stars were pale step by step while the sun rose on the far horizon. Above, the yellow sand was brighter and brighter, and the red sky turned orange and golden yellow. On the right and left was dull, mysterious, and smoky fog, climbing and snaking on the roof wrinkles as if it felt and horrified the coming day. It was quiet around in the sky and on the land, as in the human's heart at the prayed morning time, only sometimes the cool north wind was blown. Caroline dressed up, descended the stairs to the small yard, and looked around. She crossed the blossom flower garden; it was full of morning flowers. She smelled the greenery aroma and admired with early-morning dew on the roses. Next to the exit on the clear green field, the girl saw Raymond and his servants. He was dressed in white; his bright gown was hanging down to his knees. The hakim was shooting on small plates that were flowing in the air. This kind of sport his majesty picked up not so long ago when he came to know that in the United States, mafia leaders

They like to do it because they become very good marksmen. His heart was beating hard in his chest because he felt that very soon, he might have a combat, that a lot of his people could die and probably himself too. The servant, with a look, pointed at the young woman standing quietly behind his back. Raymond turned around, and a slow smile spread his lips when he met with her forest green eyes. They were smoky darker today, maybe because of her interest in his business. Raymond made a sign to his people to follow him. Caroline was still unmoved. The hakim came up to her so close that he almost touched her forehead. He took her arms in his and brought her to his lips for a slight kiss, still admiring her magnetic eyes. The girl gazed at him under her low eyelashes, checking if he was still angry after yesterday's conflict. But his watchful eyes were bright and lively.

"Caroline," he carefully called by her name. "Are you ready for training?"

She smiled back at him nicely, and her little earring with a white pearl waggled. Caroline flinched away from the sudden thought, and her little pearl glittered in the sunlight, as a tear ready to drop.

"Yes, Ray. I'm ready." Her voice was soft and confident at the same time.

"Ok, then let's go," he said, holding her by the arm. He made her follow him obediently.

They were walking without any rush just simply holding hands. The wet grass whispered in the breeze under their feet. Raymond and Caroline came close to the rack and took some missile knives. The servants set the target for them quickly.

"Ok, my friend," Raymond paused and took some deep breaths. He continued, "At last, the time came when you had to show me what you learned during this year spent with my teachers."

Caroline became serious, and her eyes darkened when she tried to imagine instead of the target of those mean men who murdered her family. The girl raised her hand holding the missile knife and rapidly threw it. The knife jabbed sharply in the center of the target's circle. She was given seven attempts and all of them were passed successfully. The guy narrowed his eyes, raised his eyebrows in surprise, then took a handkerchief and freshened his face.

"Wow, that was cute!" Nervously, he smiled and breathed out slightly that she didn't screw up the lessons.

Caroline turned to face him and proudly said, "Well? Did I pass your test?"

Raymond, squishing his lips and narrowing his eyes, said, "I want you to show me your nice whip use."

Caroline slightly tightened and shrugged, barely dropping her jaw, that she didn't receive a lot of praise for her shown skills. But she quickly kept her temper and followed Hakim into the stable where his snow-white horse was playing. Out of the box, Ray pulled out the whip and threw it to her, she grabbed it in the air. She took it hard and gave a freedom to its leathery and blazing tip. She caught the tip's end with another hand in the air and asked Raymond, "How do you want me to show you that I can master it?"

The servants put twenty-five clay jugs on the ground some distance apart. The hakim pointed them out, saying, "These clay jugs here, you need to smash each of them step by step, and I want to see your dainty," he crossed his arms on the chest.

Caroline turned her head, pulled out from her pockets the black leather mittens, and neatly put them on her arms. She took the whip's handle hard. With a right hand, she raised it above her head, her left hand she put on her hip and slowly moving, she crashed jugs with the whip's tip. The whistle in the air roared more often as the whip's tip swished: it smashed the sixteenth, eighteenth, and twentieth, and then Caroline made a somersault and a pose with a whip. She continued to smash the jugs from side to side, moving to the starting side. When she was done with this test, she stood in front of Raymond and gazed at him with a treacherous look. Caroline rapidly curled it in its primary way and threw it to Raymond's feet. It landed in front of him on the hard ground floor. With almost invisible surprise, he looked at her. Caroline was sweated to death from such exercising; she put her hands on her hips and asked Hakim, "Well, what is my mark? My lord…"

The hakim, without turning to his people gave them signs to clean up everything here. Then he looked into the girl's eyes and, with a light smile, said, "Let's go and have some lunch. It's getting late…"

Brian is sitting in his high leather armchair next to the fireplace, putting his chick on his fist and staring at the fire. His sister Victoria is lying on the sofa, spreading along the whole couch she was busy with the grapes.

A long hush came over the room while the sister broke the silence, asking, "Brian, what kind of fight did you decide to organize behind your father's back?"

He nervously shrugged in his seat and, crossing his legs, answered, "We decided to attack our enemy very unexpectedly; he beat us and stole our ship. He hides his face, but revenge is the best dish that is served cold."

"Well, I see and who will take part in this fight?" She asked with a sultry voice.

"Me, Martin, his people, also my friend Jason, I think his team too, and Chris Wren, well, actually a lot of us will be there."

With curiosity, Victoria bit her lower lip and again took the discussion up with her brother, putting a small grape in her petite mouth, "Are you sure that you will have success?"

"Our belief and trust will bring us a triumphant day," self-assured Brian said in a cold voice. "The enemy isn't so serious, despite the fact that he has our crack weapons. If he uses it correctly against us, then we're done, but we think he's stupid because he's a fucking Arab."

Victoria had known her dad's business since she was twelve. The mafia was something like a medieval kingdom, where the influential barons were united and treated the most powerful and strong lord in the war, who they admitted. But, like that old baron, the powerful leader was supposed to treat and share a haul from the fight with his subordinates. John managed them without force.

He ruled them, uniting their different interests in one source so it would bring some benefits to all of them. John Fury tried to be very careful with them. Everyone had their own connections: assassins, suffocates, poisoners, well, long story short, those who were very respectable in its special murder. He always tried to be prepared for unexpected attacks; he wanted his best friend Trey Parker to take leadership while youths were still silly for taking such responsibility in their hands. Those mafia leaders were also not silly people; some were really very treacherous heads in Chicago. They were not angry that John made his power stronger and more influential – they just believed and trusted him. Nobody ever guessed what kind of craziness he had. But this was a different story.

Brian looked at Victoria with some kind of interest and asked, "Why are you so interested in this?"

"Just curiosity, nothing more."

"Maybe you want to participate in this adventure?" Easily asked her brother.

"Life in my twenties is too important for me; I don't want to be buried so early."

Brian grinned, looking at his sister with some kind of suspicion. His cold facial expression changed into a derisive smile, "Well, and I can die being so young?"

Victoria looked at her brother in perplexity, "So, you will grow up in Dad's eyes when you haven't yet reached the age of majority. Well, you'll recommend yourself good after winning the fight…"

"And what about Martin?"

"Huh… Martin is older than you, only a year, but he doesn't have a real man's power; I can't tell he's a coward because he's actually very brave, but like a man, he needs to grow up."

Victoria took a middle-high glass and poured some mineral water to wet her lips and get lost in her thoughts. After drinking it all, she looked at Brian. She had this soft, maternal look while she was talking to Brian. Every day, she noticed her brother growing and changing. Their real mother, Adeline, paid too little attention to her children; she was a terrible mother, wife, and lover, and even worse in business. Adeline was spending her time at somebody's house drinking tea with her girlfriends, and she was chattering about her girlfriend's life, husband, and almost never home. So, all the kid's responsibility was given to Victoria as the oldest in their family. Victoria saw the world in harmony and its disharmony; she concluded that not really as sweet and nice as writers usually describe in their love novels. All of these things are just tinsel. Nice stories are just people's desires, where there are just a few pieces of truth. Victoria has a hunt for real happiness, true love that could fulfill her completely. She was greatly disappointed in everything, and after that, she dropped into adventures and travels looking for happiness until she met a man. She fell in love with him so much and completely.

To their conversation, joined Martin. Like a magpie, he brought a fresh new on his tail.

"Hey guys, our friend Jason got a girlfriend…"

Brian and Victoria exchanged confused looks, trying to digest the piece of information.

"Such a silence," continued Martin, "What's up?"

Brian, collecting his mixed-up thoughts, asked, "Doesn't this mean he will try to leave us before the real fight starts?"

Martin frowned and innocently shrugged his shoulders, "I don't know…"

"So, you have to get information about this," Brian said with a command in his voice, "No excuses!"

Victoria lifted up from the couch and crossed her arms on her chest.

"Who is she? Do we know her?"

Martin smacked his lips and shifted his eyes away, feeling that he said something odd. Brian was sitting still in his armchair and nervously waggling one leg.

"Well, Martin, we're waiting for an answer..."

"I doubt if you know her; she seems to me like a totally brand-new person. She doesn't know anything about us."

Brian looked at Victoria, puzzled, and she pulled a face, "Did you see her?"

Martin's eyes were jogging around as if a scared small animal, which was supposed to be eaten right now; he was thinking about one question, "To say or not to say?"

Brian frowned in the desire to hear an answer, "Come on, Martin. Tell us the truth..."

"Yes, I saw her. Are you satisfied now?"

"Ok, and where is Jason Parker himself? We haven't seen him for a week."

Martin lowered his eyes, being shy, "Jason's red road "Jaguar" hurtled straight on a freeway at top speed along the shore across Santa Monica, passing Hollywood. It was warm, even hot. In the air the petrol's smell mixed with evening sent. Jason's car was rattling up to eighty miles. His appearance was some kind of a sloppy racer. His side-view and his black mittens looked so spectacular."

Jason was a really good-looking guy: elegant, pleasant, and graceful. He was not too tall, but his shapeliness filled with awe and warmth in every woman's heart. His light-brown eyes shininess dragged in a green marsh where you won't find an exit. So much dragged that Giovanna Shrimp and Chris Wren's sister Julia Wren, those two vamp ladies of our generation, fell alternately in love with Jason, and after breaking with him, hardly ever sank in tears. That was Jason's glorious past.

But today, he is hurtling on the love-wings to his girlfriend, Helen Dee, who won his heart and mind. Helen Dee – a blue-eyed blonde from a simple family in Santa Yanez, California. Her parents took her to Chicago to visit their relatives last week. In one of the local cafes, she and her relatives decided to spend a pleasant evening. Helen had a terrible thirst and left the table where her parents were. And came up to the bar table to order some mineral water. With the corner of her purse, she shoved a neighbor guy and apologized to him, but it was not enough for him. Jason turned his attention to her; he liked her humble and shy look when she sat on a bar chair. Generally, when she looked at him under her lowered eyelashes, their eyes met since then, and between them was born an unspeakable bond of sympathy for each other. Later on, the chemistry between them was quite obvious. And, right now, Jason was ready to break any distance between their hearts for even a short meeting, just to see her. This unexpected flow of Jason's feelings brought sadness to his friends.

"Life can be treacherous and, in the most unexpected moment, can bring you a nice or a terrible surprise," sadly said Brian, thinking about Jason.

Victoria and Martin had no comments.

"Well, my dear friend, it's time for you to show me your master horseback riding," said Raymond, looking at Caroline.

The girl smiled back at him and answered, "With my great pleasure."

She whistled out loud, and at the stable, her mustang neighed. Raymond slightly raised his eyebrows in uncatchable surprise.

Less than a minute later, Caroline's horse was standing next to her, sniffing and expecting the next command. The hakim observed the animal, pointing special attention at the horse's legs. They were tiny and graceful. Caroline was worried a little:

"Is everything ok?"

"Yes," he nodded. "Everything is fine. How did you name him?"

Raymond looked at her, trying to touch a horse.

"Flash... Flash Magnifico," easily answered Caroline.

"Hum.., it fits him."

"Not bad, huh?" The girl was interested in his opinion, trying to catch and guess Raymond's thoughts.

"We'll check it now," and the hakim ordered his people to prepare his white Suleiman and bring it to him.

Caroline caressed the horse's neck. Raymond took a harness and put it on Flash.

"Will you ride him without a tack?" He questioned. Ray was curious.

The girl nodded positively to him, and he shrugged his shoulders, "As you wish."

The snow-white Arabian stallion was brought to Raymond. He looked at his horse amazed, smiled, and gave him a treat. He mounted Suleiman very quickly and prepared him for racing. Caroline was no longer on the ground herself. Gracefully mounted her Mustang, raising him up on its hind legs. The hakim looked at her, trying to explain the game rules.

"And now, listen to me. Behind us, there is a horse pen, and we need to jump through it, then the desert is coming, sand and dust. It's easy to ride there; we need to delay only one mile and a half so as to be next to that hill where my troops start their way."

Caroline lowered her head, nervous that her Mustang wasn't ready and would lose this quest.

"Don't doubt in your horse's strength," he exhilarated her and commented, "He's stronger than you think."

The girl looked at Raymond. He winked at her.

"Savory!" He exclaimed to the black servant, "Shoot in the air when the horses be ready. I'll give you a sign."

The man bowed to him and raised his hand up in the air, holding a gun.

The horses were nervous. They neighed and tried to calm down and focus on the competition. Caroline put a scarf above her head and wrapped her nose and mouth so the sand wouldn't do some damage.

The horses took a silence, and their lords prepared for the start. Savory rose up his hand, and the strong, loud shot roared. Like two tornados, the stallions, side by side, took off their race, climbing the dust behind them. Flesh took the leading part, and Caroline crouched low so close to the horse's neck that he jumped through the high pen. Her heart was beating fast; her fear was breaking down under her mustang's thirst for speed.

When the desert started, Caroline's stallion took it easy while Suleiman took the leading part, galloping hard. He was not far from Flesh, only three meters ahead, leading his position. Of course, for Arabian Raymond's stallion, it was common to gallop in the desert. But when he ran a few meters, Suleiman lowered his speed, feeling tired and discomfort. Caroline took the reins of her horse, firmly holding them and closing her eyes in fear that she'll screw up this final test and everybody will laugh at her. Breathing hard, Flesh got relaxed from his last easy galloping; he put some force in his strong front legs and rushed at a great speed like the wind. The wild bay stallion plucked his hooves; the dust billowed out behind him; he felt a winning time against his Arabian competitor. Caroline arrived at a finish line before Raymond in ten seconds. The hakim rode close to her with a wide smile on his tan face. In his eyes, Caroline read his admiration and fascination. He is glad that he has an apt student.

He shook her hand and offered her to have a celebration dinner for this wonderful occasion as she successfully passed exams.

Caroline slightly breathed out and gave him a nice smile, showing off her white teeth.

"I love this idea," my dear teacher. "Let's go!"

# CHAPTER 12

*The will is a beast of burden. If God mounts it, it wishes and goes as God wills; if Satan mounts it, it wishes and goes as Satan wills; Nor can it choose its rider... the riders contend for its possession.*

### *Martin Luther*

The night started to cover the sand mountains, and you can sit here in silence and simply do nothing, see nothing, and treasure your silence. Yet through the silence, something throbs and gleams. The desert tells a different story every time one ventures on it. But you know what? In the desert, in the pure, clean atmosphere here in silence, you can actually find yourself. This was probably the main reason why Christ escaped from the desert so he could be himself and reconnect to a true identity. Around the celebration table at the Moulay Ali's palace were dancing people, reels, and loud music. Caroline was sitting next to Raymond and spying on him under her low eyelashes.

"Father, my young apt student has passed all my exams successfully!"

"Oh, yeah," Moulay Ali spoke in a drawl, "That's good, very good."

Uncle Ali smiled at Caroline.

"I'm so proud of my niece. She is such a smart girl, after all."

Caroline bit her lower lip, feeling nervous because she knew that only Jewish women could go around freely without covering their faces, but only in their territory called Mellah – the special Jewish quarter. Caroline tipped to Jain Mozhardin's ear and whispered, "Tomorrow morning, I want you to take me to the public market; I want to find material for making a new fine outfit."

"Why do you need another one? You already have them a lot!"

"I want one awesome and special," winked Caroline.

Jain Mozhardin lowered her eyes and looked at her hands, and her face turned pink.

With a great appetite, Caroline ate everything on her plate, and she was waiting for family members to put an end to the dinner.

Raymond caught Caroline's gaze at him and offered her to go to the in-yard for a couple of new songs.

Caroline agreed with pleasure, and she loved Raymond's singing.

They apologized to the guests and family, bowed, and left the table in a hurry. They came to their hide, out nice and quiet place. Hakim shifted his look from Caroline into the dark sky brightened with stars.

Breathing hard, he said quietly, "The East, as it is better to say, is our childhood, and if we want to know it, we don't need to ignore the early human civilization life."

The girl looked at him with interest, trying to guess what he wanted to say.

"Have you ever regretted you were not born here?" Raymond was very curious. He wanted to know her feelings and thoughts about this matter.

"Well, I am pretty satisfied with what I have. I was born in Marseille, and that's fantastic. I'm French."

Raymond didn't say anything about it. He took a guitar and slowly, like touching a woman's body, plucked the strings of it with his thin fingers; he tried to choose a suitable melody for his new song. In half voice, he dragged a song:

- *Many beautiful women have their eyes like shiny stars at night.*

*Loving them sweet is so dangerous for us.*

*But better, of course, our young lives.*

*Gold will buy four wives at once.*

*Nice horse has no price.*

*It will win a strong wind blow; it doesn't betray and doesn't lie.*

He was playing really well, looking into Caroline's eyes. The girl was staring at him with a wonder face. She tried to memorize each minute spent with him.

Deep in her heart, she was afraid to face one day a hard truth of hers. When the moment comes, she is able to leave him. And who knows if they see each other again. Half of her wants to stay with him forever and never face a revenge promise, but another half wants to find family murderers and put an end to them.

He stopped playing on his guitar and tried to concentrate on a new song but the girl interrupted him and offered to sing together their first song. That was her favorite one and the first that she heard from Raymond. With pleasure, he agreed, smiled, and plucked the strings rapidly.

When Raymond finished it, they laughed and she slowly put her head on his strong shoulder, closing her eyes. His cheek lay on her gold hair; he felt the scent of it. She was not even suspecting how much she wanted a man's warmth and was looking for reassurance in him. Caroline trusted Ray because she knew he never betrayed and upset her. Caroline loved him; it was not easy for her to fulfill Fillip's place in her heart which was empty for too long. She lost her brother, but she found Raymond. He became her "Brother" and "Father." She knows he loves her, too, with all her "Bugs." He can forgive her everything except betrayal. For all of their dynasty history in their society was no such a woman who pretended to be a warrior who was ready to fight for a people's freedom and for its own sake.

Brave and fearless, mild and affectionate, tender and mean; it's pretty interesting how she could be such a person simultaneously. He loves her not for something specific but despite everything.

Raymond shepherded his hand on her hair and heard her snuffling. She fell asleep on his shoulder, slowly going down on his chest. Raymond carefully picked her up with his strong hands, stepped across his guitar, and carried her to the palace. It was too late already; all the members of the family were asleep. Going up slowly and carefully by the stairs, he tried not to wake her up. Hakim entered her bedroom and slowly laid Caroline down on her silk bed sheet.

Caroline was sleeping deep after full of adventures in her day, she just opened her lips a little in a sweet dream. Raymond admired her for a long time, then he lowered close to her face and slightly touched her lips with a kiss as if trying its taste. She didn't feel anything; she was a dreamland. Hakim admired her neck and bust; he got the courage to touch her tender and soft skin. He had a passionate desire for her, but he nipped it. He knew he couldn't do stupidity. Raymond decided to escape as soon as possible; he wanted to save their friendship. He is afraid to lose her. Not waiting even a minute, he left, making a pause at her door he threw the final glance at her once again.

The sun started rising above Morocco; the morning promised to be bright and clean. Jain Mozhardin entered Caroline's bedroom, so they went to the local market as she asked her yesterday. Caroline was already dressed up. The last thing she did was her eyes. She made this really beautiful makeup in the cat's style and covered the face below the eyes with a lightly see-through purple-black veil. So, you can see her light green eyes only, and right now, they had this nice shine which was sparkling with some unforgettable brightness.

They didn't want to stick around in the palace for long, so they just rushed out through the door and went to this crowded place full of gossiping people.

Jain Mozhardin bought a basket of vegetables and fruits at once for cooking dinner while Caroline stopped at the table with different materials and accessories, too. She was looking for something she needed so badly. And luckily her view stopped on this special hard material in snow white. She touched the piece of material and decided to buy it at once three meters exactly. The seller did her order and rolled the material in a piece of paper. Caroline gave him money, took the change, and joined her friend Jain Mozhardin. They were moving slowly, watching the right and left counters. The girl's attention was attracted by the sandy-hilled platform shoes made out of suede. They were not on a too-high hill. It was medium, though. So, Caroline decided to try them on, and they fit her perfectly. She bought them. Jain Mozhardin watched Caroline with slow and burning curiosity, "Why do you need them?"

"For special occasions," she simply answered, smiling.

"What are the special occasions?"

"Look at this!" Caroline pointed out the navy green dress made from silk and ornamented with Indian shell jewels.

Jain Mozhardin was admired for this dress.

"Oh yes, it's awesome!"

"Let's buy it!"

"Raymond will be all yours when he sees you in this dress," said Jain Mozhardin, letting her friend spend more money. "He loves that color."

On the way home, they were talking in great joy, satisfied with shopping. Caroline's face was showing calm and impassive conviviality. With great pleasure, she closed her eyes and bit her lower lip, looking forward to a new suit that she was going to sew. Caroline knew that her future image would be shocking.

Hakim had never seen such a dressed-up woman as she was going to dress. Despite this, she knew what she wanted, and nobody could stop her from doing this. Today, Raymond decided to do a dance and song competition, so for women, it was a lot of work with cooking and cleaning because an influenced family wanted everything to be perfect.

Three days had passed since the Fury guys talked about Jason, who was gone from Chicago for several days because of his new love. His friends were assured that this unserious behavior would not last long and, like any other, fail, but not today and not now. He came back at last and was not alone; he was with her. At this very time, his best friends were sitting at the round table and playing poker. Victoria watched Brian from time to time with her face calm. Martin was fumbling under the table, shuffling cards in his hands and putting some of them to his brother. Chris was watching how one brother was fooling another, and he would not even notice that if a curly head pointed at it. Henry Dylan was a short loser of a big time. He never had a serious job and was always pointing out people's mistakes, while he had many of his own, and it was pretty much hard to count all of them. He joined their bravo team rapidly. Brian didn't care for him at all; Henry was just his wish dealer, just a second card in his sleeve.

The friend's faces were dull and unhappy; they were missing Jason's jokes and Jason himself. Suddenly, the door opened wide, and Jason Parker entered the hall, greeting everybody. He was with Helen. His face expressed a warm smile and joy.

He gave a hug to all of them. Victoria came up close to him, hugged Jason hard, and kissed his cheek. Her eyes were shiny and bright, and she was glad to see him again. She loves Jason like her brother. Helen looked at her boyfriend with curiosity and waited for explanations. Jason smiled and introduced his beloved one, "The lady of my heart, Helen Dee, please don't upset her."

Martin got an opportunity to make eyes at her, "Nice to meet you," he shook her hand, "Martin Fury."

The lady smiled nicely at him and looked at Jason back.

"You have to be careful with this guy. He's a playboy of a high caliber," whispered Jason into her ear.

The most intriguing was another guy with this burning, cold facial expression.

Brian Fury, "He said quietly."

Jason introduced her to other friends that were sitting with sour faces and recently having a pain in the asses. Honestly, they were shy, actually, that's why they didn't say a word. And at last was Victoria's turn. She didn't even shake Helen's hand in response. Jason lowered his eyes to the floor, embarrassed by Victoria's behavior. That's easy; she just didn't want to let anybody else enter their family space, and right now, she couldn't avoid it because Jason wanted everybody to respect his decision.

Jason invited his friends to have some drinks for his reunion case. It seemed like everybody was positive except for Victoria. She grabbed her Prada white purse and left through the door without saying bye. Jason tried to stop her, but it was too late. With squealed tires against the road, she left the car parking lot. Hopelessly, he covered his eyes with a hand and moved uncertainly toward his friends.

On her way home, Victoria was clasping the car's steering wheel with anger in her heart. She was thinking about this stupid situation coming up: 'This Helen Dee appeared not in a proper time when we're preparing for a fight. I can give a hundred dollars bet that attacking Morocco will take long and this guy is going to take it easy. I know if Jason falls in love with somebody, it will take a long time for him to put an end to this. And where the hell did this innocence appear from?"

Victoria drove by one of the main streets and turned right to her car in the underground parking lot. She parked her classic tan Mercedes and got out of it with ease. Victoria entered the building and went up the stairs straight to the elevator. She opened her apartment's door with a key and quietly entered the hallway, taking off her shoes from tired feet. When she finished with her shoes, a pleasant man's voice called for her, "Victoria? Are you at home?"

She entered the living room and saw him. He was resting on the sofa with his white headband.

"I'm sorry, dear. I was late today," said Victoria with a sweet voice, "Let me change your band, sweetheart."

He was gazing at her like a baby.

"Where have you been so long?"

Victoria brushed her fingers through his wet, dark brown hair and looked at him softly.

"I visited my brothers. I wanted to talk with them. And how do you feel?"

"I still have a headache," he paused, "And my leg was in pain, too."

"What can I say, honey? The doctor said you have amnesia; you hit your head so hard, and we need some time for it. We have to wait until you can feel much better."

The silence between them filled up the room. But she broke it immediately, "But I will take care of you, don't worry."

Their eyes locked in a gentle gaze at each other in a loving way. He slightly tilted his head to the side and licked his lower lip, "Promise?"

"I give you my word," she returned him a smile.

"Victoria, can you show me my passport, please?" I want to try to remember something.

She lowered her eyes on her hands and looked back at him, "Let's do this tomorrow. Ok?"

The guy nodded positively to her and brought her closer.

"Love you!"

"Me too."

Brian was sitting with his friends at the large square table and thinking about Jason's new fad. Helen was sitting on Jason's lap and hugging him. Martin was telling interesting stories from his life experience, while Chris and Henry were admired by his goofy tales. But Jason was a real actor. He made such a face as if he was interested but only wanted to know about Brian's thoughts. His curiosity won, "Brian, I think we have to talk, shall we?"

He smiled foxily and answered, "You're right."

"Maybe let's have a walk or something?"

Brian wrinkled his forehead, unsatisfied.

"I'm pretty good here," he relaxed, sinking in his chair, "I'm interested in your further actions. Will you join us in our quest that we have to endure, remember?"

Jason shrugged a little, and concern overtook his thoughts. Some sort of a long pause hangs between them, and then he softly replies, "What if I die? I'm going to marry very soon."

Brian showed an irony on his face. "I'm not kidding, Jason. I'm serious right now."

"I'm serious, too, Brian," answered Jason, feeling a boiling anger.

Brian crossed his legs, self-assured, and gave the word back, "Maybe I have to freshen your memory about your sister's honor? It's marked."

Jason lowered his eyes on the floor, and he was nervous; you can tell this by his shaking leg.

He was thinking about Brian's words.

"Personally, me," Brian continued his speech, "If I was in this situation, I would beat his ass for Victoria. I'll never allow anybody to mark her honor. She is my sister, my blood. Did I say it clearly?"

"Quite enough, so I got it," answered Jason back.

"You have a mess in your goddamn head. I really hope you'll not betray your best friends and will not leave us in trouble here, especially now when it's in your interests, too," Brian insisted, "You're older than me. You know your behavior is so immature."

It was so unpleasant for Jason to hear such words from Brian. He perfectly knew that he was right, and by slowing down and postponing the attack, they couldn't anymore. Jason admitted his mistakes, and the guys decided to attack Raymond in seven days. Helen didn't like this plan. She was afraid to lose Jason. And she was annoyed by the fact her beloved one was in tight connections with mafia men; they never deliver anything nice but dirty money. But he was a part of this team, and she understands that. They need him. She could read an opportunity here for him to become a real man: strong-minded, willed, a man who needs a woman complimenting his spirit, supportive, forgiving, and understanding. Unfortunately, Helen didn't have these qualities.

The deeply red sky symbolized a late evening. The palace was crowded and too noisy. It was a Muslim Christian family, so women were allowed to be in the same room with men. The fresh dishes were served along the long, low table. Ali and Moulay Ali were smoking shisha gaily, talking about government achievements as well as inside issues. Politics is always in honor. The young Eastern dancers were dancing in beautiful costumes all over. Around the low table were surrounded by many silk cushions, they were embroidered with golden strings. Upstairs in her room, Caroline was preparing for dinner. Deep in her heart, it was so calm and quiet, like before the storm on the seas. She didn't react to anything until two short servants mixed up in her tights at the back. The dress was in European style and servants didn't know how to tie such clothes. Caroline helped herself. The girls lowered at her jewelry box and pulled out an awesome necklace from three leveled moonstones. She put it on her neck and then pulled out beautiful gold earrings and put them in, too. When she was done, Caroline was walking accompanied by her girl servants. Her eyes met with Raymond's eyes. His fiery pupils were attracted to her; it made Caroline raise her head proudly. For dinner, they served silver dishes with sewer milk, where floating meat cakes rolled in grape leaves. Because of too much sauce packed with onions, saffron, and black and sweet red peppers, the table looked colored with green, yellow, and red marks. Until late evening, one dish went after another: roasted muttons on the spit, barbecued doves, beans – and everything was seasoned with spicy black pepper.

Finally, late evening arrived the time for professional dancers and singers. The light flute music and drums made dancers take their position, and they were dressed in light, colorful skirts and silk blouses, and clinking with their pieces of jewelry, they started dancing. On their open faces were fake blue tattoo signs. The women were circled around with their backs to each other that dance was called "Aidy," a symbol of love. Their skin was perspired and shimmering from sweat. Their closed eyes and half-opened lips expressed a sensual desire. Men were amazed by their talents and beauty.

From the engaged staring audience, she felt such a heavy sensation that Caroline lowered her eyes. It really gave her a headache. People were captured by a sweet, loving rush.

From a distance, just a few steps in front of Caroline was a young Arabian fellow. He was staring at her open face. That was one of the young officers from the garrison, Raymond's father's nephew. Caroline noticed his classic Greek nose; he had dark bronze skin and looked like an antique statue at night. On his face sparkled two shiny eyes and white teeth when he replied back to Moulay Ali's compliments. He didn't shift his eyes from a young French girl whose face was so white and unique.

Her body shivered when she read a flaming and masterful call in his eyes. She saw his thick lips trembling. Caroline searched for Raymond, who was sitting next to her a few minutes ago, and didn't find him. "Didn't Ray notice that a man is staring at his shiny star?" But Hakim went somewhere, and probably his absence gave courage to this young fellow. Caroline turned away and closed her face with a cover.

The lamps and candles were darkening in the hall. In the dark, the dancing girls moved slowly and were falling down one by one.

Everything was so annoying to Caroline; she got up from the cushion and ran to the stairways. She was all trembling from the nervous excitement, but at the stairs, a young fellow crossed her way, and he was staring at her for so long. When her burning skin was touched by a cool palm, she shivered in deep, scary fear. In the light, she recognized a triumphal face that was cached by passion.

"You lost your mind!!!"

She felt his hands touching her hips and waist. His muscled hands grabbed her body in the iron ring. Caroline pushed him against her and gave him heavy slaps against his bronze cheeks. He roared with lough, and his voice changed into a light cough from excitement. He grabbed her closer in the desire to get her body. She felt his hard push in his pants; she screamed out loud, so he became deaf a little. Suddenly, like out of the ground appeared Raymond's guards and Raymond himself. Caroline's face grinned, and she ran up to Ray and nestled into his strong hand. His look was full of fury, and he was ready to cut his head. The guards grabbed the fellow and took him away.

In the morning, while it was not so hot, Caroline was riding her Mustang being dressed in amazon. From the thick tree brunch of an old silver olive was hanging an executioner. The body was hanging on the legs. Under it on the ground were fire oddments; its head and shoulders became coals. Caroline twitched reins. She couldn't find the will to turn away her eyes from this terrible act. She was sure on a hundred percent that this deceased belonged to that chocolate bronze fellow that crossed her way by the stairs.

Caroline heard the hooves' noise approaching behind her; the hakim rode close to her, sitting on his light gray Arabian horse proudly. She slowly turned her face to him and looked at his satisfied grin.

"Why did you kill him?"

"I couldn't allow him to do something terrible to you," my dear friend. "Your safety is my priority."

"The law will punish you."

"The Law?!" Ray roared with laughter and majestically threw a look of satisfaction at Caroline. "I am the law. My lands, my laws," this time, Raymond calmly answered. "He forgot what I taught him during these years: knowledge needs to be practiced, not only carry the theories. Apparently, he forgot everything. Who wouldn't? Look at you…"

Caroline heard the lyrics of irony.

"What have you taught him?"

His lips stretched in a sarcastic smile, "You have never wished for somebody's things if you are not sure you can take it."

Caroline didn't answer anything; she spurred Flesh and galloped into the palace's stables.

When the girl opened the door to the hall, she saw her friend Jain Mozhardin. She was thinking about yesterday's events.

"Jain Mozhardin," said Caroline sharply, "Send me in our tailors, please."

"Ok, they will come now," said Jain Mozhardin in a humble voice.

Caroline opened a patterned chest and took out her newly purchased material.

"What do you have in mind?"

"This will be my new costume," stated Caroline, looking at her mirror reflection.

"Do you think Raymond will like this?"

"I don't know, but personally, I do, and that's enough for now." Caroline gave her an enigmatic smile.

"I'm sure you're up for something, and my gut tells me it's tricky," strictly said Jain Mozhardin, crossing her arms.

"I just want to please myself;" she smiled back and innocently blinked.

Caroline took the material side and laid it on her breast, observing it in the mirror. Jain Mozhardin was watching her carefully and trying to read the girl's mind. 'What does this girl have in her thoughts now? Why does she need a weird-looking costume for? She has never worn such clothes before! Oh...! Allah!!! Please watch for her for all our sake. Don't let her make silly things because I can see it is coming.' They heard a knock on the door, and after their invitation, the tailor and two assistants walked in.

"Who asked for me?" asked a tall man with a dark face and black beard; he was dressed in a golden yellow caftan and wore long golden nose shoes without heels, and that made him look like rich townsfolk from the Middle Ages.

Jain Mozhardin pointed at the girl.

"Miss." He said, bowing with respect to her, "What is your wish?"

The girl raised her head and replied to him, "I need you to make me the costume."

"What is the style, Miss?" The tailor was already interested in his new order.

Caroline pulled out the magazine of the exclusive West Styles. She placed it in front of him on the bed, indicating the specific page and the picture number.

The man opened the page and was searching for the costume, trying to give a mark to the different styles. He was surprised by the Western clothes from other countries. With an interested look, he looked through and then looked at his customer.

"But Miss," he shook his shoulders, "but where are our traditional dresses?"

"That's the point. I don't need these dresses," Caroline, cleared the situation.

"So?" He pointed at the magazine's picture, gazing at it with confusion; "this is practically a white jacket, white trousers, light booties, and a hooded cowl?"

"Not exactly like that," softly said Caroline. "Well, this is 'Shinobi shozoku.' I need a cloth that can give me some space for moving freely. You see, I'm a very active young woman."

The tailor listened carefully and quickly made some notes.

"Oh, yes." She added, "I almost forgot. Can you sew a bolero to it with a long sleeve? It will zip in the front."

The tailor fixed everything in his order notes and then asked, "How soon do you want your order?"

"As soon as possible. All the expenses you can forward to my uncle Ali."

"Okay. We need to take measurements." Reminded himself the tailor.

His assistants quickly measured Caroline and wrote down the numbers for him.

Jain Mozhardin was stunned with an unexpected surprise. She raised her eyebrows. When they were done, the tailor and his assistants bowed and went through the open door, taking the material with them.

"What are you doing, Caroline?" Jain Mozhardin was angry.

"What? I can't?" Caroline looked at her strictly.

"What is this masquerade for?" She raised her voice, demanding an immediate answer and at least a reasonable explanation.

"I'm sick from your black robes and too many underneath unnecessary garments," hissed Caroline through her clenched, perfect teeth. "This stupid robe that covers a woman's skin beauty, I'm sick of wearing it. At last, I'm Christian and not a Muslim, and I will not break my principles anymore."

Jain Mozhardin widened her eyes and decided not to give up:

"Just respect us… Raymond had allowed you too much already. Your name is rumored everywhere. Women are talking about you in every corner of our region.

Jain Mozhardin resent waving her hands up in the air.

"Let them talk; it's their business to wash bones till they are clean and shiny."

"Caroline! Stop it, now!!!" Jain Mozhardin exclaimed, "Uncle Ali will be embarrassed and disappointed."

A glint of anger sparkled in her eyes, "I know what destiny you prepared for me. You want me to take Muslim and marry Raymond, right?"

Jain Mozhardin shivered and round on rising Caroline's serious anger.

"I know your plans for me. I'm telling the truth here," continued Caroline, "do you really think you can make me exist like your women in Islam? I think it's supposed to be in the blood," grinned Caroline, "All of you are so naive!!!"

Jain Mozhardin's eyes were looking for something specific, and she was silent.

"I despise these women without freedom locked up under key; women who are unable to do something independently, and let them go, they will wither like roomed flowers."

Jain Mozhardin felt her mistake in making an argument with Caroline; she decided not to deepen the already flaming conflict with her and left the girl alone with her concepts and attitude. As soon as Jain Mozhardin left her alone, Caroline understood that her opponent had broken down, and she ran away from their 'battlefield.' The triumphant smile appeared on her face. Caroline decided not to waste any more time and went downstairs to see Uncle Ali's library. She has never visited before to find something for her nice leisure.

Caroline took the doorknob and was ready to open it but suddenly stopped for a moment and then decided to enter. In front of her was spread a large and high library. It had so many bookshelves where there were ten thousand books. There were a lot of them, her eyes ran through. She didn't know what to choose. But she was curious about Moulay Ali's, Ali's, and Raymond's wisdom. Probably, they got their wisdom from books. Caroline felt that she also wanted to be so smart like them. She put her finger on her lips and was thinking about choosing a book. She went through one of the bookshelves and stopped, her attention was attracted to the thick black book with intriguing pictures that she tried to understand. Finally, she pulled it out and turned it round in her arms, then opened the first page and read the golden letters "Kama sutra." At that moment, she froze, thinking about the meaning of this word. Then she opened the middle pages of the book where she saw pictures of the nude couples and at the bottom the description of their activity. Caroline turned the page and suddenly let it fall.

"Oh, here you are, my bird. I'm looking for you," said Raymond, smiling at her, entering the room.

He shifted his curious eyes from her face to the fallen book.

Caroline was standing close to the table, holding her hand on her chest, she didn't expect Raymond here. He raised his eyebrow, surprised by her presence in the library and unusual behavior. Ray came closer to her and looked into her eyes, and she was hidden from him. Being frozen as an antique statue, Caroline didn't make any sound; she was waiting for another action. The hakim tilted and picked up the book on the floor. Once again, he glanced at her and raised her head slightly, touching her chin. Ray noticed that Caroline's eyes fogged a little by an inexplicable emotion.

He frowned and made a serious face, then asked, "In the morning, you were more gain. What happened with my princess?"

Caroline didn't answer his question. Only her cheeks and hands got hot. The guy lowered his eyes to the holding book, turned it around, and read the name of it. He abruptly looked at her back.

"Caroline, do you know what kind of book this is?" Quickly asked Raymond.

The girl didn't say anything; she pushed him away and ran out of the library. She ran quickly to her bedroom upstairs. Raymond followed her, holding a book in his hand. Caroline entered her room, closed the door hard, and locked it behind her. She was breathing hard, nestling to the door with her back. She closed her face with her palms and cried, embarrassed. She felt so much shame, and right now, she doesn't know how to look into his eyes. Caroline ran up to her bed and lay on it crying.

Raymond came close to her bedroom door and knocked. But she didn't respond, and he knew she was there.

"Caroline, open the door!"

She didn't respond.

"If you don't open the door right now, I'll force it…"

Caroline got pissed and shouted, "Go away!!!"

"I want to talk to you!" He insisted.

The girl turned away from the entrance to her room and turned her face towards her balcony. Raymond didn't give up, "I'm not kidding; I warn you here the last time if you don't open the door for me, I'll take it down."

Caroline made a grin, jumped up from the bed, and ran up to her closet. She opened it, pulled out the long square towels, and connected them together hard.

Raymond's patience ran out of control. He kicked the door with his leg and then kicked it one more time with his strong, iron-thick shoulder. Caroline threw out her balcony, connected in knot towels, just like she did in her childhood. Raymond crashed the door at last and let himself in her room. Searching around for her, he didn't find Caroline's presence. He frowned, then ran up to her balcony, and saw her running in the backyard. Raymond wasn't thinking too long. He found the courage to pursue her.

At this time, Jain Mozhardin had just walked into the backyard carrying a basket, and suddenly, she saw Raymond climbing down from Caroline's balcony. Being in shock, Jain Mozhardin shook her head. He winked at her when he landed safely. He knew where Caroline rushed, so he followed her straight to the stables. Raymond almost caught her up the hand, but she pushed him again. Being unfocused, Caroline tripped against the small bench and fell on the stack of hay. Raymond covered her on top. He laid on her chest and forced her a little when she was struggling up. He squeezed her arms above her head. She tried to push him against her, but his muscled chest didn't give her a chance to get up. Instead, it was pressing her down. It was fun for him and something new in his experience.

The young man was smiling at her and teasing her. Caroline felt that she couldn't take him down and slowly was calming her nerves down, looking into his eyes that were so close to hers that they almost touched each other's noses. They were breathing on each other heavily. An inexplicable feeling of attraction to him appeared in her heart. Raymond was watching her with a mystery gaze having a little smile at the corner of his lip. He approached her face more closely. She noticed that and just slightly closed her eyes and relaxed under him. Raymond looked at her parted lips in desire and gave himself into his passion. He nestled to her half-open lips and froze, waiting for her kick. But she didn't do that. Instead, she replied to his kiss.

It was light, so aerial and pleasant. This kiss wasn't too long or too passionate. Moreover, it wasn't recited. It was natural and sweet. Raymond relieved her arms and they slightly and slowly rested on his shoulders. And then slowly went down to his back straight to his thing waist. His broad shoulders covered her trail body. Caroline raised her head, and his kisses covered her neck. She uttered a sigh of pleasure and dragged Raymond closer in desire to discover something else sweet. In his head were thousands of fireworks, and her body was shivering from excitement. He looked into her eyes and saw the width of her soul, and in her chest, he felt a passionate heart pulping. From awakened pleasure, Caroline threw her leg on top of his without even noticing it, and a dizzying stream of sensuality took them deep into the sensations.

# CHAPTER 13

*Life is like a pudding:*
*We need sugar and salt.*
*Then it goes to be good.*

Our wonderful world with rainbow dreams that are cast with a glimpse of shine; all of this is out of fashion in our generation when the people's souls are dark, gray, and hungry for money, wealth, fame, power, and recognition around the world. And what does a common man need with its simplicity? Only a small wish is to be happy in this cruel world. And how hard it is to catch the bird of happiness by its tail, especially when it's in front of you, and you can just reach for it, and it's in your arms. But it hurts when she's playing with you, and you start realizing that all the wonderful feelings that God gave just seem like a mirage, a cruel game on your nervestrings. And life after all of this is seen as an error that creates a burr on a sharpened blade that serves to make notches on the line of man's life and destiny.

The Ancient East says that a man has the power to change his destiny, but only with the efforts of his will can a man achieve the desire. Some of you will probably ask, 'How?' Just decide what you want, fix your achieving goal in mind, and move forward, despite everything. Remember that thoughts become things if we have faith. Only then will you feel that you are the great architect of your destiny, that so unpredictable and insidious. Smile in her eyes and wink at her with joy, and after that, it will kiss your footsteps.

"How are the preparations going?" Brian asked Martin, putting his arms on his belt.

"Not bad so far. Our people are training very well: running, shooting, visiting the gym," rather looking up, said Martin.

"Do you think we'll win a steak?"

"I've never taken anything seriously, thinking about losing."

Brian grinned, surprised by their brother's calmness.

"What kind of confidence do you keep awake?"

"In this world, there's no confidence, only possibilities." Martin bit his lip.

"To be honest with you, I like your attitude. With such a mood, we'll show them our big shot."

"Don't doubt in our guys," Martin confidently patted his brother's shoulder.

They were standing in silence for some time, watching guys training through the large panoramic window. With a corner of his eye, Brian stole glimpses of his brother. Martin seems so serious; he looks totally different when he is concentrating on something particular, and it's so rare to see him like that. Brian was pleasantly surprised. Suddenly in Brian's jacket pocket rang a cell phone. He smoothly pulled it out and answered, "I'm speaking."

"Hey, son!" His father's voice boomed, "Why do you mute guys and don't call me? What's going on?"

Brian swallowed and placed his palm on the phone's speaker, saying in a whisper, 'Dad.'

"Ah… We don't want to disturb you from your work. We know you're always busy."

With a calm voice, John asked, "How're you doing in the company?"

"Pretty good, thanks."

Martin turned around to his brother's conversation with dad.

"And how's my fellow Martin doing?"

"He's busy as a bee," Brian grasped.

"Oh, I see," said John with a tired voice, "me and Mom haven't decided yet when to come back home, so it's still up in the air. So, probably we will fly in a few months."

Hearing these words, Martin happily pulled his hand in the air. 'Yes!'

"Dad, you're already six months into the business trip. Don't you want to have a rest?"

"With pleather son, but work is work," quickly said John, "Ok stud, good luck!"

They finished their conversation. Martin smiled slightly at his brother. Brian replied with a light grin. Their company joined Chris Wren with its jokes. But Martin didn't even smile at his goofy story. He was standing quietly and observing training with his hands in his pockets.

Brian dialed his sister's number.

"Hello," languidly said Victoria.

"Sister, will you join us in the gym?"

After thinking for a while, she replied, "Unfortunately, I'm busy today."

Brian was upset and modestly lowered his eyes, "So, we will not expect you?"

"Yea. But don't get mad," softly said Victoria, "tomorrow I'll give you my attention."

The woman turned off her phone and placed it on the coffee table.

Victoria's lover reached for her, and she sat down on his bedside, lovingly stroking his hand. She smiled softly at him and asked, "Want to swim?"

He shook his head.

"You will. You have no choice," she said sternly.

He slyly smiled at her, "Come on..."

"Is this a challenge?" She confidently asked.

"Yes," he replied firmly in return.

Victoria gave him a foxy look and smiled mysteriously. She slowly got up from the bed and went to the kitchen. He looked at the ceiling, thinking about her behavior. She came back with a plate of water and splashed it on her lover. As if scalded he jumped from the bed, taking off his wet clothes stuck to his body. Victoria laughed at him, but when she saw that he rushed to her, she spun around and ran to the bathroom. She quickly closed the door, but he grabbed the door handle and, forcing it, pulled it. In the end, the door handle was left in his hand. Victoria opened the door and let him in. He picked her up, holding his hands around her waist, and pressed his lips against hers. She wrapped her arms around his neck and, with great pleasure, responded to his kisses. Her look was tender and full of some elusive mystery. Something trembled in her legs, and his hands went numb. She tilted her head in a proud stand, in desire of hot kisses. He bent over and bared her gentle silk on touch shoulder, which was a little frozen in anticipation of his subsequent actions. Their eyes met, realizing that they wanted each other. They hugged each other very tightly.

Breaking the silence, he proposed to her, "Let's take a shower together?"

Full of feelings, her eyes blinked approvingly. His hands smoothly slid under her dress and took it off, gently kissing her neck and shoulders. Clinging to his muscular body, she planted a kiss on his chest. His scent was tender and bittersweet. Victoria gently touched his arms and placed them on her bra.

"Take it down, babe." She murmured, gazing into his brown eyes.

He licked his lower lip in a desire to find out more about her. His fingertips gently removed her bra, and her firm breasts obediently landed in his palms. Her eyes were focused on his, and she breathed out slowly. The nipples of hers in between his fingers got firmer, and Victoria's arms traced a circular motion around his round firm butt. His boxers slowly fell off, and he closed his eyes when she lowered in front of him with a slightly shaken voice of hers. 'Time to bathe, my cherry.' The wave of feelings caught them both.

Brian and Martin said goodbye to their friends and walked outside to the street. A red Jaguar drove up to them, and with a friendly smile, Jason took off his glasses.

"Hey, Die Hard! How are you doing?"

Martin shook Jason's hand.

"We're preparing for the battle, man." Brian, in greeting, stretched his arm for a handshake and winked at Jason.

In response to one, he nodded and smiled slightly. Martin's look was a little tired and lost.

"Get in, man. I'll give you a ride..." Jason suggested.

Martin took his sit comfortably next to his friend. He put on a seatbelt and asked his brother, "Are you with us?"

Brian shook his head, "No. I'm going to the office first."

"Pass them all my regards. And give a kiss to your secretary. Tell her that it is from me," he winked to Brian.

"I'm already on my way..." sarcastically replied Brian.

Jason started his Jaguar, and its engine roared slowly and then quickly departed from the sports club.

Martin looked at Parker and inquired, "How is it going? Are we playing at your wedding soon?"

"No. So, is this your wish to have fun at my cost, hah?" Amused, Jason asked.

"I hope you don't expect me to be the first to depart my bachelor life," he smiled enigmatically.

"Most likely, Helen and I are going to dance at your funeral first, then your wedding," Jason said, carefully turning the wheel of a car that was on speed of eighty miles. The wind blew in their faces and ruffled their hair. For a short time, the guys were silent, imagining Martin's funeral.

"I see you driving a car more often than usual, and you look like a professional car racer?" Asked Martin.

Jason glanced at his friend, "I forgot to tell you..."

"What is it?"

"I am interested in car racing now," Jason said with a note of confidence in his voice.

"Great!" Exclaimed Martin, "You decided to become a new champ, better than Schumacher?"

"You're a horse racer! I don't even know how they accepted you; you're pretty tall to be a jockey!!!"

"I paid to be accepted."

"I knew that…"

"And you're a bonehead," flared Martin.

"What's up, man?"

"This is very dangerous. You want Helen to be a widow soon?"

"She will be a widow sooner if I take part in the battle with Arabs," Jason expressed his opinion, "I understand that supposed to because of my sister."

Martin shook his head, tapping on his leg nervously. "Do you love Helen?"

Jason smiled pleasantly, thinking about her.

"What a stupid question! Of course, I do, too much. I'm ready for her. She is my world now."

Martin looked at his friend hopelessly as if he lost his mind and shook his head again, understanding that his best friend was in a woman's trap.

Meanwhile, Caroline was kissing Raymond, running her fingers through the soft, wavy hair that went sideways to his forehead. In his stall, Flash was neighing very loudly, throwing his head up and pawing his hooves on the ground. Caroline, as bewitched, jumped to her feet and walked away from Raymond lying on the straw. Gathering her feelings together, she woke up from the heady sensual feelings.

Hakim looked at her anxiously, "What happened to my birdy?"

"Do you realize what could have happened if Flash hadn't stopped me?" Strictly asked the girl, with a sense of hoarseness in her voice.

Raymond Moulay Ali smiled at her and said, "Since I saw you, all my dreams have become associated only with you. I waited for the moment when I felt the taste of your lips, the heat of the kiss, caressing your hands, the scent of your body..."

"Shut up, shut up immediately!"

Raymond laughed sarcastically, "Inside of you is a sleeping woman who resides, waiting for her true love..."

"Shut up!" Cried the girl, closing her ears with her hands. "I hate you, I hate you!"

He laughed again and said, "You don't feel much towards me but to yourself. You're afraid that one day you'll have an experience of love, and a woman will wake up ready for love work."

The girl, shaking, looked at Raymond. Her eyes were sparkling with fierce. "You're trembling, you are afraid."

Caroline's lowered her humbly eyes and bit her finger.

"I will not touch you, I promise," he said, gritting his heart, "until you ask me."

Raymond reached for her hand, and she placed it in his. Like a king and his queen, they left the stable, holding hands and going through a flower garden to the palace. They walked quietly, without a word, accompanied by cries of peacocks.

Caroline closed her eyes heavily with the thought of a strong and deep burden in her heart. He became not only her friend but a brother and someone more than all of them together.

"What are you thinking about?" Asked Rey.

The girl sighed and looked up at Raymond, "Most likely, there is nothing, but about whom?"

"Whom?" Waiting for her answer, asked Hakim.

Caroline gently smiled.

They both knew the answer, and there was no sense in saying that out loud.

Raymond closed his eyes and slowly said, "Heart? Can you open me your heart?"

"Before I give you my answer, tell me this, Ray," quietly said Caroline, hopefully waiting for the right answer.

"You are well captured, my soul. The words of love are hard to say when you truly feel it."

Caroline waited for an answer, just looking into his eyes. A long silence hung between them. The silence was heavy and unbearable. A crucial moment came for them.

"Caroline, I love you, and I desire only you with all my heart and soul," Ray's trembling voice broke a long silence. "I want you to be mine, and I want to be yours."

After this phrase, his breathing paused, and he waited for her reaction. He noticed how gentle and nice shadow fell on her cheeks from her long lashes as she lowered her eyes, looking at his hands.

He took her shaken hand and placed in her soft palm a golden ring.

"Marry me!"

Caroline was very surprised, she opened her jaw, no man had done this to her, and this was the first time in her life when she got a ring from a man and a kiss on her hand. She didn't know what to say. It was shocking.

Jain Mozhardin saw them out the window and called them out for dinner.

"Look, I know it's hard for you to agree on a marriage with me, but marriage is something more in this life. Marriage - what I call are two aspirations in a desire to create something that is more than creating it. The same reverence for each other, as though two people of the same aspirations. That is what should be the meaning and truth of your marriage."

Caroline thought about his words, 'What is it? Raymond is serious and is unlikely to back down just in front of my "NO!" At dinner, Raymond told everyone he made the proposal to Caroline. The impression is that all of this is long-awaited, especially Moulay Ali and Uncle Ali. Jain Mozhardin was interested only in one question: 'will the stubborn girl agree?'

Raymond's father stood up from the table and spoke to his people, sharing it, "Oh, people! Fear your Lord! Who created you from a single being and created its mate,

And from them spread many men and women.

And fear Allah that you love each other to beg,

And avoid relative relationships.

Truly, Allah is the overseer of you."

Caroline sadly looked down and swallowed her food.

Raymond looked at his father competently and revered. Caroline sat quietly on a cushion, motionless. After Moulay Ali's speech, people drank wine and twittered like magpies on the tree.

The day passed quickly. Lunch was replaced by dinner. Very soon, the tailor's assistant came to Caroline to try an almost finished outfit. After they left, she made a promenade riding Mustang and, at the end of the day, went to bed exhausted.

Time passed relentlessly fast when it was busy or was going so monotonous and very calm. Caroline finally received her new costume that she liked, but she didn't show it to anyone. Often, in the mornings, she went to the green areas and was busy practicing yoga.

Everybody thought Caroline accepted a marriage proposal to Hakim, and they started the preparation for the wedding and turned Caroline to Islam. But the Universe didn't think so and decided to manage Meknes people's lives in a different way.

Caroline went out of her room to the balcony and smelt the smoke up in the air that the wind brought from the desert. She suddenly heard the news downstairs that foreigners attacked them, and the peace was over. At the bottom of her balcony, she saw soldiers serving in the Hakim's army. She suddenly wanted to meet Raymond and ask him the permission to join him. Very fast Caroline went downstairs and ran out of the palace. The common people, especially women with children, were running back and forth in the yard, looking for a safe place to hide.

Caroline found Raymond and ran out close to him, "Ray! Ray!" She called for him, crossing the whole yard full of people.

He was sitting majestically on his horse, ready to go to the battlefield, where, by his command, were waiting for his armed people. Hakim turned around and saw Caroline running toward him. He was glad to see her, but he was scared to lose her, and this fear was tearing his heart apart. Anyway, he rose up his head proudly and was ready to meet her.

"Raymond, what's going on?" She asked him in a worried, concerned voice.

"American tribes arrived at the northern-west part of the country. Their numerous armies are moving to our city," with a trembling fury voice, he said to her, "and we must stop them!"

Caroline opened up her mouth, "But if you can't?"

Raymond bit his lower lip, "Well, then we'll have a great war."

"I don't want to lose you!" She exclaimed, understanding the whole danger of the situation. She clutched the reins of his horse. He looked at her above, "I'm not ready to die yet. I still have to win your heart!" He pulled out the white envelope from his pocket and gave it to her. Then he turned his horse.

"Go to the palace! Wait for me there! Do as I said," he told her in a raised tone, "otherwise, I will be angry, Caroline, if you disobey me."

On her finger, under the sun's glare, sparkled a white diamond, given to her by him on the engagement day. Seeing it on her finger, he relented, "Go away, hide now!"

In his voice, there was the strength and confidence that she understood - it was impossible not to comply. Caroline gasped and took off. Breathing heavily, she stopped at the tall white door, holding the iron rail hard. She accompanied him, moving away from her eyes. Raymond Moulay Ali looked proud and supremely confident on his magnificent snow-grey horse. Squaring his broad shoulders, he held his head high as if disdaining any call in advance that he could throw. He is a real man, a great worrier, but unfortunately Muslim.

Caroline sadly blinked off and ran into the palace, clutching his envelope to her chest. Quickly up the stairs, she rushed into her room. She took off her whirlwind vase on the chest with a napkin and opened it. In this patterned chest was rested her spotted outfit with a long black coat, a hat, and a fingerless black kit. She pulled out the black high, soft boots she had bought at the market with Jain Mozhardin. And the entire arsenal she quickly put it on. Caroline's curiosity overcame her will, and Hakim's prohibitions and visionary 'never show you yourself.' She also wanted to take part in a historic moment and get a taste of the massacre. On the belt, she put two holsters with guns, which it had once borrowed from Raymond. So, not to be seen, she got a bandage on her mouth and nose and tied it on her face. Moving fast, she brushed and tied her hair in a braid and pulled on the hand mitts. Without hesitation, she put on her boots, took an envelope on the dressing table, and slipped it into her boot.

Not leaving the palace through the main entrance, she went out through the balcony. Caroline quickly untied the long curtains and instantly went down. Women in the yard ran around in panic, clutching their heads, begging and calling for God to help them and protect them. Jain Mozhardin was led by Moulay Ali. He dragged her to the palace to lock her in a room, which should shield them from the unwelcome invasion. Jain Mozhardin fell on her knees and called for Caroline, with tears running down her face. Her clothes turned dirty and untidy. Caroline took her eyes away and abruptly grabbed a gray whip hanging on a fence's hook. She secured it on her belt, which glistened in the sunshine. The young woman jumped on the stables' roof and mounted her Mustang.

The stable doors swung open, and Caroline rode her stallion to the war field. The wind was blowing at her back, and because of this, she was riding faster. The horse under her smelled the smoke and felt the upcoming bout. He went confidently, moving his hooves, kicking up the dust, heavily wheezing, and looking forward to a clash with his other rivals. They climbed up the sand hill. The August air, warm and calm a few hours ago, now was shaking from fiery rage.

The amazing contrast was between the opponents. On the left side are enemies in cars and all-terrain vehicles, and infantry are ahead, and on the Hakim's side are horseback riders, well-armed.

Caroline shrugged her head; just now realizing in what kind of action she involved herself. A smart girl would do otherwise - launch a horse and would return home. But then it wouldn't be Caroline. Stallion threw his head up and kicked the sand as if still torn apart between "Let's go" and "Whoa." But she double-clicked her tongue, and the horse threw his head up again and reluctantly stood frozen for a split second. All around them, it was quiet, only the wind howling in the distance over the sand. There was a talk between the enemy and Raymond's people. But nothing, not a treaty, the Hakim ordered the attack. Both sides rushed to each other.

The moment - as short as the seagull's cry - horse and rider stood motionless, looking at the military groups. She tried to determine the head of the invasion's team with her narrowed eyes. Her attention was drawn to the massive black-terrain vehicle, and there were two men in helmets.

One of them nearly jumped out of the car, waving his fist threateningly to soldiers who were marching ahead. Finally, he jumped out of the car with weapons and joined the ranks. In the car left one of his friends, carried away by events.

"Come on! Come on, Martin! Attack these savages, I'll cover you," he cried hard, jumping up.

Caroline, seeing him alone, squeezed tight the reins and decided to attack him behind. She tossed Flesh and put him into a gallop. They flew down the sandy road, like a hawk in his sky, past rocky peaks. Caroline pulled out her Beretta from the holster and was ready to shoot.

Jason heard a strange roar and hoofs clatter; he turned around to see what was going on and saw a rider in a black cloak. Caroline was ready to shoot a weapon, but she couldn't get a shot.

The guy grabbed the machine lying on the seats and opened a fire. Several bullets whistled overhead of her. Suddenly, in front of Flash appeared a deep pothole. Her horse hesitated - and jumped, waving its tail. Jason didn't stop shooting; she dodged bullets and moved the stallion so it wouldn't be hit. When he was out of bullets, the guy threw down his arms and jumped out of the car, running to the side of the desert, struggling out of the team. Caroline prepared to shoot, but to kill an unarmed man was above her, and she didn't.

Jason was running hard, trying to break away from the rider. But she spurred her horse, and she rode faster. Running on the sand was absolutely impossible; he, exhausted with fatigue, tripped and fell on the hot sand, facing the enemy. Resigned to the inevitability, the guy looked at the rider quietly, pondering his next steps. Caroline overtook Flesh and stopped galloping, kicking him several times on his legs around her victim. She stared into the guy's eyes, marveling at his calmness and coolness. Jason drew attention to the horse and its owner, so beautiful and graceful viewing them together. For the masked face of the enemy, he noticed green eyes and how skinny and light is his opponent.

Caroline boldly reached out, clutching tightly the pistol aimed at Parker. He didn't move even once, quietly sitting on the sand with drooping arms on his knees, but in anticipation of the moment when he could disarm the enemy. The girl was surprised by his behavior. It was hard to shoot him because she had never killed a single person in her life. To pretend doing it is one thing, but actually doing it is another. She jumped off the horse and, without dropping a gun, walked closer to Jason to find out about the purpose of their arrival. The young man very playfully jumped up from the sand and knocked down with his feet the weapon from her hands. Caroline wasn't scared of being lost. She bounced and rolled over in the air and got up again in a combat position when Jason tried to knock it down.

"Not bad," he said, "More."

Caroline shook, as from a whip hit, stood up, and gave Parker a look, just a lightning glance. She grabbed his fist on the fly when he tried to hit her in the face and slumped back on the sand, pulling him along and slinging over her opponent.

She jumped to her feet and took a new stance. Between them struck up a close fight. Neither he nor she gave up on each other, but at one moment, when he showed her his finesse, she was already on her back and doubled over in pain in the abdomen, making a subtle muted sigh. Her lips quivered in spasms and tearing pain. Jason jumped up on her stomach, pulling off the black armband and hat from the enemy's face. He tugged at the unexpected surprise for him:

"Woman! My God!"

Caroline was breathing heavily, coughing, and typing in her lungs, gasping for more air. Her look was soft and, at the same time, tough. Jason got off the girl and gave her a hand.

"Come on, baby, come here!"

Caroline gave him her hand and, rising sharply with full force, drew him to her, pushed it close to him, and without delay, climbed on top of him, pressed his neck with a whip, and said, "Now listen to me and answer my questions, or you'll die, understood?"

The horsemen and the infantry clashed in battle. In jeeps, snipers demolished opponents. Raymond's people sitting in shelters were shooting Fury's group of people. Brian shot with a rifle at

Hakim's people. Martin was fighting hand-to-hand with the chief's army, Jalal al-Dina.

Some people died, and some were left wounded. The number of victims grew rapidly on the side of the young fighters. Brian was not himself; he didn't expect those people to be born for war, and he wanted to share his impression with Jason, but looking around, he didn't spot him anywhere. Pushing Chris, he asked:

"Where's Parker?"

He just opened his mouth and raised his eyebrows.

But the fight went on and more and more momentum. In the fight back against the back, Raymond faced with Martin, and head in the head, they met. Martin stood still, observing the famous Hakim of Meknes. In the moment of silence, they looked at each other, rocking from foot to foot in anticipation of a new fight. Raymond finally broke the silence with a question:

"What is it, Fuego?"

Martin laughed with irony in his eyes. He finally said, "You are well aware, Hakim!"

"Of course." All of them just say, "Fuego is handsome, tall, slender, black eyes like a mountain gazelle has, sees you through ..." Tensely said Raymond.

"Are you afraid?" He smiled with an unexplainable side grin. It was enigmatic at the same time.

Raymond shook his head.

"No! How about meeting an equal here?"

Martin's face became serious, and the full, cunning smile was gone.

"Give our weapons back to us," demanded Martin. Thief...

"Take it first," Hakim laughed, causing the opponent to duel.

Their focus on each other was interrupted by the distant rumble of approaching riders from the southwest. People on both sides of the enemy looked around.

Caroline looked at Jason with rudeness, but the noise behind forced her to pay attention to the valley of the hill, from which black ants crawled local thieves, wanting to regale new victims.

"What's going on?" Jason asked anxiously with a worried look.

"Rogues, bloodthirsty savages," she thoughtfully said, with her eyes wide open, full of fear, sliding from the guy. Caroline got up and straightened as if she was hit. Jason sat up and looked at the back of her new enemies. Under her lowered lashes, she watched him.

"So, what now?" He asked.

"Run. These assassins. They cut mercilessly. It's time to flee, confidently replied the girl." After these words, Caroline put her foot in the stirrup and sat on the horse, turning it in the direction of where they came from.

Jason looked around, searching for his team, but they were too far away. Reaching them on foot will take much time. The situation was hopeless. Caroline is removing gradually, without turning around. Jason ran to his friends but fell sharply on the sand, as his feet stuck in the sand and gradually began to absorb. Realizing this quicksand, the man called for help.

Caroline galloped her Mustang not too fast but, for a while, heard a shrill cry for help. She stopped the horse abruptly and turned her head back with a worried expression. She noticed that man was in distress and in need of salvation. Rapidly expanding the horse, she rushed to help him.

Taking off from the saddle and lariat, she ran it over her head. Carefully, Caroline threw a loop around the guy's waist. Jason grabbed the whip tighter and made every effort to get out of this absorbing abyss. Flash backed up, and with its help, the guy was saved. Jason fell with his face down on the sand and caught his breath with fear and anxiety. Caroline smiled slightly and raised her head proudly, holding out her hand from the horse:

"Come on, I'll help you to escape."

With great hope in his eyes, he looked at her and said, "Really?"

"Come on, We're running out of time, and the bastards are coming."

Jason climbed on her horse from behind and grabbed her by the waist. Caroline commanded Flash, encouraging him with a slap on the horse's neck, "Well, my friend, it's all on you!"

Flash raised his head and rushed into the path indicated by his mistress, climbing up the dust.

The interference of the third party in the battle forced Raymond to gather the troops and adopt the position of the observer. The command "Take cover!" by the Moroccan soldiers quickly resulted in the execution. The riders turned their horses and were followed by their leader. Fury's army was in an escalating position; Martin, Brian, and Chris left the ATV and fled in a tank. There, they were pretty safe.

"Raymond," the commander of the army, approached Hakim, "they are stealing our opponents."

The guy raised his hand in silence and nodded approvingly, "I know."

"Long time since we want to get even with savages. Let's take a moment and shoot the robbers," suggested Erebus Nazareth. Erebus is Raymond's best friend and right hand in the army. He's the one who helps Raymond in any super difficult situation; he is beside Raymond's back in every battle they take and go through.

Raymond, with a cold expression on his face, looked incredulously at his friend.

"What are you afraid of?" Asked Erebus. "Look, our snipers survived, and now we are in the shelter. We will defeat third-party opponents easily."

"No, I think we have to let them kill most of the American tribes; too many of them. They have a good chance to beat us and take away our weapons and our pride."

"But it is not ours, and the Americans came after it!" Outraged Erebus.

Raymond took a deep breath and stepped back a little from the trustee.

Erebus looked into his face, "Why is our Lord silent?"

"Did you know that Fuego is there?"

Erebus's face changed into a grimace of surprise, "The famous Illinois boy?"

"Yes," calmly replied Hakim.

Raymond cheered, looked at the assistant, and said firmly, "You can now play around with the robbers; give an order to our snipers, open fire, and destroy savages. Leave Americans to us."

Erebus Nazareth stood up and said, "Right away, lord."

"Father will cut our heads off," excitedly said Brian, referring to his brother.

Martin waved at Brian and again played a fool, "Come on, brother! But we – are the soldiers and had a taste of war. I know for sure we're so grown-up after the victory!"

Brian gritted his teeth and grabbed Martin by the shirt, "Are you a dunce with a capital letter? Are you blind and can't see that our army is struggling? I wasn't counting on this. Shit went crooked."

Chris interfered in an argument between them, "Come on, guys! You're going to kill each other. That's enough! Enough!!!"

"We won't see tomorrow's day. We were almost buried alive, just simply razed to the ground." In rage and anger, Brian was gesturing in front of Martin's nose with his dirty fist.

His brother dropped his guilty eyes and bit his lower lip, "Yet we should act by Jason's plan. It's too late. That idea was more feasible."

Step by step, Brian was calming down. His ocean-blue eyes were still focused on his brother.

Chris frowned and, gazing around, spread his arms, "We don't even know where Jason is. He's gone, vanished."

Martin shrugged, and his eyes widened from unexpected surprise. After Chris's words, he also looked around them and exclaimed, "What? What happened? You want to say that Jason ... He's ... he's ... dead?"

Brian and Chris looked at each other and, in disbelief sighing out.

"We couldn't lose him. We have to find him," Martin said sadly, his eyebrows met at the bridge.

Brian put his hands on his hips and added, "Come on, Martin, take some excavations. You're the bravest, so start searching for him."

Martin looked at his brother, raising his eyebrows, "I hope you're joking. After all, this was just a joke, right?"

"No," uttered shortly Brian. "I'm pretty serious."

"But it's a suicide."

"I know." Calmly replied Brian.

"Where's Jason?" Martin asked excitedly.

"Where the hell he dissolved, knows only God," with straight features on his face said Chris.

"I feel that we are going be buried here, and here's the end of our lives." Brian sighed sadly. "And I'm still a virgin."

Martin grinned after those words and said in an invigorating voice, "Life is full of surprises, but hope never leaves us completely, even when we narrow squeak."

Chris and Brian looked at Martin suspiciously, and then Chris commented, "Your stupid head doesn't give a rest to your feet. Why did you drag us into this shit?"

With gleaming black eyes, Martin laughed and said, "Because the thirst for acting tormented me, I love to play dangerous games!"

"Those are not games, Martin. People are dead, and most likely Jason, too." Mumbled Chris, firmly staring at Martin.

Brian glanced sharply at his brother, "You're not afraid to lose and suffer through it, are you? Can you at least stop for some time and live and let live to others? Man, you will lose everything."

Martin held his arms out to the side, "I have nothing to lose except my life."

In Martin's pocket, the phone rang. He answered, "Yes!"

"Mr. Fury, I have news for you about the progress of military operations," reported the young Canadian.

"What now?" Martin replied nervously.

"Hakim Raymond Moulay Ali attacked the invasion of the savages, and they rode to the northwest. I'm afraid they will attack our fleet at Rabat."

Martin looked down, carefully listening to his assistant, and then replied, "It is necessary to inform Miss Fury about it. Tell her about his actions now, damn it!"

"The troops of the Arab savages don't attack our people anymore. They quit."

"What does that mean?"

"It seems he wants negotiations, sir," hesitantly replied Wrigley.

Martin bit his lower lip and said, "All right, let's talk to this Arab monkey. Give the order to stop the battle."

The guy was excited and confident, "Did you decide to give up?"

Martin put a hand on his forehead and said, "Let's see what he wants."

"But, boss…"

"Just do it!"

Martin interrupted their conversation by turning off the cell phone with a thought, 'What the hell he wants this hakim? Why his people don't finish us? '

Brian looked incredulously at his brother and decided to ask, "What is it? Did Hakim Raymond decide to capture us? Wow, we played a good game: lost the battle, lost the friend..."

Light breeze circled the finest grains of sand. The sun was beating down and mean to the skin of these strangers. In the middle of the day, the sun's rays are more dangerous to humans, and you need shelter and protection. The heat and the warm air are exhausting; they were tormented by thirst, and had just slight thought of a little water to moisten their lips.

Too much time had passed since they left the battlefield; she tried to overreach the way home until Caroline realized she got lost on the way back. Flash fingered his hooves hard; he felt pain in his body. Caroline tried not to demand from him too much, as she understood that it is very hard to carry both. She heard his heavy snoring and growl of discontent; they had appeared in such an awkward situation. The girl glanced at a guy who was sitting behind her. He looked exhausted, as well as she. And his bowed head was resting on her shoulder. From beneath lowered lashes, Caroline watched him. This stranger seemed so mysterious and cute at the same time. His dark, straight hair flowed down on her shoulder. His slightly golden-toned skin is so suspicious about his origins. But the fact that he's American was misleading.

Caroline stopped her tired Mustang and dismounted it. Strictly looking at Jason, she said in English, "Get off, we're going to walk."

Jason once again gave her an appraising look; he dutifully dismounted from the horse. The girl took Flesh under his reins and slowly stepped onto the sand. She led him away. The guy followed her. He walked confidently without raising his head, but his mind was spinning the same question, 'Why did she save me?' Jason guessed that Reina was talking about her, about a girl with eyes of the sea color, that her fiancé preferred more than her. And it's not surprising that Hakim's choice fell on her because Arabs are addicted to white skin and Western women, which was not his sister anyway. She has the same appearance as well as her brother, a father and a mother. Mexicans! Now, Jason understood Raymond and was not surprised by his choice.

Jason obediently followed Caroline as long as he slowed from fatigue. The girl looked back and saw him sitting on the sand. She stopped and asked, "What's up, you're tired?"

"I'm thirsty."

Caroline nervously bit her bottom lip and looked sympathetically at the young man.

Jason decided to ask her a long, tormenting question, "Why did you save me?"

"Get up. At any moment, the bastards can show up." Commanded the girl.

"And you are not afraid of them?"

Caroline indifferently averted her gaze from the guy to the valley of sand hills, where the eye could see faint greens. Without turning her head, she replied, "Decide whether you go with me or die here." And she kept walking.

Jason got up from the sand immediately and followed Caroline; she moved slowly but surely, with measuring steps. She felt the ruthlessness of this scorched desert, and she dreamed of finding something similar to the oasis. Jason obediently followed the girl, trying to talk to her less because he noticed her unfriendliness. He was deeply surprised by this beautiful stranger. He could not understand what is she doing here, in a place where the weaker sex was literally burning their lives serving men and being just a piece of furniture. He didn't deny the fact that she was attractive and full of some irritating charm. They have been walking both in silence for two hours at least. Caroline was hungry and thirsty so much, but she knew there was nothing with her.

She stopped abruptly, hiding. Jason didn't realize what was going on till he saw a snake on the road. A nervous grin crept across his face. The girl pulled out a gun and shot the snake's head.

Caroline smiled with contentment and said, "Here's our lunch!"

Jason raised his right eyebrow, looking wildly at the girl.

"And are you going to eat this?"

Caroline smiled sweetly and said, "Do we have a choice?"

"...No," said the guy quietly.

"Do you smoke?"

"Sometimes."

The girl looked around in search of something.

"I need a fire."

She looked into the valley of the desert and saw the rising wind and the sand dust. Caroline went cold from a terrible feeling; she anxiously waited for what would happen next. She heard the buzz and shooting. Worried, she grabbed Jason's hand and they quickly climbed on the horse and galloped away, where she saw a green canopy. Fortunately, it was the desert paradise, where they hid in the bushes and sat in the shade of ferns. She put Flash on his knees and made him lie down so nobody could see him. Jason and Caroline lay on their bellies next to each other and gently spread bushes, waiting for some events.

The screams and gunshots noticeably became closer; it was a little group of robbers who were heading to the port city to bolster their forces. The couple was unnoticeable thanks to God, and the robbers sped past, climbing up the dust.

Jason cocked up his eyebrows and asked, "Is this a third part of opponents?"

Caroline barely turned her head toward him and made a muffled sound, "A..?"

The guy did not say anything. He got up from the ground, grabbed the snake's tail, and dragged it to cook. After gathering the dry leaves and tree branches, he slightly folded them all together, then pulled out a lighter and made a mini fire. Well, Jason tried to cook a dinner for them, if it can be such.

Panting and tortured by the heat, Caroline stood up and went to look for water. Carelessly stepping, she slipped on the wet green stone and fell, bouncing like a ball into the water. Her clothes got wet. She felt the coolness of the water and let out a sigh of relief. She has never felt so great!

She took plenty of swims, laundered all her clothes except boots and a hat, and waited for daylight to dry laundry and breeze the rest. She washed not only her body but also her long hair, dirty from the sand, and it had lost its usual brilliance; she experienced a true pleasure, feeling like they come to life again under her fingers.

Late lunch was ready. Jason, rubbing his hands with delight, went for the girl to get her but didn't find Caroline on the spot where he had left her before. Looking around, he stepped slightly to the side of the breeze and saw her lying on a small, flat stone, and the rays of the sun kissed her body, dried droplets of water. From such a landscape, Jason's mouth fell open slightly; she was lying on a rock bathing in the sun.

The guy slightly sat down, watching his new stranger. He'd seen half-nude girls before and not only seen but also experienced close physical communication with them. All this gave him great pleasure and enjoyment. But the body of this young woman was the most beautiful one he had ever seen during his dating time. Jason crouched when the girl lifted from the rock and jumped into the waters to make the final plunge. She rose and wiped the water from her eyes. Jason noticed the beauty of the girl's legs and slender hips. Her hips were comparable to the ancient vase. The slim waist was elegant, and the flowing water drops made her waist slenderer.

The girl's breasts were similar to a couple of large hills. Her hair got wet and seemed darker than it was. The tips of the strands caressed her neck and chest. Next to the girl, Flash greedily satisfied his thirst.

Jason had nothing to do but swallow saliva and watch the stranger. He felt his hard little friend in his pants. That monster was bugging him; he barely reined his desire to go to her, to touch, to squeeze into his arms and take her in case she would hang back and resist. Oh, yeah, Jason is American, and he was raised by his father like a gentleman. He can't behave like an animal. No, no, he's not that type of man. All of a sudden, he remembered the pictures of her hard fists in front of his nose, and the desire turned off on its own. He put his hands in his pants pockets and walked away, feeling it was time to disappear so she wouldn't even know he watched her.

Caroline stepped close to Flash's saddle and started dressing up. She quickly ducked into her white undergarment, put on pants bolero, pulled the boots, and threw on the shoulders her black cloak. She glanced at herself in the water reflection and put a hat on. She turned to her horse, picked up his saddle and bridle, and went toward the campfire smell. As if nothing had happened, Jason was standing in front of the fire with his cute smile. In his eyes, she could see a dim light. Caroline suddenly realized that he had seen her when she was bathing. She was confused, but then she said to herself that it didn't matter.

Jason decided to interrupt the long silence between them, "Lunch is ready."

Caroline looked at him and calmly asked, "And what are we going to eat?"

Like a schoolboy, Jayson was playing with ash in the fire but gave her an answer right away, "That snake you killed, remember?"

The girl sat down on the nearest stone and grabbed a piece of palm dish that Jason gave to her.

He watched as Caroline skillfully cut up her prey and was enjoying its taste. Carefully, Jason had a bite of snake's piece of meat. With a sharp sense of hunger, he tasted the flavor. After making sure that the meat was tasty, he began to eat.

The girl finished her piece of snake and gently looked at her enemy in the desire to thank him for the food and get to know him closer. Maybe he isn't that dangerous. She lowered and then raised again and again her thick eyelashes. Jason noticed her slight flirt with him and gently smiled at her, cutting off the silence between them, "I'm more than positive you are a foreigner. European chick."

Caroline gently bit her lower lip and asked, "How do you know?"

"It's easy to guess; you speak English with a French accent, which is unusual for this area."

After a pause, she said, "Yes. I'm French. This isn't my home. I am not a Muslim either and don't wish to convert my faith to Islam."

Remembering his sister's story about Raymond's bride, Jason decided to make sure whether she was the one - Raymond's new bride.

"Do you want to be a part of this world?"

"No," sharply girl hissed through clenched teeth.

"Then what are you doing here?"

Caroline looked down and said, "My parents wanted me to be sent to Meknes to stay with my Uncle Ali, and my meeting with Hakim was just an accident. That's what I thought at first, and later on discovered that it was all planned. They want me to marry him and take Islam."

Jason nodded to himself. Her story spilled the beans on the situation here, and his suspicions were verified, but then he had no idea that she didn't want this marriage.

Caroline looked at him, "You're American, right?"

Jason slightly smiled and said with pride, "Yes, I am."

"How's the life in America? Is it nice?" Caroline's curiosity can't leave her alone.

"Yes. It's a beautiful and stable country," Jason caught himself on the thought that he would like to take her with him to the US with pleasure. But thoughts about his sister bothered him too much he wanted to find out the truth.

"So, has Moroccan Hakim been engaged before to somebody else?"

Caroline frowned, remembering those days, "Yes. It seems to be. I'm not familiar with her, but I heard that she was never nice to me. I wish she marries him and makes him happy. He deserves happiness and simplicity."

Jason nodded his head, knowing that his sister was still that little thing. She has a beautiful voice, which almost all the time sounded lyrics of vanity - she loved to take what she wanted. Sometimes, it seemed that she was a stuffed fool, though, at times, it was shocking that she wasn't. Yes ... she still had that.

"So you don't know each other?"

The young, beautiful stranger got up quietly and, without answering his question, walked to her horse and stroked his mane, gently purring as if talking to him. Jason glanced in her face.

She looked back at him and said, "I think your team will show up soon. You will stay here and will wait for them, and I have to go back home. I can't take you with me. I'm sorry."

Jason raised his eyebrows, "Why?"

"Because Raymond will kill you. You are our enemy."

"All right. Then why didn't you kill me? Do you have a gun?"

"I'm not a killer," quietly replied Caroline, "it's not my lifestyle, but I need ..." she cut her words off, remembering her own enemies, whom she was looking for.

Jason wanted to know who she wanted and what happened in her life that her facial features changed so much, "Who do you need?"

Caroline jumped into her saddle, which had just been placed by her on a horse, proudly raised her head and said, "Goodbye! Wait for your friends..."

She turned her horse around and set off in a full gallop, raising balls of dust behind him.

Jason looked at her trail, watching her admiringly. His gut was alarming him. It wasn't their first and last meeting, after all. The future is so unpredictable, and one day, their paths will cross again, and he'll have the pleasure of speaking with her, hopefully under different conditions, which may be more pleasant.

# CHAPTER 14

*The biggest tragedy of life is the utter impossibility to change what you have done.*

***John Galsworthy***

The guys got out of the tank and decided to talk to Raymond just to find out what he wanted. The armed horse riders surrounded the rest of the American army; they were quietly awaiting the master's order. Brian, Chris, and Martin looked around, searching for Jason. From the armed men group, Raymond Moulay Ali came close to the guys sitting on his grey stallion Suleiman, who was dressed in a white robe. Men all together paid attention to Raymond, observing him from toe to head, trying to mark his appearance. The Hakim's face expressed impregnable steel and cold. Brian felt the distance of his opponent, the same pride and arrogance as he was. Raymond was moving on horseback, looking contemptuously at Brian, commenting on the appearance of enemies, "Those who have bought life for the nearest future, they're mean and disrespectful, and they will not be helped," Raymond was speaking beautifully in a clean Arabic ancient dialect.

His people started to fuss a little but smiled after Raymond's speech.

Brian pursed his lips and looked at the enemy with a hostile. Martin glanced suspiciously at his brother without understanding what the hakim had said in Arabic.

Raymond was staring at Brian, looking into his eyes, "How can it be that every time a messenger comes to you with what your soul did not desire, you are arrogant? You announced some liars, and you killed the others. And for the disbelievers is always a painful punishment."

Brian looked down and unconsciously rubbed his chin.

Raymond continued his appeal; he noticed that his opponent understood his speech.

"Don't you know that Allah has power over all things? Don't you know that Allah dominates the heaven and the earth, and you have no other God than Allah, nor closer or helper?" Ray grinned. "What good you have prepared for yourself, find it with Allah because Allah sees what you do! Only to Allah belongs the East and the West, and wherever you turn, there is always Allah's face."

Martin got tired of this speech about nothing, and he approached to Hakim in English, "Stop your Twittering. It's useless, and tell us what you want from us. Our world is not yet ready for such wisdom!"

Raymond kept his coolness, turned his horse to his people, and ordered, "Take them!"

The order was executed. The guys and their team were captured by Arab forces. Without thinking too long, the conquerors moved to the southeast, back home.

Meanwhile, Victoria was on the board of their frigate "Phantom," her brothers and friends arrived. Victoria stood on the deck and enjoyed the view of the sea and pier. Her eyes wandered over the sea. The wind caressed her skin. She felt a vibrating phone in her pocket and answered the incoming call. Her brother Martin informed her that they lost the battle and were captured by Hakim and his people. They also lost their friend Jason on the battlefield. Martin gave the order to escape; he also said that local bloodthirsty pirates are moved to the fleet destination, and he wants them to be saved in an open sea. After that, he ended his call, and Victoria was stunned in a scary shock for quite a while. But she is stubborn. She didn't want to leave now. She was going to find out what happened to Jason. Victoria tried to call Jason's phone several times, but there was no answer. All of a sudden, their Canadian scout, Wrigley, called for Victoria from his deck.

"Miss Fury, Miss Fury!!!"

Victoria turned around and answered back, "What? What is it, Wrigley?"

"Come," he was waving to her, "you have to look at this!"

Without waiting even a minute, Victoria ran down to her captain's wheel in the cabin and took binoculars to see what was going on. "Shit," Martin was right; there were black horse riders coming to them. She gave the order to be ready for fire.

The sun goes down, and the warm wind changes its blow on a cool breeze. The air isn't that hot anymore and the salty freshness charmed tired Caroline. She is positive about the fact that she is lost, and she's confident about Raymond's punishment as well. The country isn't that big, so Hakim will find her anyway. But does she want it? That's another question. She is riding Flash, and the horse seems unusually quiet. Caroline didn't know whether the battle had finished or not, but all of a sudden, she heard screaming and shooting behind her. She turned her head around and saw a crowd of thieves riding horses behind her. Caroline made Flash gallop as fast as he could. They were not as fast as her, so they tried to shoot at her several times. She screamed from fear and hit Flash unexpectedly for herself and felt guilty for this action. The horse ran furiously. Caroline felt tears on her face streaming down. Obvious death was breathing in her neck. She knew if they catch her she is done, anyway. They never leave anybody alive. Finally, Caroline saw a coast with a huge massive frigate on the waters. She waved her hand to it and screamed, 'Help!'

Behind her back, she heard horse's hooves and a terrible horsy, deep voice; "A-Ha! Catch it! Catch it now!"

Then, a couple of gunshots whistled, and Caroline fell from the horse, dragging Flash with her holding reigns. Caroline felt the ground under her hip and back and saw darkness. Her eyes closed, and terrible heaviness fell on her knees. She lost her consciousness.

"Fire!" screamed a woman's voice.

The frigate fired several times, and the rest of the riders were killed, and silence hung around. The helicopter landed not far away from Caroline. The lady in the leather jumpsuit stood her ground and came closer to look at the first rider lying on the sand.

"Oh, shit!" She said to herself.

She saw a passed-out girl lying on her horse.

Then she glanced at an animal, and it seemed to her alive. She tried to touch it, and all of a sudden, it grinned and tried to bite her.

"Damn it! Calm.... Th...!" The lady said.

Victoria took the horse under the reins and made it stand up. Flash wasn't hurt; he just tried to protect his mistress from anybody. He noticed that the lady was nice to them and let her see his rider. The girl was not hurt as well. She just passed out. She seemed so young to Victoria, probably a teenager. Victoria waved her hand to a man in the helicopter and asked for help.

"Are you serious?" Replied a man, "We can't take them on board. We don't know her, and she might be wild like those idiots here."

"I don't care what you think. I'm a boss here, do you understand? And I'll never leave them here without help. She doesn't look Moroccan; can't you see she is white as snow? We're taking them on board." Victoria turned to the helicopter and left a man.

All night was a nightmare for Caroline. She slept hard but was talking in her dreams. Victoria was sitting next to her and tried to make sure that she was alright. Suddenly, she heard her last name and looked at the girl's face with concern. 'How does she know my maiden name? That's impossible. There's nothing common between us. What the hell?' Thought Victoria.

But Caroline whispered that word in anger in her dream: 'Fury, Fury...'

Victoria left her cabin early morning, confused and full of questions.

At the cabin upstairs, she saw Dawson and told him about the girl's nightmares.

"Listen," she approached to Canadian scout, "Never in her presence mention my name, don't say Miss Fury, just call me Victoria."

"Ok, no problem," nodded a man.

She looked through the window at the ocean and thought about her father. 'There's something that I should find out. My dad has never been an angel, and he probably did something to this girl or related to her. There's a secret hidden from me. And maybe my brother knows it too, but I'll not bother him with this. I will try to win her heart. Maybe through friendship with me, she will tell me her secret, which bothers her so much.' Victoria nodded to herself and left for her captain's cabin. The decision was made, and she will make it through.

She was taken; she didn't know where she was and what was going to be in her life again. Did she lose her mind? From now and forever, Caroline knew her life would definitely change. She is young, beautiful, and smart; all of these three features are leading her ahead. But she can't come back to Morocco and be in prison; now it's over, it's up to her to decide what's next. Neither Hakim, Uncle Ali, nor Grandpa has an influence on her anymore. Holding a cup of coffee that she found next to her in the cabin, she felt warm and comfortable watching waves. She knew now she was on board the ship.

"Oh, I see you already enjoying your way?"

Caroline turned and faced a beautiful woman with just gorgeous brown hair and amassing dark eyes that scared her a little. No, that's not because she is scared. It's just because she felt that she had already seen them before. The woman was widely smiling and Caroline couldn't answer her rude.

"Yea, I am."

The stranger came closer to Caroline and stepped beside her. She looked really nice, the way how she was dressed; the clothes on her were definatly from some famous designer.

Caroline couldn't hold her curiosity anymore, "Who are you?"

"My name is Victoria," she answered politely. "And you?"

Caroline softly replayed her back, "I'm Caroline."

The woman smiled again.

"So, do you remember what happened last night?"

Caroline was confused, she didn't really remember what definitely happened, just terrible heat, thirst, and riding Flash.

"I ... I don't really," she lowered her eyes, feeling embarrassed, "seems strange, yeah?"

A woman shook her head and became serious, "That's okay, especially after that shocking stress that you went through. I would probably feel the same. But, anyway, you're safe and on my board under my command."

Caroline, with widened eyes, opened her mouth.

"Oh... What? This is your boat?"

"That's right, my dear." Nodded Victoria. "Welcome to Phantom!"

Caroline felt unhelpful. She didn't know what to say, and she was just speechless. The girl looked into the woman's eyes again and felt weak.

"What?" Victoria noticed some confusion on the girl's face.

"Your eyes," Caroline barely pronounced the words. "I have a feeling that I've seen them before. But I can't really remember who that was..."

The woman smiled back at her and replied, "That's ok, everybody says to me the same thing too many times."

Caroline smiled, too, "Yeah."

"So, where are you from?" Victoria wanted to know about this girl as much as possible.

"Am..mm," hesitated Caroline, licking her lower lip. "I'm from France originally."

"Oh, yeah. I can tell."

"Really?"

"You have this French accent, like my boyfriend."

"Mm," nodded Caroline.

"I love French men. They know something about love."

Caroline's cheeks flushed.

"Do you have a boyfriend?" asked Victoria, smiling.

"No," Caroline lowered her eyelashes. "And never had."

Victoria bit her lower lip in provoking was still glancing at the girl from toe to head, "I see... Well, I want to inform you that tonight we're going to have a good dinner with my friends here on board, and I know you have nothing to wear, so you can find some outfits in the dresser in your new cabin."

Caroline nodded, adding, "Oh, I want to thank you for everything."

"That's all right, I'm sure we'll be wonderful friends, take your time. I'll see you later."

The mysterious women left. And Caroline was alone with her thoughts. 'Oh my God, she's so sweet! Wonderful friends? I even had never had a girlfriend before,' thought Caroline,' where are we going? Dinner? Who is going to be there? What should I say, and what shouldn't? Where's Flash?' And the shower of questions gave her a terrible headache. Caroline decided to come back to her cabin and take a nap.

Meanwhile, Victoria came to the captain's room and made a call to her brother.

"Martin, are you alright? Did you guys find Jason?"

"Hey Vicki, yes, we're fine. Raymond captured us."

"Oh my Gosh! Are you serious?" She was worried. "How can this be alright?"

"Me, Brian and Chris are waiting for Raymond's answer. We don't really know what he's going to do with the rest of us. And Jason, we still don't know anything about him either. No news. Are you on your way home?"

"Yes, I am. We shot a couple of Arab animals last night. They wanted to attack us, but we were first."

"Oh, good!" sighed Martin with relief, "Call me later, okay?"

"Sure."

Martin hung up and looked at Brian and Chris. There was something irritating in this entire situation. Something really changeable. They all have a feeling that they will soon go home. This silence without news helped to listen to the second feeling. They are sitting in a wide, cool room more looks like a hole for interrogation. It is wide, with white walls and huge big columns, no pictures just nothing. Guys didn't talk to each other, so nobody could listen to them, they tried to be careful. All of a sudden, they heard somebody coming, and it was Erebus. They looked at him without any expression on their faces.

"You have to follow me now," finally said this muscled man with a voice that broke all possible objections.

Martin was the first who made a first step, than Brian and Chris followed him. They have been walking through a long, wide, and light tunnel. Erebus opened a massive brown door in front of the guys and let them come in. In the center of the room was sitting Raymond. He had a serious and worried look on his face. The guys saw Jason alive. He was sitting on a high eastern pillow. Martin slightly waved to Jason and smiled, glad that he was alive and safe. He knew that Jason was close to Raymond through his sister Reina. So, friends were not surprised to see Jason in a privileged position.

"Fuego."

All of a sudden, Raymond approached. In echo, this word went through the room. Guys turned around to see who that was. But Raymond was staring at Martin. And Brian with Chris glanced at Martin with confuse.

"What?" answered Martin hard.

He was damn serious, like never. Where was that stupid look of a fool that he always had? It's gone; friends had never seen him before like that. He looked like a different person.

Raymond placed between him and Martin a distance like to his equal.

"I have to apologize," started Moroccan Hakim, "I made a big mistake when I took your weapons."

Martin folded his arms on his chest and raised his head. He had a look of steel.

"Go ahead."

"I will give you your weapons back and my frigate," said Raymond loudly so everybody could hear.

Martin smiled slightly, nodding, "That's smart. Finally, the right decision!"

"You're free and can go back, Fuego. I don't want to do any business with you and your people; I don't want to see you on my land either."

Raymond looked at Jason Parker and talked to him, "I don't have to marry your sister. She chooses her own way."

Jason didn't interrupt him, and he wanted to hear Hakim's version.

"Reina doesn't love me; she left me and my lands. I wanted her to be with me, but it was up to her, unfortunately." Raymond lowered his eyes to his feet.

Jason Parker wasn't satisfied with this speech.

"What about the other one?" He questioned him, trying to catch his emotional look.

Raymond's eyes sparkled, "What?"

"My sister told me why she left you. You shamed her with the other girl," said Jason abruptly.

Martin smiled, "Oh, a second chick? Huh... I see, Hakim. You don't waste your time."

Raymond circled and got mad, "Islam allows us to have a second wife and a third..."

Now Jason god mad, too, "Hey, my father took from your father a promise that his daughter would be the only one in your marriage and no other women, you forgot?"

Raymond looked at Jason with his open mouth trying to say something in to his protection. But Jason insisted, "Yes, I see you have a short memory. I also remember that she promised to be a good wife and bring you a son you want so much. She even agreed to become Muslim. But now I don't want her to have you like her husband."

Hakim squeezed his fists and looked into Jason's face, "I will kill you talking to me like this."

Jason replied back, "Yeah? Since when did you become a naval on this Earth?"

Raymond stepped back and answered, "It's easy for me to burn you up!"

"You know Raymond, you need to get down to Earth a little. Stop being an ass!"

The silence hung in the room between them. Nobody tried to say anything. Martin was staring at Jason, Brian, and Chris were waiting for something stupid from Hakim's side. While Jason was so cold with Raymond, "I'm sorry," finally, Jason said, itching the bottom of his palm, "but you will never get either my sister or the other girl."

"That's enough," roared Raymond.

In the room, Ali entered and approached Hakim in Arabic. While he was telling him something very important, and you can tell by his face's reaction, the guys winked at each other. They looked at Raymond, and he was so pale, like his walls in the palace. Jason understood that something terrible. Hakim called for Erebus and gave him an order.

Then he turned to Jason and said, "Maybe you were right."

Jason gazed at him with a rising upright eyebrow, "About what?"

He didn't answer him back just walked away to the balcony and looked through the window. Raymond looked fed up, and he was silent and speechless. He didn't look that brave and scary anymore. He was broken by something that Ali had told him.

The seawater was sparkling on the surface of the moonshine. And pleasant water sound under the ship just relaxed an exhausting Caroline. She woke up and looked at the electronic clock, and it was five-thirty. She just remembered that Victoria invited her that night for dinner and she said something about clothes in the dresser. Caroline came closer to the dresser and opened it. She really found some nice pants and shirts, some jackets. The variety was not that large, so she chose a white-pinkish shirt and dark brown pants. Also, the girl found high shoes on a low hill. She put them on, and they fit her. Caroline gently combed her hair and was ready for dinner with Victoria. She had too many questions, and she needed answers on them. Caroline came closer to the door and finally opened it.

The hall was white and light. She looked in on the right and left, deciding which way to pick. She moved to the left side and saw some young guys talking to each other about nothing.

"Um... m," made a sound Caroline.

Guys looked at her.

"Hey, what's up?"

Caroline got confused and shy, "Can you tell me how I can find Victoria?"

"Sure, she is upstairs. Just go straight and turn left. You will see the stairs and go up, and she is going to be there."

"Thank you so much!" Caroline smiled slightly at them and followed their directions.

She climbed up to the second deck and saw Victoria through the glass. Caroline knocked her on the window and waved. Victoria opened a door and let her in.

"Hey, what's up? You look nice in these clothes," noticed Victoria.

"Thank you! I know they're so nice and so comfortable," admitted Caroline.

"Sure, they are, it's Ralph Lauren!" exclaimed Victoria.

Caroline raised eyebrows and asked, "Who? Who's that?"

Victoria widely smiled and said, "Oh, that's an American designer!"

Caroline lowered her eyes in embarrassment that she didn't even know any except famous French designers. She has never been wearing any designer clothes. Mom and Dad earned pretty good, but they had never really paid attention to expensive stuff from big malls. And Caroline, together with a sister, never insisted.

"So, are you hungry?" changed the subject Victoria.

Caroline nodded.

"Yes, I am."

Victoria came close to her, put a hand on her shoulder, and softly said, "Come on, let's have some meal. Follow me."

They came to the dining room and everything was already on the table, cooked and ready served. They sat in front of each other. Victoria broke the silence first with a question, "Wine?"

Caroline looked at her and bit her lower lip.

"No. I don't drink."

Victoria placed a jar on the center of the table and put on her plate thick steak and some mashed potatoes. Caroline picked fresh vegetable salad and some fried salmon on her plate. They start eating slowly from time to time, glancing at each other. Victoria was the first who give away her curiosity.

"So, tell me about yourself."

Caroline was chewing and then stopped, adding, "There's nothing much to tell."

Victoria didn't give up that easily, "Do you have any documents with you, Caroline?"

She sighed, "No more. They left in my room."

"We have a course to New York," said Victoria.

Caroline moved a little on a chair, "Are we going to the US?"

"Exactly," she nodded.

It seemed to Victoria that the girl's mood improved.

"So, you need documents," continued Victoria, "I want to help you with this, so you better tell me something about yourself."

Caroline realized she had no choice, and Victoria was right. She needed to tell her at least something. She doesn't know how to start. There was too much to tell.

"Can I trust you?" asked Caroline.

Victoria nodded.

"Sure you can. I know how to keep secrets, especially if they are not mine."

Caroline told her about her childhood, a nice time in Marseille back in France. She also told about her twin sister and brother, mom and dad.

"Everything was not that bad until all of them were killed and burned in our mansion one terrible night," tears stuck in Caroline's eyes.

Victoria opened her mouth. "What?" She barely said, "burned alive in their house? Oh my God, that's so mean... What did the police say in this case? Did they find murderers?"

Caroline swallowed and took a glass of water, "Nope."

Victoria couldn't believe this and continued her emotions in words, "But how? Why have they never been investigated?"

"Do you know why? The police said that something was wrong with the gas in the house, and it caused an explosion; my grandpa believed that murders paid the police good money."

Victoria exclaimed, "That sounds more like the truth! So, what did happen to you?"

Caroline lowered her eyes to her food and bit her lip, "I was sent to Morocco by my uncle Ali to recover from this shock. My granddad said that I have to find killers and take revenge for my family. This is the only purpose God saved me for."

Victoria nodded positively, "Yeah, you have to. If I were you, I would search for them and, if found, kill them all." Then Victoria made a pause and killed her thirst with the rest of the water in her glass. "Man," she said, "you have to find them for sure. Do you know where to start?"

Caroline looked at her and smiled, "Yes, I do." Her voice sounded cold, full of decisions.

"Well," said intrigued Victoria, "What is it?"

"The US," said Caroline confidently.

Victoria raised her eyebrow, "Really? Why?"

"Murders live in the United States," said Caroline in a strong voice, "their leader is John."

Victoria didn't move. She froze on her chair like a statue. Meanwhile, Caroline continued her unspoken speech:

"Their name is Furry. I'm going to find John Furry and his team, and when I find him, I will forget about my kindness." Caroline's eyes sparkled when she said these words.

**"You are the masterpiece.**
**Of your own life.**

**You are the Michelangelo**
**Of your own life.**
**The David you are sculpturing.**
**Is you.**
(Dr. Joe Vitale)" – read on the wall Brian and smoothly rubbed his chin.

Martin walked closer from behind to his brother and said:

"Those people are crazy about lyrics and poetry, as well as songs and nice dances."

"I know," answered Brian. "How do you think what made Raymond so sad?"

Martin smiled and said sarcastically, "Women!"

Brian turned to his brother and met his eyes so close to his face, "I'm serious."

"Me too. In this world, my brother, it's all about bitches!"

Brian got mad, "Stop talking about women in such a disrespectful manner!"

Martin lowered his head to a side and leaned against the wall of their temporary room.

"They're all the same to me, falsely sweet, deceitful, and dishonest whores."

Brian walked away from his brother on the opposite side of the room.

"You disgust me."

Martin laughed out loud, "It's not my fault you don't like the truth. Listen, I was dating a lot of women and can tell that they're all the same, nothing new."

"Look at Jason and his girlfriend; they have a beautiful relationship, and it's rare," confidently, said Brian.

Martin did not object, "That's true, no doubt. I wish I could have something like this."

Brian slightly smiled to the side, "Not with you. You have too many sins."

His brother didn't answer this time; he was standing with his back to Brian and was facing the balcony with beautiful dark red curtains. He went outside and looked at the horizon, where the eye could catch some sparkling stars.

Brian noticed that Martin concentrated on something, looking at the sky. Only now, he noticed brother has nice legs and a thin waist with wide shoulders. Brian has never paid attention to his older brother; he had no interest in him in person, but now Martin is completely occupied with his life and mind. He came closer to Martin and asked him, "Why did Raymond call you Fuego?"

Martin turned a little so he could see his brother with a corner of his eye.

"Fuego means flame in Spanish; I think he associates me with fire. That's my nickname."

Brian smiled a little, "Weird. Our dad gave us a good education," Brian noticed unexpectedly for himself.

"How many languages do you know, Brian?" asked Martin.

"Well, let's see... My English, then German, French, and Arabic."

Martin sighed lightly, adding, "Nice."

Brian looked at Martin and asked his brother, "And you?"

"Hmm.., Spanish, French, and Russian," said proudly Martin.

"Russian?" Brian was surprised. "How? Where did you pick up Russian?"

Martin lightly smiled and turned his muscular body to his brother, "From my nanny. Our dad used to take me to France, but mom never went with us, so father didn't want to leave the little boy alone. He got a Russian nanny for me, and she taught me to read and write in Russian; she was a beautiful girl with fair hair and deep blue eyes, and she also spoke French."

Brian was pleasantly surprised with his brother.

"I didn't know anything about that."

Martin continued his peasant memory story, "Her name was Alena, yes..., that's how she introduced herself to me. She brought me this funny wooden doll, and I told her that it was ugly."

Brian opened his mouth, trying to say, "A wooden doll?"

"Yeah," nodded Martin, "And Alena explained to me that in Russia, this doll symbolized different sides of women. That wooden doll is contained inside the new and smaller and smaller doll that hides in a big doll. The meaning after that was clear to me."

"What is it?" asked curious Brian.

"While a woman grows from a little girl, she changes in different sides of life."

"So, you liked your nanny?"

"She was cute," admitted Martin, "I was a boy, but even then, I already saw the woman's beauty inside and outside."

"What?" exclaimed Brian.

"She had a nice soul. Probably, in my life, my Russian nanny was the best honest woman." Smiled, Martin was pleasantly surprised by his discoveries.

"Wow!" said Brian, "how long did she stay with you?"

Martin scratched his head, trying to remember, "Oh, let's see. I met her when I was five, and then every year, we spent some time till I was nine. Then we moved to Chicago for a long time, but I got nice letters from her, and we became pen friends. Then, on my birthday, father bought a trip to Marseille for us with mom, and I met her there unexpectedly. Back then, I was sixteen."

Brian nodded with a pleasant smile, "I can imagine her face when she saw you after seven years."

Martin laughed quietly, "Hah, she said in Russian, 'Just look at you! Such a big boy!' that was the first time when I got embarrassed."

"Why?" The curiosity was killing Brian.

"Because I liked her a lot, and I asked her for dinner, and she said, I will say yes if you agree to speak with me in my native language," Martin pressed his lips tight.

"And? What did you do?" Brian put his elbows on the table that he occupied."

"I told her, OK," sadly said Martin.

"And what happened then?" asked Brian.

Martin looked at him and frowned, "You're asking too much!"

"You were the one who brought her up into this conversation. How old was she?"

Martin turned his back.

"Twenty-eight. She was older than me by twelve years."

"Knowing you, I think it was a wonderful dinner," slightly smiled Brian.

Martin got angry and almost roared, "Shut up!"

After these words, the brothers quit. The room got a little cool. Curtains were slowly moving from the blowing wind. Brian was staring at his hands on the table, and Martin tried to make a bed to spend the night. He feels tired after all the events that happened in their lives here on a wild land.

Unexpectedly, Martin mumbled, "I want to go home and take a bath and drive my hot car."

Brian didn't answer. He was not with his brother now. He was too far from this place with Victoria on board of their frigate. He imagined her having dinner, eating delicious food, relaxing in a captain's cabin, or just staring at the stars.

Victoria couldn't sleep that night. She is sitting in her captain's room and staring at her favorite perfume, thinking about Caroline's story and feeling goose bombs on her skin: 'How can this be possible? If John Fury really did that murder, how did he live with such a sin? He should be insane. I can't tell this every time when I look at my dad. But in my life, I know only one John Furry who visited France so often, and if he really did that, all I can say is that he's worse than an animal.' Victoria sighed. 'My father is a killer, killer from the capital letter... The orphan is looking for him to kill, to take revenge for her family. What should I do?' Victoria questioned herself. 'Shall I hate him and help her to kill my father, or shall I let her go her own way after helping her with documents? What should I really do?' Victoria bit her lip, looking around for someone who could give her advice, good advice. She is positive about the fact she can't share with anybody about this matter. She made a promise to a girl to keep her mouth shut.

So, all she can do is figure out by herself what to do. 'I will make a call tomorrow to my friends in the embassy and order documents for Caroline. I will help her to get a passport and send her to college so she can get an American education, will help her financially to set up a life, and then she will decide what to do next. I'm out.'- Thought Victoria. 'I feel responsible for her life now. I took her on board. My dad killed her family, so I should do something good for her, and it's my problem as well.' Victoria took a hairbrush and started combing her long, deep, dark hair. Then she smiled to herself in the mirror, looking at her dark brown eyes, and whispered: 'Dark eyes are always full of shirts.'

Meanwhile, Raymond is walking back and forth waiting for Jain Mozhardin. As soon as she entered the room, she shed her tears. Raymond saw her and let her come close.

He looked at her with cold eyes, knowing no sorrow, "Why?" He asked angrily. "Why did you let her leave the palace, woman?"

"Hakim, it happened so unexpectedly, we haven't seen her, she just slipped through the window and took her horse, Ali was forcing me to the palace inside and didn't let me explain anything. I'm so sorry," and she started crying harder.

Raymond was still mad, "It doesn't make sense! Woman, tell me everything, and don't blame men!"

Jain Mozhardin looked at him with blurry eyes, "My dear Lord, our 'Sea Pearl' was always wild and did whatever she wanted. She considers you her only friend and wants to help and take part in this battle, so she dresses up and leaves a palace invisible by her horse.

I and all of us were hidden in the palace tunnel in case we were under attack, and..."

"Enough," Raymond moved his hand up, "like Hakim of this twenty-first century in Meknes, I will not punish you through execution," he paused and then added, "No food or water for three days."

Jain Mozhardin fell on her knees and grabbed his arm, "Merciful hakim, thank you! Thank you!" - She was crying while Ali came up to her and helped her stand up.

Raymond looked up at Ali and lightly nodded to him. Ali took away crying Jain Mozhardin.

The Hakim proudly left the huge palace's hall, rustling with his jetting white clothes; he made a decision to visit Jason before he could go to bed.

A knock at the door interrupted Jason's thoughts.

"Yes," he said loudly.

The door opened, and his eyes met with Raymond's eyes.

The Hakim broke the silence first, "Jason Parker, I'm fascinated by your audacity; you're a foreigner here and never afraid of me."

The guy smiled widely, "My Lord, we live in the twenty-first century."

Raymond nodded, "Thank you for reminding me. Because of you, I didn't execute a poor, honest woman who dares to this family."

Jason raised his head, pleased. "That's a big progress in this middle age."

Raymond came closer to Jason and said politely, "Tomorrow, you will leave this Land, and I want you to deliver my sincere apology to Reina; she can come back any time to share her place with me."

Jason nodded with respect and then slowly said, before Hakim could leave, "Sure, I will. So, you didn't find the other half, did you?"

Raymond turned his head fast, "What?"

The guy continued when he saw Raymond's worried look, "She is an outstanding beauty! I saw her. Nice choice."

Those words took Hakim's breath away, and he seemed to look nervous. His lips were trembling, and he couldn't talk. He was shocked by Jason's words. But finally, he took himself in his hands and said, "Where? How? When?"

Jason became serious, feeling his compassion towards Raymond's feelings, "She was on the bay horse on the battlefield. She attacked me and saved me from bloody riders. She let me know that she has never been a killer, and she can't cut my throat."

Raymond sadly nodded, "I know she had never killed anybody."

Jason looked at Hakim and sadly asked, "She lost? She never came back?"

Raymond shook his head, "No. We're still looking for her. But no signs of her anywhere."

Jason put his hand on Raymond's shoulder, "Never give up! Remember that, my dear friend."

The next morning, Caroline woke up early with a question: 'Where is Flash?' She realized her last action and remembered her falling on the ground. Raymond must be looking for her. Jain Mozhardin, her best Moroccan girlfriend, must be crying for her.

Caroline felt guilty. She is so unserious. And then she remembered a white envelope that Raymond held to her before she left. She checked her vest's inside pocket and found it. Caroline, with a trembling hand, pulled it out and opened. She took out a small letter and read: *"Caroline Sauvage Roux, I love you! Whatever happens today I want you to know in grave or in life, my feelings are always devoted to you! Raymond Moulay Ali."*

A knock on her door cabin made her jump from unexpected motion. The girl came up close and opened the door.

"Good morning," said Victoria.
Caroline smiled a little, "Hi!"

"Dress up. I want to show you something," said Victoria in a voice with no objection.
Caroline closed the door and rushed to the dresser; she grabbed black pants and quickly put them on and took a long sleeve shirt with some ruffles on a chest and buttoned it. Took a dark leather belt and fixed it on her waist. High shoes finished her look.

Victoria was waiting for her behind the door, and when Caroline showed up, she turned to her.

"Let's go," said Victoria.

Caroline followed her with so many questions holding in her head. But Victoria's mood was not ready to listen to none of them. Then she stopped and asked the girl to open the white door.

"What is in it?" Caroline worried.

"Open," said Victoria with a cold voice.

Caroline did what she said. The room was not bright, but there she saw her Flash. He came up close to her and tried to show his happiness.

"Oh my God!" Exclaimed Caroline, hugging the horse. "I thought you were dead..."

Caroline turned to Victoria with a wide smile on her face, "Thank you so much!"

Victoria crossed her arms on her chest and smiled back, still gazing at the young woman, "The Mustang is pretty tall for his normal size, but I can tell he's a young fellow still. How old is he? Like two years old?"

Caroline was rubbing her head giving an answer back, "Yeah, something like that."

Victoria gave away to her curiosity, "How much did you pay for him?"

"I didn't pay any money. That was a gift for my birthday," she smiled back to a woman.

"Nice gift," said Victoria, "I'm glad he's fine and healthy."

Caroline turned back to Victoria and asked her with a worried voice, "How do you feed him here? You don't have any food for horses on board, do you?"

"Yes, we do," unexpectedly said Victoria.

"What?" Caroline was deeply surprised.

"My brother used this boat before, and he transported some good-looking horses from Spain, and the food left after it, nobody cleaned it, we had no time for it," said Victoria confidently.

Caroline pleasantly smiled and thanked Victoria one more time. "What's his name?"

"His name is Flash," shortly said Caroline.

"It matches him; he's reddish as fire, very nice," admitted Victoria.

The woman left Caroline alone with her pet for a while.

Caroline was talking to him, kissing and rubbing his chick, giving some sugar from the sack that was hanging on the door. She is so pleased and grateful to Victoria for being so kind and nice to strangers. Caroline likes Victoria a lot; she is different from all the females that she has known in her whole life. When Caroline finished with Flash and gave him some rest, she tried to find Victoria. It was not that hard because Victoria was always at the captain's wheel.

"So," said Caroline when she saw Victoria with binoculars on the deck, "how far are we from the target?"

Victoria gave her a warm look, "Some couple of days, and then we will see the Liberty Statue."

Caroline smiled, and Victoria noticed some charming dimples on her cheek. 'This French girl is so cute,' thought Victoria looking at her. 'Even without her make-up, she is still so attractive. I like her wavy long hair and those eyes...Oh my God! Those eyes!'

"I ordered your documents this morning," added Victoria.

Caroline raised her fair eyebrows, "Did you?"

"Yeah, it is going to be ready when we arrive."

Caroline didn't know what to say.

Victoria is too kind to her, "You will get your document and what are you going to do next?"

The girl shook her head without answer.

"You know," continued Victoria, "You have to be serious if you want to be successful. You must get an education and a well-paid job, otherwise you gone."

Caroline sadly said, "Education? I have no money for that."

Victoria glanced at the teenager with a caring look, "Ok, first, never say this to nobody because words can materialize and you will never have money. Second," said Victoria with a teaching tone in her voice, "I will help you with that."

The girl nodded, "You are too kind to me, why?"

"My dear," said Victoria, slightly smiling, "I like you a lot and understand your position. I have a lot of money, and instead of wasting them on bullshit, I want to spend them on you. You have been under my protection since I met you and decided to take you and your pet on my board."

Caroline didn't know what to say; her words were like catching rope, and it was too much for her pride, but she understood clearly that this woman was right, and there was no objection. She has to take everything that life offers her that was the way how her dad taught her.

Her thoughts were interrupted by Victoria's question, "So, what do you think?"

Caroline agreed, "I have no objections."

"Well done," said Victoria, smiling.

There was nothing else to say, everything was already said. Victoria is a strong woman. Caroline realized that immediately. It would be hard to show her temper, she will cut it off. Now it is clear that she is going to be under her support and depend. Caroline sighed hard, and she went through different hands. Caroline knows she's smart enough to get a suitable education. She can learn and speak other languages, loves music and dance, knows history, and is keen on literature. Sometimes, in her free time, when she has her muse in visit, she can even make her own poetry.

Her father was a lawyer and would love to have a child to follow his steps, but Caroline isn't sure if she wants to do law. It's a very responsible job, and you have to be a bitch sometimes. Caroline isn't also sure if a judge mask will suit her as well. No, she doesn't want to be anything like that. She loves traveling and adventures. Danger is a little scary but enjoyable after a good finish. She shook her head and bit her lip.

Now the work with dolphins like she dreamed seemed so silly to her. And then she realized that she grew up from being a child. She looked at her reflection in the mirror and noticed how beautiful she was. Even without making, she was simply noticeable. She liked about her appearance everything and never wanted to change anything. Caroline sat on a bed, took off her high shoes and socks, and felt her feet sore from being closed in tight shoes all day. She looked at her toes and, for the first time, noticed that they were pretty and just the same size, not ugly like Eastern people have.

Caroline smiled slightly at this thought and opened a drawer near her bed. She glanced at her old clothes and took it out. She tried to smell it and wrinkled her nose - it stunk with her adventures. She felt something hard under her finger and tried to see what it was. She raised her eyebrows when she saw a gold marquise ring with a shiny diamond in the center. The tears stuck in her eyes. Janie's gift! 'It will bring you luck!'

She just remembered her words. 'Yes, it did,' thought Caroline, holding a ring. She put it on and hugged close to her chest. 'Thank you, Janie, for everything. I will write you a letter for sure when I come to the States. She came up to her window and looked through, but there was nothing except waves and a blue horizon. The frigate moved quickly, and you could hear the stubborn waves under it. Luckily, Caroline never felt seasick and she is absolutely comfortable on the deck when outside or inside.

# CHAPTER 15

*Sometimes, in some strange ways of life, everything starts getting better by itself.*

***Max Frye***

The Moroccan sun was not that burning today and the procedure to move stuff on the ship was smooth. Martin and his team packed everything left after the battle and the heavy weapons were already on board in the safe place. Brian and Chris were so happy as never. They are coming home back alive and safe. Everything is done, and Jason is also alive and came to an agreement with the Moroccan Prince as well. Martin was inside the palace's garden passing by high bushes as he saw a middle statue in the center of the fountain. That was a figure of the white woman holding flowers in her arms. He came up to see her close. She has a beautiful face with long wavy hair and if she were in color, probably he could even guess her eyes color, but the statue was pale and white. He frowned and tried to concentrate on her face in particular, and she seemed familiar and far at the same time. Something about her touched his soul. He wasn't sure what yet.

"She is beautiful, isn't she?" Suddenly, he heard the voice behind him.

Martin turned around and saw Ali coming to him.

He nodded, "Yes, she is gorgeous."

"The modeling is fresh as well." Ali admitted. "I see you know something about this art."

Martin gave away his curiosity, "Who is she?"

Ali smiled a little with pride in his eyes, "My niece."

"Your niece?" Martin was deeply surprised by his answer.

"Yes, she is only eighteen, so young and wild," said Ali.

"Why have I never seen her in this palace?" asked Martin, giving away his obvious curiosity.

Ali sight and said sadly, "She is not here anymore. Only Allah knows where she is. She ran away."

Martin widened his eyes, "I thought that your women were always afraid of everything and hid in the palace with their men."

"But not her. She's not from here, and she's European."

Martin was struck by his words, "You must be kidding me!"

"No," Ali said sadly again.

"What's her name?"

"We call her "Sea Pearl," but her real name is Caroline."

Martin heard something about it from Jason's story, but it has been unclear to him.

"How?" He asked Ali.

"Well, our hakim wanted to marry her soon and even engaged to her, but she never loved him, I guess," sighed Ali.

'Good for her,' thought Martin, nodding to this grey old man.

"My niece ran away, and we're still looking for her, but there are no signs of her presence anywhere, and I'm afraid that the worst could happen to her."

Martin looked at Ali and put his hand on his shoulder, "Don't worry, man! I'm sure you'll find her safe and sound."

Ali smiled back at Martin, "Thank you!"

They left the garden, crossed the palace's yard, and took a car. The trip to the coast took nearly two hours until they reached the target. Martin came out from the massive car and saw Raymond talking to Jason. They both were dressed nice and had a kind look.

Jason was the first who approach Martin, "Hey, man! We're ready."

Raymond nodded slightly, and a wide smile showed up on his face.

"The frigate is full, and you were the only one whom we were waiting for. What took you so long?"

Martin made an ironic smile and answered back, "Nothing, just curiosity."

He grabbed his leather sack from Jason's hand and asked, "Where are the guys? Brian and Chris?"

"Oh, they're on board already."

Martin and Jason turned to Raymond and shook his hand. After that, they left him alone, climbing up the stairs to board. When they were inside, the machine took the ramp up, and the frigate under the name "The Mask" raised the American flag and set sail from the marina. Martin turned the wheel, and the huge boat's nose set the trip course to the west.

Then Brian showed up next to Jason and informed his brother, "I called Victoria and told her we were coming home."

Martin nodded and agreed, "Good Job! How's she?"

"She's fine, and soon we'll see her," added Brian.

Martin concentrated on the horizon and asked Chris to update the weather advisory.

Chris checked the computer and immediately informed, "Sunny all day and at night, supposed to be cloudy without rain, temperature between seventy and eighty."

"Excellent!" smiled Martin.

Now, he is pleased. He finished his quest here, but it was disappointing with too many people lost and missing. He has to figure out the report for Father and the rest of the 'shots.' Of course, John Furry will be happy to get weapons and the new frigate, but at what cost? John was on a business trip to Casablanca with his wife. So, he might come back in a week or so, and by this time guys need to make a report at the company. Maybe Victoria will give them some ideas. Who knows? Yesterday, they were almost dead and today, they're coming home safe and with the catch on the hook. 'What a fortune!' - thought Martin Furry.

The night was silent, and no scary waves on the Ocean. The guys took turns sleeping and controlling the frigate.

"One more day," silently said Victoria to herself, holding a map and sitting on a chair with her legs crossed.

Caroline looked at her without words. They were at the captain's cabin eating their lunch. Victoria seemed busy with her bossy responsibility, giving instructions to the people all the time. They're working on a deck doing different kinds of work, never resting. Caroline did nothing, just eating, sleeping, and waiting for the coast to show up. She was thinking and trying to get to know her new friend - it was terrific, Victoria wasn't the same every time, her mood changed every hour. But she is a stable woman of nearly twenty-seven years. Caroline learned about her one pleasant thing: if she gives a word, she always keeps it.

Sometimes it seems, that people like to work for Victoria, they never argue with her and she's flexible in making decisions. Pleasant at any conversation they had with her. She's mature and so smart. Caroline never asked her what she was doing for a living. She just guessed.

"Victoria," all of a sudden said Caroline, "what's your real job?"

The woman turned to her with her eyebrows raised, "Well, I'm working for my father at a big company, and I'm responsible for training new people who were just hired."

Caroline slightly nodded, "I see..."

"I helped him since I was twenty-one," she added.

"And what did you do before?" asked Caroline.

"I studied at the academy," said Victoria with a confident voice, "that's what you're going to do and will be busy for six years, and then you will see what you want to do."

Caroline didn't say anything to her words, and she knew that Victoria's right.

"Do you have brothers or sisters in your family?" Caroline tried to talk to Victoria about something else.

"Yes, I have younger brothers, but we all spread up," answered Victoria carefully.

"Oh," sighed Caroline, "that must be hard for you not to see them often."

Victoria's lips stretched in a charming smile, and she replied, "It doesn't bother me much. Of course, I miss them."

Then Caroline looked at the world's map and slightly smiled too, "So, you live in New York?"

"No, that's where our port is. I live in Chicago."

The girl smirked, "The gangster city!"

Victoria laughed out loud with a sweet voice, "Oh, come on! That's legends and history, and people made them terrible for the public! Right now it's a safe city, and you will enjoy it a lot. Even Flash will love it. We have beautiful stables and nice green fields, and the weather is really nice there."

"Really?" Caroline came to life in her eyes.

"Yeah, you won't see the desert like in Morocco and dullness unless you can go to Nevada or Arizona if you miss the desert," smiled Victoria. "Which I doubt you would."

Caroline shook her head, "No, I don't like a desert; it reminds me of death. Nothing grows there, and it's cold or super-hot. No, that's definitely not me."

"I knew you were going to say that. You grew up in a picture-rescue country. So, you have to love green nature."

"That's right," agreed Caroline.

Victoria had a call and she rushed to the higher deck, and Caroline followed her to see what worried her friend that much.

"Low the engine!" Yelled Victoria to Wrigley.

"What is it?" asked Caroline with worry in her voice.

Victoria looked through binoculars and gave it to the girl to see, "We have to be careful, see..." she pointed, "some wales coming up, and it's the whole families, and we shouldn't hurt them."

"Wow!" Caroline exclaimed with surprised.

"Yeah, they're sometimes blind. I think we have to give them a way to cross, and then we can start moving again," said Victoria in a thinking voice.

She dialed Wrigley and told him to wait for Wales to pass. He agreed, and they were waiting, crossing their hands on a chest. Caroline looked in the binoculars again and couldn't believe how big those animals were. They came closer and crossed in front of the frigate, making hard and deep noises. Caroline was amassed by those animals, and she had never seen them before in her real life. When they left, the ship's engine started again, and they flew on the water surface. Victoria came up close to Caroline and asked her opinion, "How do you like our ship?"

That was surprising for Caroline to hear this question, "It's really nice." Admitted Caroline, "Not a cruise, looks like a military frigate."

Victoria turned away her eyes and answered, "Yeah? Thank you!"

They didn't talk to each other this late evening. Victoria was too busy and Caroline spent her time in her room reading a book that Victoria left for her on a dresser the other day, so the girl wouldn't be bored that much.

Meanwhile, Moulay Ali and his son Raymond Moulay Ali Hassam took a decision finally to inform Mohammed about Caroline's behavior.

*"Dear Mohammed Hasaan, you were always nice to us, and thank you for the invitation to your tent." Jain was very nice to your child, Caroline. Unfortunately, we lost her. Americans attacked us in Meknes, and your stubborn child ran away from the palace. We're still searching for her but no results for now. We want to bring you our apologies for losing her; we couldn't take care of her as we promised.*

*Hopefully, she is fine and somehow shows up. My dear brother, I'm so sorry for everything. "Sincerely yours, Ali,"* - whispered to himself Mohammed holding a crispy letter. 'Well, here we go,' thought Mohammed, 'she shamed me with this stubborn child.' Mohammed turned to his fireplace and threw the piece of paper into the fire. He watched it burning and after sighing, he slowly walked to the kitchen and poured some water from the tall glass jar. He drank it and took a sit at the table. His arms were lying on his knees, helpless. 'I was going to inform her about money that was received for the house insurance, but it will not happen, my Caroline had gone… This country is very cruel to lonely women.' He sighed again. Mohammed didn't want to believe that Caroline just simply disappeared just like that. He felt her alive, and maybe those people were not nice to her there because there was no other reason to escape.

Mohammed also assumed that Caroline vanished on purpose just because she had to do her own things and make up her future; he guessed that they were close to engaging her with Raymond, and she would show her attitude anyway, so she did what was better for her. Maybe she got a new friend helping her with her goal or probably, she saved some money for a trip back home. Sure, his house's door always opened for her. Only Caroline knows what she is doing.

Meanwhile, this naughty girl is resting in the comfortable bed in her cabin on the "Phantom" board. She is staring at the ceiling of her temporally place, thinking about Janie and Hakim. How pissed and mad he can be right now with her. She is far from them and can't see their faces, just little she felt guilty.

She knows that she writes them a note and lets them know that she's fine. Caroline has another bothering thing - it's her education, she has to choose her future profession. 'Maybe to try science?' Caroline thought, 'No, that's not my strong point.

Hmm... May be law? Like my father... No. You have to be smart enough. That's not me. Mm... Acting? Hollywood? No, then everybody will find out my story.' She moved to another side of her body and got mad with no idea coming into her head. 'How about writing articles and doing photography for some glamorous magazines? Like my mom. Well, I can do it.' Caroline smiled, being glad with any idea progress.' If not, I can try something else interesting,' then she rose up from the bed and walked back and forth. This time on the ship was different. On the one side, enjoyable, on the other side, boring. She took a jacket and put it on her shoulders; opened the door, and went outside to breathe in fresh air. It was autumn, and she was a little chill. She looked around, and the deck was empty. Employees just vanished somewhere. Caroline came close to see water, but really nothing was there. She raised her head to look at the sky and noticed different star positions. They looked quite unusual, not like in Morocco. She wondered what time it was. She forgot to look at the alarm in her cabin. Never mind, she isn't hurrying anywhere. All of a sudden, she heard a strange noise on the other side of the ship. She hurried to give away her curiosity. Caroline's eyes opened wide when she saw beautiful fireworks in the sky above the Liberty Statue. So many flashes spread everywhere, making the sky bright like in the daytime. She smiled and waved to those flashes. Above her is Victoria. She was smiling, too.

"Victoria!" waved Caroline.

The woman looked at her down and yelled, "We're in New York!"

"What!!??" Caroline couldn't hear Victoria's words.

"New York!!! We arrived in New York!!!"

Caroline happily exclaimed, "Wow!!! Yay!!! That's so cool!"

And tears rolled down her cheeks, she was happy to arrive in the United States. Her heart was going to jump out from her being glad. She jumped like a little girl; Victoria was watching and smiling at her. 'She is such a child! I love her!' – thought Victoria.

It took them an hour to approach the dock. The ladder was adjusted to the board, and several men close to Victoria met her with hugs, pleasant smiles, and handshaking. She passed to her other friend, who was dressed in an officer form. He was taller than her on a head and older, probably by several years. Caroline was watching her from the distance, standing next to Wrigley. The man smiled at Victoria, and they shook hands. He pulled a little navy-blue book from his pocket and handed it to her. She opened it, after she closed it and put it in her inside jacket's pocket, said something and shook his hand again. Victoria turned her back to him and slowly walked away towards the rest of the noisy guys around Caroline. The girl smiled at her and said, "Sun rose."

Victoria pulled a tiny, short blue book out of her jacket's pocket and handed it to Caroline, "Here is your document."

Caroline took it from her hands and slightly whispered, "Passport?"

Victoria nodded in response, "Right."

Caroline looked back into Victoria's eyes, "He likes you!"

Victoria widened her eyes, "Who?"

"That man," she pointed her look at that tall officer.

Victoria turned her face back to him and nodded, "Oh come on, this is my old friend from school."

Caroline whispered, so only Victoria could hear: 'Old friends never have glaring eyes when they see you.'

Victoria looked back at Caroline and raised her right eyebrow. Then didn't answer back.

Caroline opened her new passport and looked at her picture with an open mouth, "Oh, that's me from the first year of college; nobody has this picture, only my college! How? How did you guys do that?"

"Shah..." whispered Victoria, grabbing Caroline's hand.

Caroline was deeply shocked and speechless. She was staring at herself in the picture in her new passport.

"Let's go," strictly said Victoria, "it's time."

They quietly went through the bridge, and Victoria's friend pointed to the wide white hall. Caroline walked there and met with another officer who took her to the window. The border controller opened her passport and asked, "How old are you?"

Caroline made a fake smile, "Nineteen."

He looked at her photo in the passport and asked again, "Welcome home, darling, to the United States of America."

Caroline slightly smiled, and Victoria met her at the exit.

"Good job!" She said to Caroline, smiling.

Caroline lowered her eyelashes with blushing cheeks and let Victoria give her a good hug. At the building exit, there was a fancy navy blue car waiting for them already. Victoria, together with Caroline, came closer to it, and two men met them and opened doors for them. Girls got comfortable inside and put their seat belts on.

Caroline looked around at the interior and noticed champagne behind frosted glass panels, nice polish doors, and soft white leather seats. The atmosphere inside is relaxing. Even iPod tables were there and a mini theater was.

"Nice car," admitted Caroline.

"Bentley was, is, and will always be the best class car," with satisfaction, said Victoria.

Caroline couldn't hold her curiosity anymore, "Who are you, Victoria? First, a frigate and then a passport picture, and now this expensive car? Who you really are?"

Victoria squeezed her hand in hers and, looking into her eyes, replied, "Just your guardian angel. Nice to meet you!"

Caroline shook her head without truly believing in her words. 'She is a big shot and all of these stories are just for the little girls, silly and naive like me.' – thought Caroline. 'She will never tell me the truth until I find out on my own.'

"Where are we going?" turned around Caroline.

"To the airport, relax and enjoy your free trip," slightly and so easy said Victoria.

Caroline felt her words burning like a slap with this answer, she didn't like the way how Victoria said that. But she has no other choice but to obey this woman. While they had been moving to a target place, Caroline tried to observe the outside streets. And there was nothing except trees and bushes.

It didn't take too much time to get to the airport. They got out of the car at the private area, and the girl saw a plane.

"I thought it was going to be big," whispered Caroline.

Victoria smiled in response, "Private jets are never big like passenger planes. As soon as we get there, you close your eyes to relax, and we're in Chicago."

Caroline sighed slightly. She didn't say anything. They got inside, and the engine was already running. Victoria suddenly went to the pilot cabin as she said she needed to check something.

So, Caroline went through the salon and placed in a cozy armchair. They were already on a speed laid running and then took off. She felt tired and didn't even notice how she fell asleep. Victoria joined her next and looked into her face. The girl was sleeping. Great! Finally, she can relax for a while.

The Atlantic Ocean was calm enough, so the ship moved smoother and faster to its destination. On board, people are working under Martin's orders. He is in the captain's cabin with his friends.

"Did anybody call my sister?" asked Martin.

Brian turned to face his brother, "Of course," he said in a strong voice.

"Where's she?"

"Victoria is on her way to Chicago," answered Jason Parker.

"She is in the plane, right?" asked Martin.

"Yeah, she is fine, don't worry that much. Pretty soon, we arrive in New York also," nodded Brian.

Martin sighed but didn't say anything in response. He took binoculars and looked through it, making sure there were no pirates ahead.

In present days, there are still so many pirates in the open sea or ocean, and they're hunting for weak victims. Money, arms, and goods are their main target to capture. They can be anywhere. At any moment, you have to watch out.

Martin looked at his brother sitting on his chair next to a table and asked, "Are you guys hungry?"

Chris, Jason, and Brian exchanged looks, and Chris answered back, "Yes, it would be good to eat something. Feel like starving."

Martin nodded. He pushed a button and gave the order to cook dinner for the captain and his close ones. Then he slightly smiled, "One hour, guys, just wait one hour."

Brian checked his computer and called for his brother, "I am almost done with the report here, Martin."

Martin came closer to see the document. He looked through it and then glanced at Brian, "Good! John will receive a report of our work soon, and I think he would be excited about it."

Jason sighed and shook his head, smiling a little, 'I will see my love soon. I'm excited about it.'

Chris glanced at Jason and raised his eyebrows, "So, when are you going to marry? Where?"

Jason looked back at his friends, "Hopefully in April. We were planning to have a wedding in LA."

Brian was constantly surprised, "Why not in Chicago?"

"She doesn't want to have a wedding there because all of her relatives are in California and for them, it would be more comfortable to stick around in LA."

"So, are we invited?" asked Martin, smiling on the side.

"Sure, you are," Jason put his hand on Martin's shoulder.

The guys were excited about this upcoming event. They wanted Jason to be really happy in his marriage, but it also meant he would drop out of their company. Martin sadly lowered his eyes, understanding that. Jason was his best friend, and now he was going to be a family guy and would have less time to see friends. Brian noticed that his brother got sad and asked Martin what it was.

Martin wondered, "Jason, are you going to quit your job at Lex?"

Jason glanced quickly at Martin; he knew the answer to this question but wasn't expecting it so soon, "Maybe," he quietly said.

Brian looked away, as well as Chris. 'Damn, this bitch is taking away their best friend. Victoria disliked her from the very beginning. She knew how it was going to end. Bitches!!! Bitches!!!' Martin has a big pain in his heart after this talk. Brian is silent. Chris made himself on purpose not to think about it. He also likes and adores Jason.

"Guys," Jason approached his friends, "that marriage doesn't make me dead for you; I'll always be your friend."

Nobody said anything in response. Silence hung in the space between them. It has a feeling of a huge wall dividing them. Martin swallowed and announced, "The dinner is ready! Let's go!"

The mess room they entered was big enough to make even a banquet. It was all arranged with elegant splendor. The dining room walls were made of gold pattern with beautiful shimmer brocade. A big round wooden table was in the center of the room, together with polished chairs around. Some dark armchairs were in the corners, and opposite them was hanging a TV on the wall. An Eastern carpet, wide and thick, was on the floor next to a sofa, and gorgeous heavy curtains finished the look of the room.

Friends were walking around, looking at every detail.

"Oh my God!" Brian broke the silence, "Just look around... It's the most beautiful dining room on the ship I have ever seen."

Martin slightly noticed, "Now I feel like a real king! And like a real lord, I invite you to share my meal."

Friends laughed and touched his shoulder, placing themselves around the table.

"Arthur," approached Brian, "We're your knights!"

Martin, Jason, and Chris roared with lough.

Chicago's beauty can fascinate everyone who visits this beautiful city indefinitely. And if you are really a city person you would enjoy night Chicago very much. Its bright lights can be comparable with The Sin City. Autumn time is really famous for its winds and amazing parks with red leaves on trees. The most attractive thing is the Lake. Wealthy people live in the northern part of Chicago, and gorgeous houses are located, not far away from the beaches. Every year, thousands and thousands of tourists visit Chicago and bring back the best memories.

The white jet with blue stripes on the side is landing. Caroline opened her eyes involuntarily and touched Victoria's hand, "Are we landing?"

Victoria positively nodded to her. She looked a little bit tired, but rosy checks presented her freshness. She checked her watch on the wrist and moved a little in the armchair. Caroline tried to look through the round window and saw the Chicago beauty.

"Gosh!" She whispered.

"What?" asked Victoria.

"It's so beautiful," answered back Caroline.

"Wait, when we land and will be in the city," smiled Victoria, "how are you feeling, Caroline?"

The girl turned to her and met her curious eyes in front of her face.

"Amazed," slowly answered Caroline.

Victoria relaxed in the armchair and informed Caroline of a plan, "After we arrive, the car will take us to the place we recently rented for you. We will leave things there and then will go to a dinner after I will take you back. By the way, can you drive?"

Caroline turned to Victoria and positively nodded to her.

"Good!" Said Victoria, "That's good news. I think next week you will go to the DMW and get your license so we can buy you a car."

Caroline was glad to hear that, her first car! Her car! She won't be dependable on Vicki like she was dependable on her parents. The fact that Caroline knows how to drive was a great plus here because, without your own vehicle, it's hard to move. She never liked to use public transport for many reasons: crowded, sweaty, and stuffy. Victoria said about her place, oh..., how it's going to look like? How much did Victoria spend on it? Caroline felt uneasy about those things.

Finally, they landed and, in a moment, were already in the car. The same beauty and luxury as in New York. This time, Caroline didn't ask Victoria about anything. Quietly like that mouse, she had been sitting in the back seat of the car. Meanwhile, Victoria was sitting with the driver in the front, talking to him all the way to Caroline's place. They have been in the car not that long but for Caroline, it seemed forever. Victoria turned to the girl and gave her a nod with words, "This is the address. Remember it fifteen fifty North Lake Shore Drive. Don't lose it, okay?"

"Yes," answered back Caroline.

Finally, they arrived, and when the door opened in front of Caroline, she saw a huge skyscraper. And her little mouth opened. Victoria came close to Caroline and, with an invigorating tone, said, "Ok, come on! Let's enter."

They went inside and the surroundings were magnificent with its richness and beauty in the hall.

"So," Caroline broke the silence, "What's my floor number?"

"It's twenty-five," said Victoria. "Are you nervous?"

Caroline glanced at Victoria and nodded, "Yes, a little."

The girls went through the skinny, tall hall to the door. Victoria stopped and said, "Hold on, I will give you the key." She opened her purse and started looking for them.

Caroline was standing beside her and breathing hard so that even Victoria could hear.

"Oh, she just gave it to me, this key," said Victoria, searching hard in the pockets of her purse, "oh, here it is." And she handled it to Caroline.

Caroline faced the door, put a key in the hole, and made only one turn. The lock clicked, the young woman went inside, and the light automatically turned on. And Caroline froze when she saw the fascinating beauty of her new place. The lobby smoothly connected to the kitchen, dining and living room. All of this time, she thought that Raymond's palace was the best, but this place was a hundred times better. She looked around and noticed the walls in silver color and the floor finished with creamy shiny tile. The ceiling was white, and the corners were finished with modeling. The living room was wide and bright; the windows went from ceiling to floor, so she could see the view of the Michigan Lake. On the windows were hanging silk dark red curtains, they matched the dark red pillows on the beige sofa standing next to a wall in front of the TV. Next to the window was placed a square brown table with three chairs around it. In front of the sofa was a carpet and a little table for magazines. On both sides of the sofa were placed stand lamps.

Victoria hugged Caroline and said, "Well, the condo you can observe later. Let's have dinner first. My stomach rumbles already."

Caroline smiled in an answer and agreed. They left the condo, and when the door closed behind, the light turned off automatically.

They left the building and came back to Bentley, who was waiting for them outside. And as soon as Victoria got in and closed the door she said to her driver, "Jerry, take us to the Palm restaurant on East Upper Walker Drive."

The driver didn't say anything, he started the engine and the car rolled on the street. In a few minutes, the girls were walking inside. Caroline has already noticed the tall glass building with green windows. Inside, everything looks pretty comfortable. She likes the beige walls with shiny redwood doors and tables. The restaurant inside was not that crowded. At the entrance, the hostess met them and invited them to take a place next to a window. The menu was handed to them and they opened it at once as soon as they took their seats. Caroline was looking through the prices first. She wanted to know if they were higher than in Marseille. Well, they were pretty much the same as in her hometown. Caroline wasn't that picky, so she knew what was going to order. The waitress interrupted her thoughts, "Hello! My name is Jain, and I'm going to serve you tonight. Do you want anything to drink?"

"Yes, just ice teas!" said Victoria and then quickly looked at Caroline to make sure she wanted the same.

"Yes, that's perfect!" nodded Caroline.

The waitress asked again, "Are you ready to make an order, or do you need some more time?"

Caroline noticed that Victoria had let her order first.

"Ok," said Caroline, "Can I have Monday night salad and Atlantic salmon filet?"

"Anything on a side?"

"Mm..., I think mashed potatoes will be enough."

The waitress made a note and turned to Victoria, "OK, and what about you, mam?"

Victoria asked for a Veal Martini and mixed green salad.

"Ok, thank you, I'll be back," said Jain. She took menus away with her.

The girls are left alone, facing each other.

Victoria's eyes were shiny, and Caroline noticed that at once.

"What?" She asked Victoria.

She crossed her arms and, with a nice pleasant smile, answered back, "I'm glad I'm home. I can't wait to see my boyfriend. Miss him so much."

Caroline glanced at her, "You have a boyfriend?"

"Yea, he's so sweet... Very nice man. I met him in France."

Caroline cocked up her one eyebrow, surprised, "Oh, really? How?"

Victoria slightly sighed and moved on a chair, "In Paris. I went there on my vacation. Always dreamed of visiting Paris, and that was a good possibility to escape from friends and parents for a while. And I was driving my car on a side road and saw a crashed car. I stopped to see if anybody needed my help, and I found a guy there with his head bleeding."

"Oh my God," silently said Caroline, "did you call an ambulance?"

"That was the first thing I did." Sadly moved her lips, Victoria. "He was just in a terrible condition. The help arrived quickly; they took him at once, and I shared my information with the police and ambulance."

Caroline swallowed hard and glanced at Victoria again, "So, you visited him, right?"

"Yes, I have been visiting him every day. And when he finally opened his eyes, he saw me. He asked if he knew me and what happened to him, and he had been asking me all the time until I realized that he lost his memory." Victoria lowered her eyes and a teardrop rolled on her cheek.

Caroline was amazed by this story she didn't know what to say.

"What did you do?" She finally asked Victoria.

"Well," she sadly replied, "I couldn't leave him alone there. I paid for his treatment at the hospital, and I told him that he was coming with me. I tried to find answers to his questions and couldn't until he touched me, and I realized that I could pretend to be his girlfriend. He was charmed by me and said that he liked me a lot and wanted to be only with me."

Caroline was hit by this sort of information, "Oh, you're really crazy!"

Victoria smiled back and giggled, "I know. I have always been like that."

The waitress brought them a meal and served them around. Then she asked if they needed something else and if everything was ok. When she made sure that the girls were fine, she left.

Caroline started chewing her meal slowly and thinking about Victoria's story. Shaking her head, she asked, "So, you brought him here? You made him documents and brought him with you, didn't you?"

Victoria moved to a side close to Caroline.

"Yes," she replied.

For Caroline, it was hard to believe that somebody could do something like that. It sounds like a Hollywood movie, and her new friend is the main character.

She just can't imagine this situation. What exactly actually has just happened to her recently? That's so crazy! Victoria has too many responsibilities. First, her French boyfriend, and now she took Caroline to her neck, and maybe there's something else that Caroline doesn't know. This lady is definitely out of her mind.

"You know," said Victoria, "I really enjoy helping people."

Caroline smiled a little and nodded, "Yeah?"

While Victoria was talking to her, Caroline was chewing her salmon filet.

"This is a very pleasant feeling to help people. And I'm grateful to God for everything he does for me and my friends."

Victoria sounds like a good person; it's so rare to be good, having a lot of money in your pocket. She helped a guy, saved Caroline and her horse from bloody killers, and continued to do kind stuff.

Caroline took a glass of her iced tea and shifted her eyes to Victoria's arms. 'This lady has manicured hands, a sweet voice, a nice look, and much money. Of course, any man will fall in love with her.'- Thought Caroline. She didn't pay attention to Victoria's words until she heard this, "When the time comes I will introduce you to him!"

Caroline stopped eating, "Me? Why?"

"Why not? I want you to meet him and tell me what you think," confidently said Victoria.

Caroline positively nodded and glanced at her already empty plate. She pushed it away and was thinking about a desert.

"I'm going to have an ice cream," said Victoria.

"Me too," agreed Caroline.

Time flew fast at this restaurant. When they finished, they took off, paid for dinner, and left.

Victoria drove Caroline back to her condo and told her that she was going to meet her tomorrow afternoon.

Caroline pulled out the key and opened her apartment. Some small travel bags are on the floor next to a fake fireplace. She moved forward to a bedroom and turned the light on. A wide bed with golden pillows and cover caught her attention at once. It was luxurious, beautiful, and very soft when she touched it. Caroline liked the golden shade everywhere in her bedroom. There was a little white carpet in front of her queen bed. She took off her shoes, and her bare feet felt the softness of it. After that, she took off her clothes and went to the bathroom. She turned on the hot water and mixed it with cold water. After that, she opened the mirror on the wall and took out the toothpaste and toothbrush. She looked at her reflection and sighed; tired eyes, pale cheeks, and dull hair.

Caroline carefully brushed her teeth twice so she would get rid of that terrible taste in her mouth. Then she walked to the kitchen and found some salt. She came back to the bathroom and, in front of the mirror, pulled some salt on her palm and then rubbed salt on her face. That was her natural facial scrub. She rinsed her face after salt and felt desirable softness. She smiled to herself in the mirror and after walked to the bath. It was already full of water. Caroline combed her hair several times and, after, plunged into the water bath. Her skin was covered with goosebumps after a pleasant feeling of warmth. Oh, these autumn days! She closed her eyes, and the wave of exciting feelings overshadowed her mind. She gave herself away to this feeling. In a moment, Caroline saw a man in her mind. He was touching her. Half dark background didn't allow her to see his whole face. She was standing with her back to him, trying to avoid a conversation with this guy. His arms lay on her shoulders, and with a side vision, she noticed his nice fingers.

Then she saw his lips touching her right shoulder trying to give a slight kiss. Caroline closed her eyes, giving herself pleasure. His lips were so soft and tender, his arms squeezed her shoulders, and she felt how strong he was. His arms went down, and he turned her around. She opened her eyes to see him, and he went down on one knee and his face pressed against her belly. She slightly touched his soft hair and noticed its dark chocolate color. And then she screamed out loud and opened her eyes quickly. Caroline turned around, trying to make sure she was still alone. Luckily, it was just a timeless mirage that enveloped her for a moment. She rose a little in the bath and felt her heart biting fast.

And then Caroline realized that she got excited from this imagination. Her cheeks started blushing.

*Sunny and warm day! Finally, one more game lasts to be won. He knows he's going to win again, one more time, and another million dollars in his pocket. What a pleasant moment. He's the best! Everybody is applauding him; he's smiling wide, showing his amazing white teeth; his sister is kissing him and hugging him. He's the best driver ever. The track and a race car his toy, enjoy and the way of living and earning money. He is drinking a glass of champagne, and the hot girls are staring at him. And he sees that, and he loves that. In a crowd, the girl got his attention. She is sitting alone and her long, wavy hair is covering her face. She is the only one who doesn't applaud his "Majesty," she seems pretty sad. He*

*wants to see her closer, but the moving crowd separates them. He's*
*trying to come closer and see her face. People push him and don't*
*allow him to come off the stage; they want to take a picture with him,*
*and they talk to him, but he's not listening to them. He's staring at*
*her. He wants to see her.*

Martin opened his eyes, irritated. He rubbed his face, staring at
the ceiling of his cabin. It was just a dream. For a couple of minutes,
he was still staring at the wall, trying to figure out her image. He
sighed, then rose from the bed and looked at his clothes on the floor.
'Damn,' – he thought. 'Who is she? I have never seen her before.
Do I know her? Her hair and her image seem acquainted. No' – he
shook his head 'I don't know her.'

Dressed, he came out of his room and went up the stairs to the
captain's cabin. Jason was there on his turn.

"Good morning, man!" said Jason when he saw Martin
approaching.

"Hey!" answered back Martin.

"You look annoyed," Jason touched Martin's shoulder, "what
happened? Did you sleep well?"

Martin smiled a little.

"As always, I see a big race, my lucky car, applauding people,
hot girls, but…," he paused.

Jason looked with curiosity at him and frowned, "But what?"

"But this time, I saw a different girl, she wasn't in my dreams before." Sadly, said Martin.

Jason Parker sneered, "Who is she? Do you know her?"

"I thought so, but not this time. Her image looks familiar to me, but I can't remember her. All I think about is that statue," said Martin trying to cover his feelings spilling out.

Jason came closer and turned his back to Martin, thinking. And then he said, "Statue? Is that statue in Raymond's garden? What are you talking about?"

Martin glanced at his friend, raising one eyebrow, "How do you know?"

"I've seen her before," nodded Jason, biting his lower lip and looking into Martin's eyes.

Martin sighed, "She is pretty; I can imagine her in reality."

Jason slightly smiled and crossed his arms on his chest. "That's what I'm talking about. I've seen her in person," and he made a pause to see his friend's reaction.

Martin shook from these words and glanced at Jason, "Really? How's she?"

"That was an incredible situation. She was on the battlefield riding a horse. We fought hand to hand; she is strong and brave with a slight shade of tender."

"Her face was covered with a mask that I had taken off at last. And she is just gorgeous," with a velvet voice Jason said.

His friend was staring at him in silence. He couldn't believe his story.

"And what happened then?" asked amazed Martin.

"When the third opponent interfered, she helped me to escape. She left me in the oasis, so since then, I haven't seen her," sadly said Jason.

Martin had a slightly visible smile on his face. Then he added, "I wish I were you."

Jason looked back and continued his speech, "I wish I wouldn't be engaged otherwise. I would try to win her heart," and he winked at Martin.

The guys spent the rest of their time discussing the plan to get home faster. They checked the map, made some calls, and by nine o'clock, had breakfast. They knew that John Fury was supposed to arrive soon in Chicago, so they tried to finish their report for him as soon as possible.

Meanwhile, Victoria woke up in her apartment with her boyfriend. They had breakfast and she told him a story about her nice trip to Spain and then to Morocco, but she never mentioned Caroline in her conversation. Victoria tried to avoid any information about her business with her brothers. She wants him to be away from it. Her life was full of adventures and difficult things to understand.

"Last night was amazing," finally, she said while she was dressing up.

"Yeah," he turned to her, "I'm glad you enjoyed it."

Victoria came closer to him and looked into his brown eyes, "I missed you so much! You can't even imagine," she kissed his lips and slightly bit his lower lip.

He looked into her eyes and responded to her kiss the same way and then lifted her up in his arms, and she screamed, "No, no ... I have to go!"

He pressed his lips to her mouth so she couldn't say anything and put her on a wide bed. He lay on her, pressing with his chest, and hundreds of kisses covered her neck. She tried to protest and slowly melted under him. He was holding her hands in his above her head. Victoria couldn't push him away; she felt the same desire as he did. Her arms circled around his body, and she allowed him to give her pleasure.

The bright sunshine came through the curtains in Caroline's bedroom. She opened her eyes and looked at the clock on her bedroom nightstand next to her bed, which showed a quarter past seven. The girl stretched her hands up in the air and put them above her head. Caroline tried to remember her last night's dream but couldn't, she had slept well and deeply after that long and exhausting trip. Flash just pumped up in her head, and she felt worried. She rose from her bed and put her bare feet in the soft white bedroom sleepers with tiny ribbons on them. The girl came to a dresser and looked into the mirror. Her reflection was satisfied. Caroline went to the bathroom and did her regular stuff. After that, she went to the kitchen and made herself a cup of coffee. She looked at the magazine on her table and opened it to have a look. During her light breakfast, she has been reading some articles, turning page after page. She looked at the cup and sight, she liked the coffee.

In France she remembered herself not drinking coffee at all; she used to like teas and different juices from the store. Milk and croissants were her favorite. And then she remembered how different it was in Morocco. They serve different kinds of teas and coffees together with Moroccan cookies and pastries, from rich almond pastries like m'hencha to crunchy biscotti-like fekkas. There's sure to be a traditional Moroccan cookie recipe to satisfy your sweet tooth. Caroline sighed slightly. Now it was far away there and not here anymore. She looked at her black coffee with a donut. It was sweet and fresh, very soft and pleasant in taste. She had heard before that Americans love different kinds of soda to drink when they are extremely thirsty, but as for her, soda was always some of a kind too sweet and, as she discovered lately, leaves an unpleasant taste in the mouth.

Caroline glanced at the magazine again; glamorous girls were staring at her, and she turned her page on the very end and read a horoscope for a week. Then she smiled to herself. Suddenly, a knock at the door broke her thoughts. Caroline looked through the peephole and recognized Victoria. She opened a door and widely smiled at her, "Hi! Glad to see you!"

Victoria smiled back, "Good morning! How's your night at a new place?"

"M…m, it was good. I had no dreams."

She let Victoria come in and have a sit on a couch. Caroline took a place at the table facing her friend. Victoria looked around and said in a calm voice, "Today we go shopping, but first we'll have breakfast."

Caroline looked at her with amazing light green eyes, "Victoria, how about Flash? When can I see him?"

"Soon," Victoria replied quietly, "he will arrive in a trailer to our local ranch with nice stables there, we'll have a ride to it, and you'll see by yourself. He must pass the vet inspection first."

Caroline seemed to have relief after those words.

"OK, I'll go to dress up for our shopping time."

Victoria nodded to her and crossed her legs. Caroline left for her bedroom. Victoria got up from a couch and came to a kitchen table to get an apple on a plate. She also picked a fresh magazine and looked through it. On the main cover, she recognized Ester, her brother's ex-girlfriend. 'Hm…, what's she doing here?' – thought Victoria. 'Another competition for Miss Chicago. Let's see what it says.' Victoria looked through the article about it and slightly smiled. She didn't notice Caroline came up close to her.

"What's so interesting are you reading?" Caroline gave her curiosity away.

Victoria glanced at Caroline and replied, "I just saw my brother's ex-girlfriend trying to win a beauty competition."

Caroline raised her eyebrow, "Where? Let me see."

"Here, look at her," Victoria pointed at her photo on a cover page.

"She is pretty," said Caroline, "so, did she win?"

"No," sighed Victoria, "she is number three. I can imagine my brother's face when I show him this article."

Caroline turned to a sink to rinse a cup after coffee and slightly admitted, "I see you don't like her."

Victoria glanced at Caroline and agreed, "I really don't. She has a weird look, and I know her family. That's enough for me."

Caroline didn't answer her back; she cleaned the table after her light breakfast and let Victoria know that she was ready to go with her. Young women put shoes on and left the apartment.

The day is so sunny, and without clouds on this autumn day. Girls were visiting every mall and each designer corner, trying dresses, pants, shirts, and blouses. They spent five hours until Victoria decided to take a break and have lunch with Caroline. Fresh beef burgers, creamy milkshakes, and crispy, hand-cut French fries were served to the girls in one of the restaurants on a square next to shopping outlets. Victoria discovered Caroline's clothing taste. She definitely likes the conservative style as well as Victoria. She bought some nice clothes for Caroline from Calvin Klein, Victoria's Secret, and Cache House. As for the casual style, Caroline was absolutely cold to it. Victoria finally got some nice blouses from Brooks Brothers and a new purse from Versace. She is planning to get some make-up for Caroline and wants to see her glamorous. Caroline's eyes were shiny with joy and happiness; she loved everything Victoria got for her.

"Today," said Victoria with excitement in her voice, "i'll take you to a beauty salon, and I want my girlfriend to make up your face."

Caroline looked at her with widened eyes, "Why? I don't usually wear make-up!"

"That's because I want to see you glamorous. I'm tired of your pail face," said Victoria, irritated.

Caroline didn't say anything in response to her new friend. She just let it go. Victoria made an appointment at the beauty salon and arrived with Caroline at exactly five p.m.

Cindy was screaming all over around when she saw Victoria entering the guest hall, "Oh my God!!! Victoria!!!"

She hugged her hard and looked at Caroline with her wide-open eyes. Cindy was Victoria's age, and she had a crazy die in orange hair, and her eyebrows were too thin on a pale white face. Her blue eyes had fake eyelashes, and her nails were long, too. The only thing that Caroline liked about Cindy was her clothes. At least she was dressed normally, not that crazy like beauticians usually do. Cindy was fast. She put Caroline into a client's chair and looked through her face and hair. She turned Caroline against the mirror so she couldn't see herself. Caroline closed her eyes and tried not to concentrate on Victoria's conversation with Cindy. They were talking loud and fast, and mostly about their past years at high school. When Cindy finished with Caroline's hair, she turned her to a mirror. Caroline opened her eyes and slightly smiled, "Oh, you just cut my hair the way I wanted it to be done."

Cindy made from her long wavy hair and some flirty bangs. And her back hair was cut accurately leaving the length up to her shoulders. When Cindy finished her last spoken word, she took the cosmetic instruments and put them in front of her. She looked at Victoria, said something in response, and started her artwork on Caroline's face. Victoria was sitting on a creamy leather couch with her legs crossed and holding a big magazine. From time to time, she turned pages back and forth, thinking and giving answers back to Cindy. It took only Cindy half an hour to put colors on Caroline's face.

"Ok," said Cindy, "I'm finished."

Caroline sighed in response. Cindy let the girl see herself in the mirror.

She had nice bronze eye shadows, black liners on her eyelids against her long curly eyelashes, and a peach color lipstick on. Her look finished with a fresh pinkish plush on her cheeks. Caroline liked the way she looked. It was not too bright or too pale. It was just perfect. Victoria offered money to Cindy for her work, but Cindy took only half of it, because of their old friendship. They hugged at the exit, exchanged light kisses, and Victoria, together with Caroline, left the place. On the way back to Caroline's apartment, Victoria offered her an idea to go to the nightclub.

"Oh no," replied Caroline, "I'm not keen on such places like nightclubs and nightstyle life."

"Why not?" asked Victoria. "I want you to meet some of my friends there and let them see how beautiful you are."

"Well, thanks for that," Caroline tried to be delicate with Victoria, "but really, I don't want to go there. We can try something different."

"Like what?" Victoria raised one eyebrow.

"Let's go to the opera or cinema!" Caroline smiled, looking at Victoria.

Victoria rolled her eyes and said, "Oh, don't be boring! Not at your age!"

Caroline looked away through the car window. She didn't say anything in response.

Victoria touched her hand and said, "Let's go to this very interesting place of mine. You will love it!"

Caroline glanced back, "What place?"

Victoria slightly smiled, showing her white front teeth, "You'll see, but you have to put on a nice dress."

Caroline's eyes were glowing with interest. She nodded in response.

'Victoria wants to take her to a nice place, but she must dress nice. What kind of place is that? Maybe to put on a dress? No. How about a shiny blouse with golden discs around it? And on the bottom pants will do…' – Caroline was asking herself during the elevator's move to the top floor. Victoria seemed to think about clothing, too.

When the elevator's doors opened, Caroline rushed to her apartment. Victoria, with a slight smile followed the girl calmly, in a relaxed way. She knew that her friend was intrigued by her. She was just a little evil! Victoria entered the apartment through the opened door by Caroline and glanced into her bedroom.

"I think you're ready!" said Victoria with a tiny voice.

In front of Victoria, Caroline appeared in a shiny golden sleeveless blouse and in tiny black silk pants. Victoria's eyes widened, "Hmm…, not bad! Put on the high-hilled black shoes."

Caroline turned to her closet, and from the top, she pulled out the box with shoes. She put them on and turned back to Victoria, "So, what do you think?"

Her friend smiled with satisfaction and said to her back, "You look great!"

Caroline was very glad to hear these words. She wanted to impress the spoiled Victoria's taste, and she did it. Caroline glanced in the mirror for a little bit quickly and winked at her reflection. Then she stopped all of a sudden and said to Victoria, "Hold on, I don't have any jacket to put on. It's chilly outside, you know."

Victoria turned back to the girl and waved to her.

"I have a jacket in the car. It will fit you and your outfit. Let's go!"

As soon as they left the apartment and got into a car, it started raining. Victoria handed a black jacket to Caroline and turned on the hitter. Only two of them were in the car, and they could hear the raindrops on the roof. Caroline put a jacket on, moved her shoulders a little, and then said, "I think it fits. You're right."

Victoria didn't answer back to her she just slightly smiled. She turned on some music and started the engine. The car roared and moved forward.

"So," broke the silence Caroline, "where are we going?"

"You'll see," answered back Victoria.

The traffic was not that terrible like Victoria expected and they got to the place right in time. Victoria went through the little gates and was looking for the parking place; she made two circles around and finally found one free parking lot. She put her car there, turned off the engine, and pulled out the key. She glanced at Caroline for a while taking off the seat belt. Caroline looks so nice in gold and black. Her fair, wavy hair lay on her shoulders; the shadow from her eyelashes gently lay on her rosy cheeks. Only now Victoria noticed that Caroline's look is so innocent, has never been seduced, she's so fresh and young. Victoria smiled to herself being surprised that she actually had never even thought about it. And then she admitted to her, "You know what; make sure that you bring your ID with you."

Caroline looked at Victoria with her eyes wide open, "My ID?"

"Yes, your passport."

"Oh, ok." Nodded Caroline in response.

They got out of their amazing navy blue Bentley and noticed that the rain had stopped. Girls holding hands quickly rushed into a building's entrance. It is warm and nice inside.

Victoria let Caroline walk in first so she could see the atmosphere there. So, it isn't a nightclub, but still, it's a club with tables and chairs and a bar stand with a big stage where musicians are playing music. Victoria invited Caroline to have a sit with her at the cocktail bar. Caroline didn't protest. She took a sit next to Vicki and looked at the musicians.

The barman hurried to serve the girls, "Would you like something to drink, ladies?"

Victoria slightly smiled at him in response and asked, "Yes, two glasses of champagne, please!"

Caroline, as if she hadn't heard Vicki, looked around with a wide-open eye, amazed by the public and atmosphere in this place. People were actually dressed here nice with taste; some were dancing slowly, and some were just eating their food. She turned her head to Vicky and saw two glasses of sparkling champagne in Victoria's hands.

"So, for Chicago?" asked, smiling Vicki, holding two glasses.

With a little shy expression, Caroline took one of the glasses with her right hand.

"Ok," she finally said a word, "for Chicago! Cheers!"

She took a little sip from the glass and shifted her green eyes to a stage. A man dressed in a silver suit appeared, holding a microphone, and he started his song. People were applauding him. Some couple of fellows invited girls to a dance. Victoria and Caroline were watching them. Time flew and more and more people were coming every single hour. The girls ordered some fruit slices and more champagne. Finally, they decided to dance. The music was rhythmic, and people were dancing fast. Caroline discovered that she could dance pretty well. Two hours later, Victoria was already talking to some guys, standing with them at the bar stage, while Caroline was still dancing.

A red Jaguar slowly parked next to a navy blue Bentley. The engine turned off, and the car door opened. Two high-heeled shoes stepped on the ground and closed the door, putting a car on a panic alarm. A woman virtuously walked to a building. She opened a door and walked in.

Caroline felt a little pain in her ankles from dancing in her shoes. She walked to Victoria and had a sit next to her.

Victoria looked at her friend, "What's up? Are you done, or you don't like a song?"

Caroline shook her head, "No, I can't dance anymore; my feet hurt wearing these new shoes. I need to break them."

Victoria nodded with understanding.

"That happens when you want to be beautiful. Beauty demands sacrifices."

"She doesn't need to wear fancy shoes to be beautiful. She is already amazing!" said one of the Victoria's friends.

Vicki turned her head to a fellow. He is six and four inches, has golden-brown skin, brown eyes, and dark straight hair. He's smiling at Caroline. Victoria rolled her eyes and said, "We are not interested in Mexicans!" And Vicki turned away her face.

The voice behind her laughed, "Really? Since when?"

Victoria heard an acquainted woman's voice to her, it was thin and velvet. Vicky turned again to see who that was. Reina came close to her and smiled.

"Reina?" exclaimed Victoria. "What are you doing here?"

Caroline shook and looked at the lady who was standing next to Victoria. By Jain's description, she looked exactly like Raymond's bride who left without any notice. Yes, she was positively sure that this was her.

Reina was about six feet tall, had golden skin, and very nice brown hair. Her eyes were light brown, and she was wearing coral lipstick.

"Well, I was bored at home; that's why I'm here," she said, looking into Victoria's eyes, "and you? Looking for new hearts?"

Victoria frequently answered her back:

"No. I'm having fun with my friend. By the way, let me introduce you to Caroline," and she turned to the girl who was sitting beside her.

Reina's eyes widened when she met Caroline in person. She recognized her right away but didn't let Victoria know her little secret: "Caroline," she pronounced her name in a weak voice - "nice to meet you!"

"Nice to meet you too!" Calmly said Caroline.

They shook hands in a friendly way. Reina was staring at the girl, trying to figure out how her groom had let this bird fly away so far. What actually happened there, and what is she doing here? All of these questions were bothering Reina. So, she gave her curiosity away: "How did you meet Caroline?"

Victoria opened her mouth in response, but Caroline said first:

"In a trip. We met on a trip. Vocation, you know."

Caroline seemed pretty confident. She didn't want Reina to discover her secret.

Victoria was biting her lower lip with a serious look on her face. 'Why did all of a sudden Caroline interrupt her from the answer?' She had a feeling of a secret between these two ladies. They might know each other, but they hide this. Pretty interesting, and now Victoria has to find out the right answer. But Reina's speech interrupted her.

"So, I'm looking forward to my main day. You know, I'm getting married soon," she glanced at Caroline to see her reaction or some motions, but nothing. She didn't react.

"Really!?" Exclaimed Victoria, "probably this season is going to be full of weddings. First, Jason, and now his sister!"

Caroline lowered her eyes and ordered a glass of fresh water, feeling unwell after champagne. Reina noticed a big diamond ring on Caroline's right hand and cocked one eyebrow up:

"Are you engaged, Caroline?"

The girl looked down at her diamond ring and then back to Reina:

"No, I'm not." She rubbed her ring. "It's just a present from my parents."

Her voice was trembling, and Reina realized that the girl was lying. So, this ring is from Raymond.

Victoria didn't even pay attention to this ring before on Caroline's hand. She glanced and saw it. It was made in a very nice shape, clear and bright, sparkling with different colors. Set in white gold.

Victoria glanced at her watch and slightly smiled at Reina:

"It was nice to see you tonight, Reina. Hope you will have a wonderful time, but it's late, and we have to go."

Caroline nodded after Victoria's words and gave her hand to Reina:

"It was nice meeting you, Reina! Have a great time here! It's a lovely place!"

Reina raised one eyebrow and shook Caroline's hand in response:

"Thank you!"

Victoria paid the bill and left with Caroline fast. Caroline put her jacket back and disappeared through the exit from Reina's curious eyes.

Victoria was driving back to Caroline's apartment not as fast as she usually does.

"What's the story with that ring?" – Suddenly Vicki asked with a cold tone.

Caroline sighed slightly and said, "Nothing. It's just a gift from my girlfriend in Morocco. I'm not engaged."

Victoria didn't want to give up, "After this meeting, I have a feeling that you are hiding a secret from me, Caroline."

"There's no secret!" said Caroline, almost with her tears on.

"Don't lie to me!" insisted Victoria, turning the wheel to the right. "I have a feeling that you guys know each other."

Caroline looked away to the road and then said, "We have never met each other before. I don't know this lady, and I don't know why she was acting as if she knew me. This is absurd!!!"

Victoria choked, "All right. May I stay at your place tonight? It's too late for me to drive back and I'm so tired and can barely see the road."

Caroline nodded in response, "Sure. Thank you for a wonderful evening. It was amazing!"

"Sure," answered Victoria.

Bentley was parked in the parking-covered garage by Victoria. The young women entered the elevator and in silence, they were waiting for their floor. Caroline pulled out the keys from her little purse to the apartment and opened the door. She took off the shoes and went to the bathroom. Victoria made herself a sleeping place on a couch and was waiting for Caroline to show up, but she didn't. Victoria looked in a corner and saw Caroline in bed. She came closer to her and noticed her sleeping hard. Victoria went to the bathroom, took off her make-up, brushed her teeth, and took a shower. After she put a white robe on and went to the living room, she turned off the lights in the apartment and lay on a couch, comforting with a pillow.

# CHAPTER 16

*You cannot get attached to people with all your heart; it's unstable and precarious happiness. Even worse - give your heart to only one man, what if he leaves?*
*And he always leaves...*

**Erich Maria Remarque**

Bright and fresh morning on this autumn day brought some white frost on the barely green grass in Chicago parks. The first signs of winter are coming and the leaves are not green anymore. From time to time, birds sing and gloomy clouds are mixed with clear clouds passing Michigan Lake. The airport is open since early morning and full of incoming and outgoing travelers from different parts of our Planet. The privet white jet appeared in the sky with its flashing lights. It is closer and closer to a landing line until it finally lands. It was moving to its parking place when a black with silver stripes on the bottom Rolls Royce drove by it. The jet's door opened, and passengers were coming out.

"Christ! Is that Dad's car?" With a little nervous in his voice asked Brian.

Martin put his dark sunglasses on and pulled out some leather gloves out of his cashmere coat:

"Yes, that's my dad's loving baby."

Jason grabbed a briefcase and went down the stairs to a car. The father's new employer met the guys and helped them to pack their stuff in a trunk. Brian together with Jason and Chris, occupied the back seats while Martin took his place by a father's driver.

"Jesus," he finally sighed, comforting himself on a beautiful lather seat, "I forgot how well it is in a nice car. I dream about my cozy bed and my loving race car!"

Jason smiled at this while Brian commented on his brother's words:

"I dream about good food and my dad's library."

Martin fraught:

"You're boring as our mom!"

Chris looked through the window and said:

"Did you call Victoria? What is she doing?"

Brian shook his head and waived to Martin:

"Yes, what is she doing?"

Martin rubbed his chin and answered:

"No, I didn't call her. I don't know. We need to see her today and find out about her business." He looked at the driver and his words hung in the air, he realized that he didn't remember the name of his father's new employer.

The driver glanced at him with a corner of his grey eye and, smiling, said:

"Ralf, sir. My name is Ralf."

Martin nervously smiled back:

"Ok, fellow. And where is our Goofy?"

"Oh, Mister John Fury sent him away to New York. He has new responsibilities now." With a calm voice, said Ralf.

The guys raised their eyebrows and exchanged their looks. They started being nervous about this little change; what if John had changed something else? On a straight grey road, Rolls Royce brought them to the Fury's big mansion. The gates opened in front of their car and let them in. As soon as the car stopped in front of the mansion's massive doors, Martin with his brother got out.

"Don't worry about luggage, sir." Said Ralf to Brian, "I'll take care of it. Welcome home!"

And he smiled, showing his white teeth.

Jason, together with Chris, followed the Fury brothers. They entered the mansion and faced their home's warmness. Bright sunlight was coming through the huge French windows with heavy burgundy curtains on. The huge fireplace is on and on a massive couch, they saw Adeline sitting with Victoria.

Brian was the first who broke the peaceful silence, "Mom."

Adeline turned her head, and her eyes met with Brian's. Victoria rose from a couch and flew to the brothers to give them a good hug. She was almost in tears, being so glad and happy to see her brothers alive. They're smiling at her and hugging. Adeline has tears in her eyes as well. She hugged Brian first and then Martin without any words.

For a while, they just stood quietly looking at each other, then she said, "Dad is home."

Martin's face got bright; Brian shifted his eyes to his brother, "Good! He's home already? How's your trip, guys?"

Adeline turned to Martin and slowly said, "It has never been better!"

Victoria was squeezing Martin's hand, trying to prevent him from something. He looked at her with wide and full of curious eyes, "What?"

But she didn't say anything. Finally, Adeline came closer to Martin and, with a caring voice, said:

"John is in the library. He knew about your arrival today. You know," She paused and bit her lower lip, "through his sources."

Martin stepped from one foot to another, being a little bit surprised. But now he's not aware of what kind of mood his father can be and what else he knows.

"Yeah," that was all that he could say.

Victoria grabbed Brian's and Martin's hand and softly said, "Come, see Dad!"

They followed her, letting Jason and Chris accompany Adeline.

On the way to the library, Victoria was walking confidently, clicking with her high hills on the wooden floor. She didn't say anything to her brothers and didn't even glance at them. They tried to read her face, to figure out her emotions, but there was nothing except her warm and kind feelings for them both. When they entered the library at the very end of the corridor hall, three of them saw John sitting at the massive brown desk, writing something with his glasses on. Martin swallowed while Brian just tried to notice any anger on his father's face. But John is too busy with his papers to express any anger. They were standing in silence and were watching him without any courage to break his peace. Even Victoria, his favorite, didn't move. When John finished his last writing, he put a pen away and picked some folders to put them away on the bookshelf. He stopped and shifted his eyes to a library entrance. He saw pale Brian, Martin, and Victoria in the middle between them. His face expressed self-confidence, and a wide smile appeared on his lips.

"Well, Well… Well," John finally broke this heavy silence; - "My children are here safe and sound! Why are you frozen there? You can't come close and give a hug to a papa?"

Brian fraught his light brown eyebrows while Martin smiled like an idiot: "Hi Dad!" And he pushed Victoria ahead so she would say something.

Victoria started moving to an armchair in front of her father's desk. She wanted to take a seat feeling like the ground going away under her feet.

John Fury seemed to be in a good mood like Martin thought, so he was the first to start his conversation with a father.

"I'm glad you're home so soon after your business trip."

John moved a little on his working chair and smiled in response: "Really? Don't boggle me, Martin?"

Martin shook his head a little:

"I don't understand, Dad."

"What are you guys doing? Why has the work never been finished in Lex?" John moved his square glasses on his nose closer.

Brian moved closer to his sitting sister:

"Lex is running successfully, and the work was done properly. Victoria goes there every day; she finishes her reports on time. There's nothing to complain about."

John's face changed into a grin, "That's true."

He rose from his working seat and came to a little bar with bottles of different spirits in it. He poured some fresh whisky into his glass and, in silence, glanced at his children again. Then he closed the bottle and, holding a glass, returned to his seat.

Martin stepped aside and said with his strong voice like a real man:

"We have something pleasant for you, Dad."

John looked at Martin and raised one eyebrow in surprise:

"What? Your excellent grades at the Academy?"

Martin sighed a little:

"It goes without saying…"

Victoria raised her brown eyes on Martin and nodded positively.

"We had done some work and it's going to be our pride. Do you remember your ship by Spain?"

John crossed his arms on his chest and sarcastically added:

"Yep, so got it from the bottoms of the ocean?"

Martin smiled back and proudly said, his dark brown eyes glowing:

"Better. We brought the stolen weapon back and a ship!"

John Fury fraught, and his face became serious: "How?"

Brian looked at his sister and his brother and then added,

"We did it together, all of us."

"I need a report," with a serious tone in his voice said John, - "where is it?"

The doors to the library were open, and Jason Parker entered the library holding a briefcase in his right hand;

"It's here."

Martin, Brian, and Victoria turned their faces. The fire was dancing in their eyes as soon as they saw Jason Parker at the door entrance.

Jason came close to them and threw the briefcase on John's table.

John Fury rose from his desk and pleasantly smiled at Jayson:

"Hah! Trey's face! Jason Parker! Welcome, fellow!"

Jason never had a fear of any of Fury's family members; John was the same age as his father. He has the same respect for John as for Trey. Jason and his sister Reina grew up without a mother, raised only by their father and nobody else.

"In this case, you can find every answer to any of your questions," calmly said Jason.

"I like you, Jason." John was touched by the guy's courage.

John looked at Victoria, and his face crossed a side smile. Victoria didn't understand the grin of her father.

"All right," said John, "I'll check this business tonight. Perhaps you guys are hungry. How about having brunch with me and Adeline?"

Martin didn't know what to say, all of them didn't expect John's reaction like this. They had nothing to do but accept his offer while he was in a good mood.

The dining room was big enough at the Fury's mansion to accept even eighty people in it. It was a huge room with a long wooden table in the middle and golden curtains decorating high large windows. The dining room was finished with different Greek statues on the side of columns that were keeping the ceiling. Victoria loved the way how her father kept the house; her mother always watched the curtains and antique treasures on table cupboards, while Martin hated this pompous. He never wanted his house to look like Dad's home; first of all, it was too big and kept too many unnecessary things that, in his opinion, were just collecting dust. He didn't want servants either because they don't do anything except gossip about landlords. Victoria hoped to inherit this mansion after her parents. Brian loved this place as well. He grew up in it and everything was too dared for him, even the walls.

Adeline was already in the dining room waiting for her husband and children to come in. The food was cooked and nicely arranged on the table. Fried salmon, with onion rings around, stuffed golden pepper, and sweet cooked green pears decorated the fresh, big ham on a huge plate. For those who like Italian Cuisine, pasta and meat ravioli was made with some nicely smelled gravy. Fresh baked bread was in the center of the table, symbolizing the main dish. Drinks were served on each side of the guest. Adeline was standing next to a window and looking through it on the golf course outside. She wore a fresh blue silk blouse up to her neck and, on the bottom, a dark maxi skirt. Her shoes had a little heel approximately three inches long. She had an image of a well-bred, educated woman with aristocratic features. Her parents were mixed, so she had Hispanic-British blood. John Fury loved the way she could keep herself in society. All his friends thought that she was royal or something. Every word spoken by her was pronounced clearly and slowly, as she had never been in a hurry. Adeline had a high degree of Master's in Arts, but she had never worked a day in her life because it wasn't needed. Her caring husband did everything for her and her children. They live in a beautiful home. All of them had high education and nice things for being kept well. She was very grateful for this to John. She didn't care about how many women he dated before or how much money was spent on living things; she cared only about her reputation in society and the prosperity of her children. Victoria Fury loved the way her mom ruled the house. She loved mom's taste.

Adeline turned her graceful profile to their guests. John let Brian, Martin, Chris, Jason, and Victoria enter the dining room first, and he finished the line after them. As the main head of the family, John took his place in the center of the table, and next to him sat Adeline and her children on either side. Victoria sat closer to her dad, while Brian sat closer to his mom, Martin sat next to his brother, and Jason with Chris joined their sits next to Victoria. When John finished placing his food on a plate, everybody started to help themselves with a portion of food. The servant hurried to John and poured him some white wine, and then he poured wine to the rest of the table members. Victoria quickly glanced at her mom and placed a white sheet on her knees.

John broke the silence first:

"Well, my dears, I'm glad that all of you are here to share this meal with us! I hope that we can do this regularly!" He took a crystal glass in his right hand and said: "For Us! Cheers!"

Everybody raised a little their glasses and, in one voice, said after John:

"For Us! Salute!"

White wine was light and not that super sour or sweet. It was just right. It tasted like dried pear and a combination of candied orange peel with lingering notes of spice. Everybody drank it a little so they could taste it better. John had a little sly smile on his face while he was watching everyone's reaction to it. Martin was a spoiled tooth, so he couldn't wait and gave in to his curiosity.

"What is this, dad? It's so nice!"

John raised his thick eyebrows and giggled:

"Guess…"

Adeline glanced at her husband with confusion on her face. Victoria shook her shoulders and looked at Brian. Martin rubbed his chin and proposed.

"I think this might cost like…a… thousand bucks easy."

John slightly grinned again:

"So?"

"Well, knowing you, it might be Columbia or Spain, I can't guess what year."

John lowered his eyes and moved a little. He rubbed his chin and slightly smiled:

"Spain. Forty-year-old white wine from Lopez de Heredia."

"Oh, Wow!!!" Everybody sighed.

Martin nodded:

"That's a truly unique and amazing wine."

Jason was fascinated by John's Fury choice. He didn't know John well, but he admitted that his father's friend had a wonderful and extraordinary taste.

The brunch finished peacefully, and everyone satisfied their hunger. Nobody said a word about their adventures in the Moroccan expedition. After noon, John left the house to see his friends and exchange their news. Jason and Chris left for their homes. Brian hid in the father's library while Martin went upstairs to take a nap. Adeline took a car and went out for some shopping. Victoria left by herself; she led herself to a living room and made a call to Caroline.

"Hello," Caroline answered.

"Hey! Are you home?" With irritation in her voice, asked Victoria.

"Yes, I am. Where else I can be?"

"What are you doing?"

"I'm watching TV," lied Caroline to her girlfriend.

"Ok, I'll be around you after lunchtime," promised Victoria.

"That's fine," answered back Caroline.

As soon as Caroline turned off the phone, she continued to type her email to her grandfather on Victoria's iPad. In the email, she told him about her presence and about Victoria, Raymond, and the American attack. She also promised to visit him one day and not to worry about her.

Caroline relaxed on her couch in the guest room and looked at the ceiling, thinking about her past; all of a sudden, she imaged herself in Raymond's palace with its inhabitants, a possible wedding, and a life in Morocco forever. She realized how lucky she was to meet Victoria; she got a little sad thinking about her grandfather and remembering Philippe. Sadder made her a memory of her parents, the house they lived in, and a promise to find murderers. Caroline's lip corner was shaken from that rough luck. She couldn't cry anymore, no tears left. All she could do was just let it go and start studying as soon as possible, and hopefully, with her good degree she can find a well-paid job. Caroline closed her eyes for a minute and didn't notice Victoria's arrival.

"Are you still sleeping?" said Victoria, indignant.

Caroline shook from her voice:

"What? You're here already?"

"Yes, it has past three hours since my phone call!"

"Oh, I probably fell asleep," Caroline got annoyed.

Victoria crossed the hall and handled a big bag to Caroline.

"Here, I brought you some nice clothes of mine. They're brand new, and I just don't fit in them anymore. Bought several years ago, when I was only a hundred fifteen pounds." Sadly, said Victoria.

Caroline rose from her couch and tried to look into a bag; she pulled out some outfits and started looking through:

"You must be kidding me!"

Victoria turned to her with a surprised face:

"What? You don't like it?"

"I like it too much! They're nice, very nice! Even amazon is here!" Exclaimed Caroline.

Victoria smiled: "Try it on."

Caroline threw her gown on the floor from her body and started putting on a riding dress. She noticed that she perfectly went through it and nothing was tight on her. She looked at Victoria with her shiny eyes: "It fits, do you see it?"

"Yes," answered her back, happy Victoria, "And now let's go!"

Caroline glanced at her back: "Where?"

Victoria smiled wide:

"To our stable to see your friend!"

Caroline hugged Victoria and rushed to her closet, where she pulled out her boots and put them on. The girls left the apartment by four o'clock of the afternoon, and downstairs, they went into the parking garage. Caroline followed Victoria in a wide walk. Victoria stopped by a beautiful car and tried to search for the keys in her large handbag.

"Victoria, look!" exclaimed amazed Caroline.

"What?" Victoria looked at Caroline with widened eyes.

Caroline was speechless, standing in front of a silver, silver-polished Maserati GranTurismo MC Stradale. It is an Italian bright luxury with high performance and super sexiest look. Finally, Victoria pulled out the keys of the car, put them in the car door's hole, and slightly smiled at Caroline;

"Get in, it's mine."

Caroline was fascinated by the beauty of it, and she knew how expensive such toys could be. Her brother used to have many posters of luxury sports cars, and he always had prices mentioned on the back, just to know the market. Philippe used to dream of buying one of the Italian sports cars one day. He loved Ferraris. As for her, she just preferred American muscle cars. But this beauty could make you forget your name…

She carefully opened the door and had a sit on the black leather seat. She looked around at the exterior of this luxury car and couldn't even breathe.

"It's my father's present for a good job I had done," finally broke the silence. Victoria, "I know what you think, but don't worry, I'm a good girl."

Caroline bit her lower lip and lowered her eyes:

"Don't explain me anything. You don't have to."

Victoria got a little nervous because of her friend's reaction. She didn't want to upset her or something, but every time she showed up, Caroline got sadder, which was not at all good for their friendship. Victoria started the car and moved it out of the garage. The vehicle drove fast by beautiful skyscrapers in the town and everyone walking on the street turned their amazed faces at the new silver Maserati. Caroline couldn't admit that she knew that not everyone could afford this piece of Italian masterpiece. Victoria couldn't handle the heavy silence between her and Caroline, so she turned on the music. Caroline, silently, was looking through the grey Polaroid window. Along with their moving, the scenery changed from high skyscrapers to fields with trees scenery. Pretty soon, they turned to a big ranch and parked under the roof. Caroline liked being inside and already didn't want to get out of Maserati. Victoria was the first to get out of it and call for Caroline. The girl sighed hard and took off the seat belt. She tried to open the door and come out. Victoria was talking to some guy at a distance from her; she turned to Caroline and waved her to join.

"I want you to meet a friend of mine," said Victoria to a young fellow of nearly twenty-six years old.

Caroline came close to them and proudly raised her head, looking at the guy.

"Caroline, this is Jerry Smith; he's taking care of our horses here," Victoria said with a friendly tone in her voice.

"Nice to meet you!" said Jerry.

"Nice to meet you too!" answered back Caroline.

Victoria looked back at Jerry and asked him about Caroline's stallion.

Jerry Smith nodded to her, smiling;

"Yes, Flash arrived before lunchtime today, and he's in a good mood, as I noticed."

Caroline's green eyes got shiny from obvious excitement when she heard about her Mustang: "Can I see him?"

"Sure," frequently answered the guy. "Let me show you his stall."

Victoria and excited Caroline followed Jerry into the horse stable. It was not far from the car parking, a light wooden stable was full of sunshine, and other horses were trying to attract their attention.

At the very end of the horse stable, Caroline recognized her Flash; she walked to him fast and started talking to him. He recognized her voice and looked at once. They were left alone by Victoria and Jerry for a while. Then Caroline came back and asked Jerry to prepare her horse for a ride. Jerry Smith immediately found a suitable saddle and other fitting tacks for Flash. Caroline expressed happiness and joy.

"Victoria, thank you so much for everything you're doing for us!"

"You're very welcome!" answered Victoria. "I know it's important for you to be with Flash. He's cool!"

Jerry Smith brought Caroline's horse close to her, holding him under his reins: "He's not aggressive as I thought when I saw him the first time," - said Jerry. – "He just has such a look as he doesn't want to be touched by anybody. When he arrived, we washed him and brushed carefully."

"Did he eat?" asked Caroline with her curious facial expression.

"Yes, like a hungry wolf," laughed the guy.

Victoria smiled in response while Caroline got into to saddle immediately. She made Flash walk first into a little corral. After two walking circles, she galloped him a little and then let it go into the open field. She tried to feel every move of his under her, his breath, his mood, and his little silent communication with her. Caroline rubbed his neck with tender, letting him show his speed.

They enjoyed the evening cool air and sunset together; she almost rode close back to a corral when her eyes were attracted by the single black stallion resting in the separate gated corral.

Jerry and Victoria were watching her from a distance. Caroline shrugged a little when she saw a black stallion; he was graceful and stunning at the same time. She just remembered the sea in Marseille and the black rider there; it was so fresh in her memory, as if it had happened yesterday. She rode to Jerry close and couldn't hold her curiosity anymore: "That horse is gorgeous! What's its name?"

Victoria looked away, trying to see what the girl was talking about, and recognized her brother's stallion. Then she rolled her eyes, looking at smiling Jerry.

"Of course!" whispered Vicki.

Jerry pointed at the black stallion:

"Is that one? Ha... Everybody loves Ivanhoe."

Caroline dismounted her horse and took him under his reins:

"Ivanhoe?" Whispered Caroline under her little nose. "It can't be!"

Victoria smiled at Caroline, putting her arm on the girl's shoulder:

"Why? This is the Illinois' famous winner, Ivanhoe Sangre Negro."

In Victoria's voice, Caroline noticed pride. She had never heard about Ivanhoe's winnings, but she heard this nickname before, and it was exactly the time and moment when a good-looking guy saved her life from the sea-strong waves. She remembered that name because when she was little, her favorite book was "Ivanhoe" written by British writer Walter Scott. Little tears appeared in her eyes. She touched her face with cool fingers, and Caroline tried to cover her feelings from Victoria and Jerry. Caroline was already quite assured that the next discovery was going to be Ivanhoe's owner. The sixth feeling told her that she won't be surprised. She lowered her eyelashes, and a shade lay on her cheeks. Jerry gave her a printed report of her horse's feed plan and asked if he could do something else for her. She said that she complexly trusts her animal to his caring hands. After horseback riding, Victoria and Caroline left to have dinner. On the way back from the ranch Victoria's Maserati was met by her approaching brother's auto. He signaled to her but she made her face as if she didn't see him. Victoria is quite positive about her statement not to introduce Martin to Caroline. The girl was very beautiful, and he would seduce her very quickly and then dump her like every girl that was met by him. Caroline was sensitive, and it would break her heart if it happened. And she didn't need that; she needed to study and get a good degree. Of course, Victoria would take care of it; that's what she decided by herself. As usual, they had dinner at their favorite restaurant, and she took her home.

Victoria arrived back at her apartment and noticed her boyfriend's absence. She went worried and tried to dial his phone number but didn't get any answer. Now she was really nervous, and when the clock showed eight past medium, she was ready to leave to look around. As soon as she put her jacket on, the apartment's door opened. She rushed to see if it was him. It was indeed him dressed in a long black coat and nice dark pants; his shoes were shiny from polished cream.

Victoria froze in cold shock, standing between the kitchen and living room. When he turned to face her, he had an unusual look on his face.

"Victoria," he finally broke the silence: "What's wrong?"

"Your clothes, where did you get them?" She asked with a cold voice.

"I was waiting for you all day, and you never showed up, I took your credit card and went to the mall."

Victoria lowered her eyes in embarrassment; she understood that she completely forgot about him.

"And there's something more." He added, "I purchased an airplane ticket to Marseille."

She shook from those words and looked up at him right away. Her eyes got a little bit wet, and she slowly moved her lips:

"Are you leaving me? Is it over?"

He came close to her and, with both hands, touched her shoulders and, looking into her brown eyes, answered her:

"I have to go and see someone, you know." The guy pronounced these words with tenderness, so Victoria sheltered under his palms. He hardly sighed and tried to explain his behavior. She turned away:

"I understand, you don't need to tell me everything. I am losing you, I understand."

"No, you don't. But I can't live in sin with you like this." His chocolate brownish eyes sparkled.

From these words, Victoria was speechless. She didn't even realize that something like this could happen between them. She stepped away from him and, looking into his eyes straight, said:

"Are you hinting at a marriage proposal?"

He tried to come closer to her, but she stretched her hand not letting him even touch her. He stopped and, without shifting his eyes from hers, answered back with a velvet voice:

"I want to be in your life, and I want people from your circle to know me. That's why I'm leaving to discover my past. I know I have something, and I have to find it."

These words sounded strong to Victoria. She isn't a boss anymore. This game of playing a house is over, and she has to let him go. Her eyes are in tears, and she realizes he's the first in her life who is leaving first. Her other deep feeling says he'll never come back. What if he's married already? What if she's looking for him? What if? And a lot of 'what if' circled in her head. Victoria squeezed her head with her arms and shook it in disbelief. This French fellow broke her heart, and a strong, deep pain inside made her cry. She rushed to the bedroom and fell in bed; she put her face on a pillow and let tears flow. He couldn't see her breaking down. He didn't like women's tears. Victoria shook when she heard the door slam. She got up and rushed to the living room to see him, but he wasn't there. Her boyfriend left. She returned to their loving nest and opened a closet of his and nothing was there, only empty hangers. Victoria got cold inside and was standing in deep shock for some time with her hands down. There was nothing that she could do or change. He left her alone, and that was a painful truth to face.

Night. Silence and cold. Darkness was everywhere. Cold bed and no sweet words of love. Victoria was circled in a warm, fluffy blanket. From time to time, she fell asleep and then woke up, again fell into deep sleep. Only in the morning, she barely woke up and slowly walked to the bathroom nude. The cold floor didn't bother her; she was cold inside with an empty heart. At nine, she has to be at work with her eyes bright and a shining smile so nobody could see her inside world. The mirror showed her pale face and red eyes, she sighed and went to the kitchen for some ice for her face. After her morning procedure, she put some green eyeshades and made black liners against her eyelashes, with dark black mascara, put some colors on her eyelashes, and finished her look with red lipstick and cold pinkish plush on her cheeks. A cream blouse with long sleeves from Brooks and Brothers laid on her perfectly, thick beige nylons covered her legs from outside cool breath, and the green blazer and black straight skirt laid on her body perfectly. She put on black middle-heeled shoes and grabbed the black briefcase full of paperwork. Before leaving her apartment she glanced in the mirror and deeply breathed in and out. After she sighed and left her home. The door locked automatically. Standing in the elevator and waiting for the ground floor she tried to concentrate on her working day and not think about her last night's nightmare. She quickly led to her car when the door opened. This time, she took her brother's navy blue Bentley, which she and Caroline had driven all the time until yesterday. Victoria comforted herself in the seat, put the seat belt on, and turned the music on.

On the way to Lex building, she constantly observed the road, looking for potential hotheads. She glanced into the front mirror at her eyes and noticed a gorgeous burgundy Aston Martin at the back of her. She smiled to herself. 'Naughty brother is driving his favorite toy.' They parked inside the car garage next to each other. Victoria got out from Bentley and closed the door softly. She put the keys in her pocket and faced approaching her brother.

"Good morning, Martin," she started the conversation; "You're damn early today, so unusual for you!"

"Yeap," Martin showed one of his outstanding smiles; "Sometimes very unusual things happen very unusually."

Victoria shook her head and rolled her eyes; Martin never changed; he's always in his repertoire. Bully!

"I didn't expect you to see at the ranch road yesterday," said Martin, looking at Victoria on their way to the building, "what were you doing there?"

"Just took my girlfriend to see our horses," simply answered Victoria to her brother.

"So, did she like it?"

"It goes without saying."

Martin glanced at Victoria and a little smile appeared in the corner of his lip: "Did she like Ivanhoe?"

"I think so. She was admired at first, but then her mood changed all of a sudden. I don't know why she got sad, but she also has a good-looking horse."

"You think she got jealous?"

"No, it wasn't about jealousy; it was something different, and I'm sure on a hundred percent she'll never tell me," said Victoria, fraught thinking about this.

Martin didn't say anything in response. Victoria noticed that today, he was dressed really nicely. You can tell by his expensive outfit from Hugo Boss. As soon as they entered the company's hall, all the women who worked downstairs started smiling at him, making their voices shrill unnaturally. Victoria rolled her eyes again being so annoyed with this zoo. It goes without saying that they all wanted him so much. They even agreed to share his attention just to get one of his flirty smiles, but Martin tried to be serious with coworkers in the company. He wanted his reputation to be clean and tried to keep gossip away from Lex. He wasn't looking for any trouble with his father. Victoria wished him a good day and left for her department right away. Martin checked his timetable at the registration and took an elevator to the twenty-third floor. That is exactly where Brian's office was located.

His brother was at his office already, drinking a cup of coffee. Brian, in his grey wool suit, looked really elegant; the grey color made his blue eyes in special deep color. They look foggy and seductive. When Martin entered his room, they shook hands and started their usual conversation about business, and then the subject changed.

"I didn't see dad last night," said Martin, his eyes glowing like stars in the night sky.

"I know, ha? I think he was drinking till midnight with his friends," said Brian, "I want to hear his opinion about Jason's report. By the way, did you contact Jason?"

"Yeah," lowed his eyes, Martin, "he left this morning for LA."

"He can't wait to see his fiancé. That's understanding." Sadly said Brian.

"All right, man, I have to go to work; I have a meeting with a client in an hour, so see you!" Martin left Brian by himself, and at the end of the corridor, he entered his office.

That is a very light room with spacious space around it. It has a large window with cream curtains and pots with flowers on the side. The writing desk with a computer on it is standing next to a window. The furniture was made in a vintage style from light wood. Martin was very accurate with the things that surrounded him. He even had a thick carpet in front of his working table. Against the wall was a couch and a huge picture above it. In front of the couch was a coffee table with fresh magazines and newspapers. He sighed when he entered his office: 'it feels like home', he thought, 'splendid atmosphere, grace, and just first class.' He sat on a couch and stretched his body, staring at the ceiling. In a minute, he glanced at his coffee table and noticed a glamour magazine with half-nude girls on the cover. A slight smile appeared in the corner of his rosy lips; he took a magazine in both hands and started reading it. Martin rose from a couch in a sitting position and was fraught when he saw his girlfriend Ester participating in a beauty contest. He found out she took third place in it, and the first place received a blond, blue-eyed chick that goes out with his car racing competitor, Mr. Ashley Eastwood. Martin's face got red; he smashed the magazine and threw it against the wall. His eyes changed from dark brown color to blue-black. Anger and fury distorted his face. He came to his desk and dialed his brother's number:

"What's up?" answered Brian.

"Ashley's blond head girlfriend won the beauty contest. She is number one, Miss Illinois," answered Martin, barely pronouncing the words.

"What?" Raised his eyebrows, Brian "That's unbelievable!"

"You can't imagine my feelings right now."

"Yes, I can," replied Brian, "So, what now?"

"I'm done with Ester," a cold tone in Martin's voice was firm. He hung up and took his place accurately after he dialed Ester's phone number on his smartphone and was waiting for her reply. She didn't answer and that made him more desperate. He made a decision to visit her place personally after work.

At lunch time Victoria organized her meeting with Caroline. They were sitting in the cafeteria in an intimate atmosphere. Caroline had a little makeup on and was dressed in a wool burgundy winter dress; she had nice earrings on and pretty manicured hands. Victoria was watching her all of this time.

A waitress rushed with notes to them:

"Hello girls? How're you today?"

"We're fine," they answered.

"What would you like to drink?"

Victoria looked at the waitress and said:

"Two hot teas, please! No sugar, Miss. Bring honey too, just honey, no jells."

"All right, I'll be in a minute."

The waitress left to pass their order. Caroline placed a white napkin on her knees and looked back at her friend:

"You look annoyed today, is everything ok?"

"No." Wrinkled her nose Victoria.

"What happened?" Caroline's eyes narrowed.

"Last night my boyfriend left me," sadly said Victoria, and barely visible tears stuck in her eyes.

"Why?" Caroline's eyes widened, and green eyes went foggy as a morning forest, she felt disoriented about Victoria. She raised her head as if she was going to hear the special complicated speech.

"He said that he needed to go back to France and see someone; he wanted to discover his past and also hint at marriage."

Caroline didn't show surprise on her face. Moreover, she seemed to be fair. She lowered her eyes, looked at her arms, and moved her head to a side as if she thought what to say. She looked back into Victoria's eyes, and her peach color lips stretched in a smile: "Are you afraid of marriage?"

Victoria didn't know what to say on this, she was totally not prepared for such kind of a question. Her brown eyes became brighter when she found an answer for Caroline:

"Too long I was single, just short dates, short romance, and nothing has ever been serious until now between me and him. I felt a deep pain in my heart when he left, and never anybody left me first. I always was the one who ended relationships."

Caroline glanced at a coming to them waitress; she brought them hot teas and took their next order. Then she left, and Victoria continued her unfinished statement:

"Personally, I don't hope to see him again. Who knows, maybe he's not single as I thought and his family may look for him. I don't know."

"What if he returns? And asks for your hand?" The expression on Caroline's face shows wonder and deep curiosity. At this very moment, she reminded Victoria of a red fox.

"Do you suggest me to think about it?" asked Vicky with a tender voice.

"You must be ready for any life surprises, just try to predict the possible situations and find solutions where they are impossible."

"You're too smart for your age," slightly teased her Victoria.

"I've learned wisdom from my Moroccan friend," simply answered Caroline on Victoria's statement.

"Hmm..." Victoria breathed out with thoughtful relief and jingled her earrings.

Caroline, in her nineteenth, seemed sometimes too naive, but in some situations, she was smart enough to survive in a cruel men's world. She had very little experience in friendship with girls and as Victoria realized later, Caroline knew men's minds better. So, from now Victoria knew who she had to ask for advice. After their rich lunch, Victoria took Caroline to the ranch so she could see her stallion. Victoria promised to pick her up after six p.m.

Brian and Martin had lunch together not far from Lex. They arrived at the company and met John and Trey downstairs.

"Hello, guys!" said Trey Parker with the same velvet voice as his son Jason.

"Hey!" answered back Brian and Martin.

"I've just finished reading your report," finally said John Fury, looking at Brian.

"That's Martin's job, not mine." Shook his head, Brian.

"Really?" In a surprised tone, asked John.

"Why? Too good to be true?" winked Martin, and his lips stretched in a charming smile.

"Well done, son." His father touched his shoulder and smiled back at him. "I want to see you in my office in an hour; I have a serious talk with you."

"Martin, you look great since I've seen you," said Trey in an encouraging way.

"Thank you, Mr. Parker!" said Martin. His golden skin sometimes confused people, and they thought he was Mexican, but he had nothing to do with Mexicans. It is from his mom, Adeline; one of her Spanish genes affected him. He gets darker sometimes when he spends too much time in the Sun, but it happens rarely. His brother Brian absolutely looks different. That's from his grandfather on his father's side. That's why when people meet them, they can't believe they're siblings.

John Fury was already at his office when Martin entered. He was frequently invited by Dad and took a seat in front of his desk. John finished typing his project, took his glasses off, and looked at Martin. For some time, in silence, they were just looking into each other's eyes. John tried to admit that his older boy matured somehow after his business trip with Adeline. He didn't hear from him silly comments, and his look was not boyish anymore. Now he's a young fellow at his twenty-three, has a degree in Science, has a car, a couple of million dollars, and tones of broken hearts. Looking at Martin, John remembered himself, but he was quite more mature and ambitious than Martin.

John was the first to break the heavy silence between them:

"Son," he said this word with a caring tone. "I have to admit your achievements in the life's field. I also want to tell you 'Thank you!' for the great job that you've done with your friends."

Martin nodded. He reached his goal in this difficult quest. He received his dad's admiration and respect, but John didn't finish his speech:

"I have to confess here the fact that you have grown up, and as I taught you before, every well-done job should be paid, right?"

"Yes, Dad". Answered back Martin.

John pulled out from his table a checkbook, and started writing on it. When he finished, he gave it to Martin:

"That's a check on three million dollars. That's yours. I hope you'll spend your money wisely."

Unexpected money made Martin speechless; he wasn't ready for such a dad's gesture. He took him by surprise. It was pleasant no doubt, but he didn't even have any plans for this money:

" Dad, I think that's too much!"

"Why, son? You did a great job! Take the money, boy. You earned it."

"Thank you, dad!"

"I'll remember your achievement, by the way," he added, "the frigate is great!"

John winked at Martin when he was leaving his office holding his check. On the way to his office, Martin was thinking what he was going to do with this money.

He counted how many people took part in this project in Morocco and decided to share unexpected income with them. Sitting at his desk he made calculations: Victoria, Brian, Jason, and Chris. Good guys helped him in this uneasy project. He decided to give away six hundred thousand dollars to each of them. He took this check and planned his appointment with a banker. After that he finished his computer paperwork and clicked the button 'send'. Then he turned off the computer, came to the mirror, and put on his cashmere long coat. On the way to his car, he made a face as if everybody had just shadows for him. The engine of his Aston Martin Vanquish roared when he turned a key and took off from the parking lot. He was going to see Ester at her place and was thinking about how it would be better to put an end to their relationship.

She lived in the eastern part of town close to the lake. To reach that place, it took only twenty minutes for Martin. When he arrived, he noticed a TV light working in her living room. Her one-story house isn't that big and hidden from curious eyes like anybody else's. He parked and glanced in the car mirror at himself to make sure that he looked perfect. He got out of Aston Martin and came to her front door. He pushed a doorbell button and waited for an answer.

The door opened, and Ester threw herself in Martin's arms:

"My love!"

She hung on his neck, and her lips pressed against his. He answered her kiss with the same passion. He picked her up with his strong hands, and her legs circled around his tiny waist. Kissing her without stop he entered the house and fell with her on a couch in the living room. She bit his neck and lower lip, pulled his white shirt out of his pants, and unbuttoned it while he ripped the color on her dress so he could reach for her neck and covered it with kisses, Ester screamed from pleasure, and goosebumps covered her body. He reached with his soft hand under her skirt and ripped her tiny bikini. His big finger slid between her legs; she breathed out hard from the desire to be taken by him. He was moving fast. She tried to open her mouth to say a word. He covered her mouth with his, his tongue went inside, and she bit and sucked it a little, she tried to scratch his back, but he grabbed her arms and put them above her head. He pressed her with his massive chest, and her hazel eyes narrowed from the pleasure. Ester tried to move her leg under him while he was biting her shoulder and couldn't; his knee moved her one leg to a side, and she yelled, feeling him inside her; Martin groaned in a deep voice from pleasure. She got a big promotion from him. Ester was happy knowing that he missed her as much as she did. He fell asleep lying on his stomach, and she was resting on top of him, hugging and kissing. She rubbed his back and strong shoulders, leaving a slight kiss.

Ester thought that she would give everything in the world for this moment not to be finished. She always hoped that he would ask her to marry him one day. It has past eight months since they were together. She offered him to move to her place several times, but he never did. On the other hand, she understood that nobody wanted to leave that gorgeous mansion where he lived with his parents. She never understood why his walking passion didn't want to share her bed with her at night. That made her cheap in her own eyes. Ester had been going out with two guys before; Martin was her third one. And she wanted to make him her last one. Marriage and only marriage was the only way to catch him. She sighed deeply.

Martin opened his eyes. His long black eyelashes almost touched his eyebrows, and he turned to Ester without any emotional or facial expressions. She smiled at him and covered her breast with a fluffy blanket:

"You bit me hard, honey, and left a bite on my boobs. I have to cancel tomorrow's modeling photography."

A slight evil smile moved in the corner of his lip: "Good!"

She opened her mouth in shock at his words. He pronounced it so deep and aggressive. He got up, zipped his pants, and put on his shirt back. Ester shook her head and asked:

"Aren't you staying with me tonight, are you?"

"No." Abruptly replied Martin.

"No? Why not?" She rose from the couch on her knees.

"Because I don't want to." Putting his jacket on, said Martin back to her, strictly looking into her eyes.

"You just had sex with me! And now you're leaving! Do you think I'm a doormat or something?" Ester was pissed so much that her face turned red.

"Look, I didn't say that, anyway I'm leaving you my mark for memory!"

"What? You're leaving me. Is this how I understand?" raised her voice Easter.

"That's right, honey. We're done!"

Martin turned his back to her and opened a door through which he just disappeared. He got into the car and started the engine. Looked into the mirror and winked at himself. He executed his break-up plan perfectly. He was delighted with his behavior. On the way back home, he drove neither fast nor slowly. He arrived at his parent's mansion and let Ralf take his car to the garage. Martin entered the living room and got face-to-face with Brian. He was sitting by the fireplace and reading a newspaper.

"Hey, Martin!" He greeted him as soon as his brother entered the room and looked at him.

"Hey, man! I'm surprised to see you here, why? Are you cold upstairs?"

"No, just want to listen to the fire's noise, it relaxes me. You look pretty confident, Martin. What's up?" Brian glanced with a corner of his eye at Martin.

His brother sat in the armchair opposite and let his shoes go off. He relaxed his head and looked away, avoiding eye contact with his brother: "I broke up with Ester."

"Did you really?" Brian put away his newspaper and looked at Martin with his eyebrows up.

"Yes," replied Martin with a slight smile.

"How was that?" Brian's curiosity didn't let him go.

" I fucked her good and told her we're done, that's it. I'm here."

Brian was staring at his brother with eyes widened. It was pretty weird to hear such things from Martin. Brian was very intelligent, and such a way to put an end to the relationship was rude. He always did things correctly and with special care.

"You're just an animal, brother." Whispered in disgust, Brian.

"I am," firmly said Martin, "I did this because I think it's the best way to let her keep a beautiful memory of me."

"Gosh," whispered Brian, "I'll not tell this to anybody. I'll keep it between us."

Martin moved his relaxed head to Brian's side and slightly smiled at him:

"As you wish. I don't give a damn."

# CHAPTER 17

*"Never hide things from hardcore thinkers. They get more aggravated, more provoked by confusion with the most painful truths."*

**Criss Jami**

Life takes people's strength and courage, beauty and years, giving in return experience and being. Some people are like real wine. With years, they become richer and more beautiful. It takes time. Time is the only best treatment for deep wounds and terrible memories. Let the angel of time take your worries and pain with it. You'll see how better you can feel afterward.

Mohammed had just finished his main duty with horses. Next to a corral, he was washing his hands with fresh water. Being old doesn't give advantages, his back cracked and he sighed deeply from pain. Now in his seventies, he started thinking of selling all these animals and letting himself rest. He took a deep breath and sat on the stairs to smoke a little. He lit his hookah and his face changes when he saw a taxi cab coming. It is moving closer and closer to his ranch. A car stopped, the door opened, and he saw a young fellow with a big duffel bag coming to him. His bad vision from being old didn't let him see clearly his face. By the manner of his walking, Mohammed recognized his grandson. His hookah fell out of his mouth.

"Oh Allah!" He exclaimed, "My boy!"

"Grandpa! Smiled the fellow back to Mohammed."

The guy and the old man hugged. Tears of happiness rolled down Mohammed's face, he was touched deep to his heart by his grandson's unexpected appearance.

"Philippe!" Well, come home! "With a shaken voice exclaimed Mohammed."

The old man looked from head to toe at his only grandson and couldn't believe his stunning grace: tall, strong, handsome. He waived to him:

"Come inside, my boy."

Mohammed entered the house first and turned the light on in the living room. He rushed to the kitchen to make some tea for both of them. When he was done, he picked up two cups holding in his hands and came closer to his dining table. He put the cups on and couldn't shift his eyes from Philippe. The guy was sitting at the table with his shiny brown eyes, his rosy cheeks burning on white like snow face, and red lips stretching in an attractive smile.

"Son," broke the hanging silence, Mohammed, "Where have you been all this time?"

"With my girlfriend in Chicago." Simply answered Philippe. He turned around and noticed some changes in the house. He tried to picture what was missing.

Mohammed frowned and shook his head:

"Girlfriend?" He tried to remember if Philippe had someone before he left for Paris. There was nobody in his life back then or he probably missed something.

"What's her name, son?" Asked curious Mohammed.

"Victoria," smiled back at him, Philippe; "She was all the time with me after hospital."

"Hospital?" Granddad couldn't remember Philippe being sick; "What were you doing in the hospital, son?"

"Recovering after a car crash," his eyes narrowed, and he shook his head, "I don't remember anything in my life…. only this place. I know that you're closer to me than anybody else, that's why I'm here, so you could help me to remember my past."

Philippe's words put Mohammed in shock. He didn't know that his grandson got into a car accident and lost his memory. All of this time, he thought that Philippe was studying in Paris, and now this amnesia. So, he probably doesn't even know what happened to his parents and sisters.

"Did anybody contact you before?"

"No," he shook his head. He and Philippe looked at grandfather with his eyes widened. He tilted closer to his grandpa: "Did something happen?"

"Yes," swallowing nodded old Mohammed; "The house where you used to live is gone. Everything has gone." The sad look made his face pale; he sat next to Philippe and put his old hand on his grandson's arm.

Philippe's eyes were shifting as if he was trying to picture his past. His House, a two-story building, was hanging on a cliff. He heard laughs and saw running twins.

"Girls," he whispered, "who are they?"

Mohammed glanced at Philippe, and his lips trampled:

"Your sisters: Emilie and Caroline."

Philippe slowly moved his shaken mouth, "Caroline, my loving sister. Where's mom? I don't see dad…"

Mohammed lowered his eyes and sadly looked at his fellow, trying to pick suitable words for explanation:

"You won't see them again, I'm sorry."

Philippe turned his pale face to grandfather, and his eyes flashed like lightning:

"Why?"

"Emilie and Mom, with Dad, died in the explosion. The house that you left that day got into the fire and exploded, and they didn't survive."

"What?" Exclaimed Philippe and got up from the chair. He was deeply hurt and shocked by these words; "That's a lie! Our house was the safest! Dad took care of it as well as mom."

"I know, I know, but that's not their fault or the house's. It's..." Mohammed bit his lip at the painful truth.

All of a sudden, Philippe starts to see clearly his previous life, he just remembered the quarrel with Emilie about feelings, and he saw an angry Caroline about her Moroccan trip to Uncle Ali and then a kiss between him and Caroline. And then he lowered his eyes in remembering it all and whispered to his grandfather: "Emilie and Caroline have never been even my sisters like they thought."

Mohammed raised his eyebrows in surprise and came closer to Philippe:

"What are you talking about, son? They are your sisters."

"No," the cold voice went with an echo in the room.

Philippe got red, remembering the terrible secret that mom was holding all these years. "I wish Rafael could be my father. He's a good man."

"My daughter didn't know any other men when she married Rafael," said Mohammed with his voice strong on behalf of his daughter.

Philippe turned with his face to Mohammed, and his eyes lit up. He raised his chin and manly said:

"Mom was in her second month of pregnancy with me when she and Rafael married. He thought all of this time that I was the blessing of their love! What a lie!"

"Son, are you sure?" Mohammed's eyes were almost in tears. "How can it be possible?"

"I know it's hard to believe, Grandpa. There's nothing that I can do about it."

"Did she tell you who your real father was?" The old man's sorrow was endless.

"Yes, she did." Lowered his eyes, Philippe; his long eyelashes got wet from little tears coming through. He bit his lips and touched his burning cheeks with hot palms.

"Who?" Mohammed's eyes narrowed in waiting for an answer. "Who is he?"

The guy looked at him with sadness in his eyes and swallowed hard, trying to let the words go:

"John Fury."

Fury's mansion rises upon the surrounding lights in its darkness. A navy blue Bentley just parked in front of the main entrance to it. Clicking with her high hills Victoria rolled a big suitcase after her. Ralf helped her with the rest of her luggage. She opened the door and entered the parent's home. In the living room, she noticed her siblings together, talking about nothing, just life experiences. Martin was surprised to see his sister with a bunch of luggage. Victoria asked Ralf to take her stuff to her bedroom; she took off her gloves and sat opposite her brothers on a couch.

"What a day!" She breathed out heavily.

"Did you leave or something?" asked confused Brian.

"No," abruptly replied Victoria. Her face expressing coldness and sadness. "I gave up my apartment back to landlords and I want to live here for now."

"I can't believe it!" Exclaimed Martin, "I thought you liked your place more than this house."

"Then you just don't know me," Victoria looked at her brother with eyes wide open, "I miss this place, and I'll leave it when a man asks me to marry him."

She had a pretty strange facial expression. It was hard to say what exactly it expressed. Confidence. Victoria has an assured look, she strictly took a decision to be here until marriage.

"You must be kidding?" Smiled Martin nervously; "You don't want to be married, sister!" And who is going to marry you?

"Why is that so?" Victoria was surprised; "Am I that ugly?"

"No, but you love freedom." Martin winked at her.

"Sometimes very unusual things happen very unusually," she smiled back at him.

"Hey! Don't steal my lines!" Exclaimed Martin with his dark brown eyebrows, meeting on the bridge.

Victoria showed him her pink tongue.

Brian laughed out loud, remembering their childhood. Three of them were happy back then, but even now, when they grew up, they still miss that time. Ten years ago, they went to school, and their only duties were studying, then college, and now work.

Martin shook his head, and his eyes went serious when he noticed that it was time for him to share some news about Dad's kindness with Brian and Victoria.

"Guys," he said, - "this afternoon John asked me to his office at work and…" Martin made a pause, picking the right words to say about money.

"So?" Asked Brian.

"Well, he was grateful for our work,"

"And?" Repeated disturbed Victoria.

"He wrote a check on three million dollars." Finished his sentence, Martin.

"What?" In a voice, asked Brian and Victoria. "He gave it to you, didn't he?"

"Yes," nodded Martin, "I want to share money between us. Each of you can have six hundred thousand dollars."

That was absolutely surprising news for Brian and Victoria; such an unexpected gesture confused them a lot. The question arises about sharing.

"I can't believe you have told us this." Victoria was pretty surprised, she didn't expect Martin to think about sharing. She was ready to take her award.

"You have really changed," admitted Brian.

"Why? I think everyone has changed after this battle, and we faced real danger. All of us faced death, and we could die there." Martin lowered his eyes

"That's true!" Victoria couldn't agree with this statement.

"So, what are you going to do with your money, Martin?" Asked Brian, looking at his brother.

"Hm.., I'm thinking of selling my Aston Martin and buying a new car." The confident upcoming decision sounded in his voice.

Brian raised his eyebrows:

"Wow! Are you going to tell it bye-bye, like you have told Ester?"

Martin's lips stretched in a smile.

"What?" Yelled Victoria, "You broke up with Ester!"

"Yep, tonight."

Victoria's eyes got round. She didn't expect her brother to be so fast in breaking the relationship with Ester. Oh, no... Ester is probably disappointed. And tomorrow she's going to call Victoria to nag about Martin. Victoria rolled her eyes with thoughts about it. She shook her head and squeezed her hands. She lowered her eyes, and an unpleasant memory about her boyfriend's leaving bothered her.

"It's probably the season of broken hearts." Mumbled Victoria, gazing at her manicured hands.

"Why?" Asked curious Brian.

Victoria didn't want to tell her story, so she just lied:

"My girlfriend's boyfriend left her last night, so she is in tears."

Martin didn't say anything about this; he had never been in love, and feelings to him were nothing but a game. Brian just glanced at his sister, and in response, she got silence from both of them. Before, her serious relationship with the French boy was enjoyable. Now, after she got hurt, nothing seemed more terrible than physical pain. Victoria lived with the hope that her boyfriend would return and make her a marriage proposal someday. She made a decision to move out of the apartment where they used to live; so, to get rid of memories about them. Now Victoria tried to concentrate on saving some money. She definitely was desperate about Caroline's education; she wanted to find out how much it was going to be – to support her little 'sister.'

She would do anything in her power so Caroline could get a nice place under the sun. In April Jason would marry and probably will move out from Chicago. Victoria looked away with sadness; 'another good fellow left their round table. Life is so unfair!'

"What are you going to do with your future money, Vicky?" Brian's voice broke her from deep thoughts.

"Em..m, I don't know yet," at least she is honest with herself.

"And you, Brian?"

"Haven't decided yet," a light smile brightened his pale face.

"If I were you, I would start a new life far away from here," noticed Martin, and suddenly he realized that all of this time it was his dream. He hated dad's demanding rules, Lex company, bitches, and high-class society in brackets. He had a lot of money in the bank and the saddest thing was – he couldn't decide to start his new life. He never had any motivation like his dad. John was quite ambitious; he was unsatisfied with his position in society, and money was never enough. John's goal was to be in the American president's chair. This was the saddest part. Martin never wanted his dad to be a president; such people as John should be far from that responsibility. How many people would be killed? John had no heart, no feelings.

"I'm satisfied with my life, Martin." Said Brian with his voice strict. "I don't want to change anything."

"It's always up to you, brother. Choices we make are the only free power we get, after all."

The next morning, Caroline caught a taxi and asked to take her to a ranch called "Westwood". When she got there Flash was feeding in the field freely. Jerry Smith met her at once, and when she asked him to tell her more about Ivanhoe, he didn't refuse.

"Ivanhoe is an American racehorse and he's four years old. He has been awarded many wins in racing at our hippodromes in different states. If you are interested in his breeding I can get you a list of his relative tree. Unfortunately, he isn't open at stud to the public."

"Oh, thank you, Jerry! I'm afraid there's no need to do this," Caroline's cheeks blushed from curiosity: "I just want to know his owner."

"Do you want to buy this horse?" Raised his eyebrows, Jerry.

"No, no," negatively shook her head Caroline, and her golden hair flowed on her shoulders like a waterfall.

"On a dashboard in our hall, you can read about horse owners, come with me, I'll show you."

Caroline followed this man into the guest hall. He pointed her attention to the white wall with the big dashboard on it.

"Excuse me, Miss Caroline," said Jerry, "I have to go and answer the ringing phone."

"Sure," she nodded to him, "that's okay."

Jerry Smith rushed to pick up the phone, and she stayed by herself, looking at the list of the horse's owners. She slightly smiled when she saw her name and Flash's opposite. All of a sudden, Caroline was pleased with this strange discovery of hers. Her rosy lips slightly opened, and her eyes got brighter when she saw the portrait of a guy sitting on a black horse. Under his photo, it was written in black ink, "Fuego and Ivanhoe". The fellow in a portrait had a cap, his visor left a shadow on his face, and by the way, he was sitting in the saddle, Caroline could tell that he was a confident man with demanding rules and high self-esteem but kind at heart. The picture was made in vintage style. The girl ran a finger over the picture and smacked her lips: 'Who are you?' she asked herself with wonder. 'I know you,' her eyelashes lowered on the floor, and she turned with her back to the dashboard and leaned against the wall.

Caroline pursed her lips and felt her heartbeat quicken; the bottom of her hands was on fire and weakness in her knees. She moved slightly from the wall and slowly walked to the open yard. Her mind was clouded, her eyes were foggy, and she couldn't see clearly so she gazed at the blue sky. Sunshine went through the little cloud, and its rays lay on her hair. Golden shine brightened around her. She feels good and warm. The cool wind didn't blow anymore, and the gloomy autumn day changed into a perfect sunny, warm morning. Goose bumps ran through her body, and she hugged her shoulders. Caroline felt a strange feeling; all of a sudden the world got colors and purpose to live.

She moved closer to the corral and whistled to her horse. Flash looked at her and ran closer; he sniffed her shoulder and licked her hair. She pulled out from her little purse some sugar and gave it to him. He crunched it and asked for some more, but Caroline spread her palms, showing empty hands. He pushed her shoulder with a head and ran around, making a circle. She smiled at him and closed her eyes in a relaxed way. The slight wind blew, moving her bang. She raised her head and let fresh air wake her from her thoughts. The girl opened her eyes and remembered about the meeting with Victoria. She checked her phone in the incoming list were no calls. Caroline dialed Victoria's number and was waiting for an answer.

"Hello!" answered Vicky.

"Hey! Are you planning to see me this afternoon?"

"Where're you?" A worried voice asked Caroline.

"Vicky, I'm at Westwood."

"What are you doing there?" Victoria got annoyed.

"Just visiting Flash," explained Caroline.

"Take a taxi and come to 'Rome' restaurant now." With a demanding tone in her voice said Victoria.

"All right," answered puzzled Caroline.

Jerry Smith called for a taxi and asked Caroline when she planned to come to visit Westwood again. Caroline didn't answer, being unfamiliar with her timetable. The yellow cab arrived pretty quickly and picked her up. They turned to a dusty road first and then drove to a freeway. At the red light stop, Caroline was staring at a burgundy Aston Martin. She gasped. The look of it classy and sporty and at the same time so sexy was to her liking. She relaxed in her seat and slightly closed her eyes, with a barely visible smile on her pale face.

Martin arrived at the ranch and got out of his car. He was free from work this morning, and in the afternoon, he had a business meeting at his office. He was dressed in winter pants and a sporty jacket, wearing some gloves and a cap, which matched his jacket color. He came close to the corral and glanced at a red Mustang in it. His eyebrows met on the bridge. Martin realized that hasn't seen this horse before; graceful, stunning, and young Mustang. He liked his black legs. The guy took off his cap and unzipped jacket, entering the ranch hall. He came to a dashboard, putting his hands on his hips, and looked through the names of the horse's owners. One of them at the very end attracted his attention.

He put the finger on a line and read it carefully: "Arrival day - (October 20, 2014) Name - Flash Magnifico; Class - Mustang; Owner - Caroline Sauvage Roux."

He froze for a minute, and his unspoken words hung in the air. Martin's eyes shifted and read it carefully one more time, 'Caroline Sauvage Roux.'

"That's impossible," he said to himself. His eyes narrowed and faded at the mention of his main father's enemy's name. Sauvage Roux couldn't be just a coincidence. There are no French people in Chicago with this name. Martin felt a dip pulse on his neck twitching and swallowed hard. "Who is this person?"

Martin hurried fast to Jerry's office and entered it without a knock.

From unexpected Martin's appearing, Jerry shook and jumped on his seat.

"Jerry!?" Martin's voice sounded cold and very sharp, like that razor blade.

"Mr. Fury, how can I help you?" The guy's face got pale from being scared that he may have done something wrong. He was staring at Martin, standing behind his desk.

"Who is Caroline Souvege Roux?"

Jerry breathed a sigh of relief and, with a slight smile, eagerly replied:

"Oh, that's your sister's friend; she comes to the ranch almost every day. By the way, she had just left in the yellow taxi cab."

Martin narrowed his dark brown eyes, and a wide grin crossed his lips:

"Victoria's friend?"

"Yes," nodded Jerry Smith. "I haven't seen her before; she just appeared not long ago. Miss Fury forbade me to say her full name in her presence, which is weird."

Jerry looked into Martin's face, trying to find an answer, but everything he could read was confusion and misunderstanding.

"All right," Martin said in a soft voice; "Keep me informed!"

"Ok, no problem," nodded a fellow.

Victoria had a girlfriend under the father's enemy's name; she brought her to this ranch and might help her with something else. Driving on his way back to the mansion, Martin couldn't get rid of these thoughts about Souvege Roux. 'What kind of game is his sister playing?' was a new Martin's focus. He died from a desire to talk to Victoria directly about this, but he knew that she would never tell him the truth. Something was going wrong, and he should find out his sister's secret. The only way he could do it – was to visit the ranch as often as possible. He slammed his hand on the car wheel with fury. His everyday work won't let him do it. Then Martin thought about Jerry Smith, that he could make him his spy. So what if Jerry told him the time when Caroline could be at the ranch, and he could appear there. The side foxy smile stuck in the corner of his lips; that's a good idea to meet her and find out who she is. At home, Martin changed his casual outfit to a suit and tie. Confidently, he glanced at his mirror in the room and left to work.

Downstairs at the Lex building, Victoria came to a reception glass room and asked Alice to give her a day schedule. Alice, a young girl of nearly twenty-four, has been working as a receptionist since her student years. She was always polite and nicely dressed. She was wearing short red hair and had amazing blue eyes; Victoria liked her much except for her freckles. Martin didn't like her appearance at all, he hated redhead people. Her personality was okay to him, but not her looks.

Victoria looked through her brother's working schedule and slightly smiled. She gave the document back to Alice, and with her face bright, she said: "Thank you, Alice!"

She put her sunglasses on and went to the parking lot. Victoria stopped by her car and opened her purse, looking for the keys. Next to navy blue, Bentley just rolled in and parked Aston Martin. Her brother got out of it and, taking off his sunglasses, smiled at Victoria:

"Hey fox!" He greeted her with a mean side smile.

"What?" Asked Victoria with an irritated voice.

"Are you leaving so soon?" Martin looked at her with narrowed eyes. He was expecting to hear her sweet lie.

"Oh," she bit her lower lip, "just a lunch time. Did you eat?"

Victoria glanced at him with widened eyes.

He clenched his teeth:

"I did at home."

"Oh, cool!" She said these words so simply that they drove Martin crazy.

He didn't move, he was standing in front of her car and couldn't believe any of her words. He wishes to go with her now. He wanted to know every single step she made. Every single secret she hid. Indeed, she was a mystery puzzle to his brain. Martin took himself in his hands and slowly closed his eyes, let his breath be normal, turned with his back to Victoria, and walked to the building. Victoria held her gaze discouraged. She started her car and practically flew to the restaurant 'Rome.'

Caroline was already inside when Victoria entered the hallway. She saw her sitting at the end of the room. She joined her at the table and tried to smile at her. Caroline noticed some nervous change on her girlfriend's face:

"What happened?"

"We need to schedule your timetable;" Victoria tried to say these words softly in a light manner as a suggestion.

"For what?" Caroline didn't understand.

"You can't visit Westwood unexpectedly," tried to explain Victoria. "There are people working, and usually, we have a lot of other owners at the stables, and when it's too crowded, it's not good for horses and working people there."

"So?" Caroline shook her head; "I can't see Flash every day?"

Victoria held her strong gaze on a girl, trying to collect suitable words for Caroline;

"Listen. I know you love him so much. You need to be organized so Flash will know when he can see you. Horses, like dogs, they are smart and have an inside clock. They know the day and time when they can see their owner. You know, they also need time for their own needs."

"I understand," Caroline whipped her lips with a napkin after her rich pasta.

"Good!" nodded Victoria and took a menu in her hands.

She snapped her finger in the air, letting the waiter know she was ready to order. The tall man dressed in black pants with a white blazer on came to her and leaned:

"Yes, Miss."

"I want Pear ricotta ravioli and Risotto Alla Pescatora, and a glass of white wine, please!"

"Sure, Miss," an Italian waiter left.

"What a nice restaurant!" lifted her head Victoria, she had a business look on her face.

Caroline in response just slightly smiled. She glanced at Victoria and her rosy lips slightly opened, she let her curiosity go away:

"Vicky," she turned to her friend, "who is that Fuego?"

Victoria slowly raised her eyes at Caroline, and her lower lip hung a little from an unexpected question that all of this time she had tried to avoid:

"Fuego? It's just a nickname for the public, it means ehm..m… fire in Spanish. A person who has that nickname has fire in side, he's hot." - Victoria didn't shift her eyes from Caroline.

The waiter returned to her with a tray, holding and serving Victoria's order. He put dishes on her side and a glass of her white wine. Victoria started with wine. She felt that she needed it, especially now, after Caroline's question, but her friend didn't seem to give up.

"All right," Caroline said and bit her lower lip, "I mean Fuego, the guy sitting on Ivanhoe. I saw his black and white poster on a dashboard at Westwood."

"Oh," Victoria lowered her long eyelashes and sighed out. She got nervous and didn't know how to explain to her that he was Martin Fury, her brother. Because if she told her that, Caroline would get weird and unmanageable. She will try to kill him like one of the Fury's family members. On the other side, there can be a lot of Furies in this city. Maybe it was just a coincidence.

Caroline is staring at Victoria at this moment waiting for an answer; she even stopped to chew her pasta.

"His name is Martin," finally said Victoria; "He is an Ivanhoe's owner and our big state winner."

Caroline's long, curly eyelashes lowed, and she slightly smiled to herself. Her guess is right. That was him – a man who saved her life at the coast. She touched her lips with cold fingers and remembered his mouth on hers when he made her artificial respiration. Her green eyes got foggy, and the memory of him didn't let her go. Caroline was so grateful to him. If not Martin at that moment, she would die.

"Is he a jokey or something?"

"No, he isn't. He has a jokey that rides his horse. Martin tried to participate in races and even paid money, but he was tall and heavy for a jokey. A normal jokey is supposed to have a right weight like a hundred pounds, and Martin is about an extra eighty, so far from this number." Finally, Victoria gave all of this information to her in one breath. She grabbed the fork and started eating her meal.

"Can I be a jokey?" All of a sudden, Caroline asked her.

"I'm afraid, no."

"Why?"

"Usually, women are not allowed to participate in this kind of competition. Jumping - yes."

Caroline smiled in response to her and looked away. She was a little sorry about the racing rules, but she was positive that she could win. Flash was fast; she saw that in Morocco when he bit Raymond's horse. But back then, she had been training him every day and now he might get out of shape a little. Nobody worked with him; he just spent his days there, eating and sleeping. And Victoria tried to schedule her appointment with him according to her likening. That was absolutely unacceptable!

At home Caroline finally relaxed being alone with her feelings and thoughts. She noticed that Victoria influenced her too much and nobody ever pushed her before. She was the only one who made people do whatever she wanted. Naughty angel, wild and innocent. Caroline came close to her window and looked through. Marseille is too far away. Chicago is outside and she is a slave of her own phantoms. She moved her golden hair to the side, straight on her shoulder, and combed with her brush. She knew she had to do it one hundred times so they would be shiny again. Caroline closed her eyes and slowly lay against the window's wall. Raymond, her only friend, was too far across the ocean led his land and palace. Her heart squeezed in sorrow, and she realized that she missed him as well as Uncle Ali and Jain. That battle is probably finished, and they won. What happened to Americans there? Her eyes brightened; she had the Internet, and it could tell her everything. She pulled out an iPad from her handbag and Google it: "Moroccan battle in 2014." Her eyes got sad when she found out there was no information about it, nothing was there... Not even a word, just history about this country. Being so mad, she put her device on a couch and slowly walking, came to her mirror in the bedroom. Caroline looked at her reflection in it. Two sad green eyes were staring at her; rosy cheeks were burning from hot air conditioning, and half-opened lips on a relaxed face showed her denial. The apartment where she lived was just a golden cage. She had to do something. Caroline was staring at herself dressed in a night-long gown. Her fingers slipped under her shoulder sleeve, and she moved it down and looked at her little mole on it. She smirked, the same mole used to have Emilie. 'Interesting, if she were alive now, what would she do?' thought Caroline. Then her head moved to a side, and Caroline looked down with thoughts, 'Martin, why did you save me for? Why did you let me see this murder, God!? *Definitely, there was a reason why the creator let her live; definitely, He had a plan for her.* All these questions were going through her mind. They didn't let her sleep. She finally got tired and drank a glass of water with one white pill so she could go to sleep peacefully. Her bed has a queen size and all the sheets were cream color. On top of it covered a beautiful golden blanket with nice patterns embroidered pillows. Caroline slipped under a blanket and covered herself. She had been staring at the ceiling for a while and then sleep overtook her.

Victoria was resting in her bedroom as well. She remembered her childhood in this room. She and her brothers used to like to play bo-peep. They always found her in the closet or under the bed. She remembered herself as not that well-skilled hider. Brian was always found in the wicker basket for dirty clothes; she sighed with a slight smile, how little they were back then. Nice memories! She didn't even know why. All of a sudden, she started thinking about it. Her bedroom was located on the second floor of Fury's mansion. Her windows faced the curly entrance gates so she could always see her friends coming through them. Most of them were around the whole country, and nobody lived in Chicago. So, among her friends, Caroline and her brothers were no one. Through the window, Victoria watched falling leaves from the tree and noticed one tear rolling down her cheekbone. She touched it with her fingers and wiped her tears off. She misses childhood as much as that candy on a stick. Victoria moved away from the window and looked at the jewelry box, standing on her dresser. She took her seat on a tufted chair and opened her treasure box. That was her Christmas present from Martin when she turned twenty-one. Her birthday was the same day as that holiday, December twenty-fifth. In the jewelry box, she found a long white pearl necklace and a matching bracelet. She tried it on and slightly smiled. She took it off and pulled out the ruby golden ring. Victoria looked through some different gemstone necklaces that she used to buy across the street from her University. Memory... Student lives: books, exams, and, of course, cute college outfits and guys' admired looks and flirty smiles. Her girlfriend's gossip at the student cafeteria, sneaky kisses from parents, and tons of broken hearts. Victoria didn't like to sleep with her admirers like her group mates did. When she was twenty, her dad used to have this cute friend from Miami, and every summer, he visited their mansion with his wife and son. The guy was one year older than Victoria and he brought her presents all the time. His name was James Abbott, a cute brunette guy with sky-blue eyes. He always had a nice smile and teeth white like fresh snow. At college, he was the best; nothing nerd was about him. He was excellent at baseball and loved to play golf with John Fury and his dad. Victoria couldn't resist his beauty and gave herself to him. She was sitting and holding his present in her hands now, the only one that left after six years – a big blue diamond ring finished in white gold. James Abbott, a Miami fellow who took her heart and turned off other men forever. A terrible feeling went through her body with goosebumps when she remembered his dad's call. John and his family were invited to a funeral. They bared James in spring; he died from a motorcycle crash. All the Fury members flew to Miami and supported his best friend's feelings. So, Victoria was engaged once in her life, and as you see, it was a terrible love end story. After James, her inside world was closed, and she didn't take seriously any Chicago's playboy. Her father, John, got along with Trey Parker; he loved his son Jason and was always positive about their union, but it never happened either. Friendship and respect for each other never allowed love to be between Jason and Victoria. As well as Brian and Martin never wanted Jason's sister, Reina. They all preferred just to stay friends.

# CHAPTER 18

*Partying means drinking. It also means playing records by Lou Reed and Chicago, which I thought was a city but is also a band it turns out.*

### Ron Currie Jr.

Europe was ready for welcoming Christmas; people decorated their houses and homes with rainbow lights and set up Christmas trees. Shops were full of gifts and bright gift cards. People were standing in a line at grocers' for December twenty-fifth, and in a week, it was going to be family meetings and celebrations. Kids were waiting for this time with pleaser they knew that St Nicolas was coming with his sack full of gifts. In some families it was a custom to leave a desired present under a Christmas tree; other members just left gifts in a hanging stocking. This was going to be the first Christmas for Philippe without his family. Grandfather Mohammed told him the whole story of what happened to everyone and, especially Caroline, his only love. There was nothing that he could do. He had been thinking of going to Uncle Ali, but as he realized later, it was just a waste of time. His main goal now was to find his biological father, John Fury. Philippe wanted to find out the truth from his mouth, what happened exactly between Mom and him, and why he was so mean to Rafael. From Mohammed's words Philippe realized that Caroline was that night in the house when it exploded. Only she held the details of that murder, and she was hunting for a killer. The saddest part was that he lost her again. Nobody knew where she was. Philippe entered grandfather's library and asked him:

"Did you check your emails, Grandpa?"

"Oh, son. You know I forgot my password to the previous email and couldn't open it, so I just created a new one, but I'm getting orders from clients and have never received anything from Caroline."

"You have to find your old password, and she might left you some news on your old email," insisted Philippe.

"I don't know how to make it." Tried to find an excuse, Mohammed.

Philippe was looking around through the papers, some grandfather's writing, as he said he had written a password on a piece of paper somewhere. Then he got annoyed and asked Mohammed to let him see the computer. His grandpa left the room and walked to the kitchen to make some dinner for them. While

Philippe took a seat at the desk, he looked through some folders and files and finally found an old password to an email. He typed the login and the password and logged in to his grandfather's account. There were too many junky ones, he looked through each of them and found Caroline's letter; he clicked twice with a mouse button on it and started reading:

*"Dear Grandfather,*

*I'm writing to let you know that I'm fine. I think that Uncle Ali had already called you and told you about me and my behavior. I'm sorry. I really shamed you, and I know that I did everything wrong. Uncle Ali, together with Raymond's father, was planning to marry me, Raymond, and take Islam, but I ran away because I didn't want to be a breeder in the Arab family. Thanks to all of them, they were nice and treated me like a real princess. When I saw that have a chance to change my life, I made a decision and didn't regret it. I have a wonderful girlfriend, and she helps me with everything. She even made my documents and wants me to start college as soon as possible. I live in a beautiful apartment in Chicago. And soon will start my college life. Well, anyway, I'm healthy and open to new beginnings in my life here. I promise to write you as soon as possible. Love you, Grandpa!*

*Sincerely always yours, Caroline"*

Philippe got up from the desk and walked in the room back and forth, with his hands in the back jeans pockets. 'That's impossible!' he thought. 'I just left Chicago, and she is there, my only one, let alone sister. She was in Morocco! She had a friend named Raymond! Marriage with Arab! Gosh!!!'

Mohammed walked into the room and looked at Philippe, "Did you find something?"

"Yes," nodded Philippe, "I left the page open for you, so you can read it. Caroline wrote you a little note."

"Oh, did she?!" Mohammed's face brightened, and he hurried to the computer screen.

Philippe glanced at his grandpa and took a seat in the opposite chair of Mohammed's desk, crossing his legs and placing his arms on a chest. After Mohammed finished reading her short letter, he breathed out in relief and said:

"At least she is all right. Nothing bad happened to her."

"I can't believe that Uncle Ali wanted to give away Caroline to Raymond!" Anger sounded in his voice.

"Why? Caroline is a beautiful and intelligent girl. Of course, she is the best gift Allah could give to any man." Smiled Mohammed, and his eyes got shiny, "In the Arab world, they even allow relatives to marry each other, like cousins, for example."

"What!?" Exclaimed Philippe, "That's absolutely disgusting!"

"The only reason why they do it is because they know the family." Positively nodded Mohammed.

"I would never marry my sister!"

"Yeah, but as I see, you're in love with Caroline, my beloved." Widened his eyes, Mohammed said, "And don't tell me, my boy, that I'm mistaken!"

With a speed rush, Philippe got up from the chair, came close to the bookshelf, and laid with one hand to it, looking away with embarrassment. Just now, he realized his grandfather's words and had never even noticed that. Mohammed was right; he was in love with his sister. He was afraid to face this truth. Philippe turned with his face to his grandfather and said, " Unfortunately, you're right. I love her too much and even forgot she is connected to me by blood through my mother."

Mohammed raised his eyebrows and let circled smoke fly in the air, "In this case, you have to be honest with your girlfriend and yourself; you can't be with her when in your heart lives another."

"I need to force myself and change my feelings for Caroline because Victoria is my love, too." He closed his eyes and put his palms on his face.

"Is she?" Mohammed said with a surprising tone in his voice.

"She is my first woman, my first real girlfriend," Philippe tried to hide his blushing face.

"I advise you to find your real father and have a talk with him." Slowly moved his lips, Mohammed.

Philippe raised his head and his eyes glowing up bright:

"Yeah, and tell him what? Hi, I'm your son, dad. Why are you so surprised?"

"No," replied Mohammed abruptly, "I know John Fury in person. He's a very responsible man concerning his children. I saw three of them when they were teenagers. He takes care of them, and you need to meet him and tell him your story and see what happens."

"I don't think he would be happy to see me and have a pleasant conversation."

"Did you see him before? Do you know him in person?" Asked Mohammed with an insistent tone.

"No," moved Philippe away, his concerned facial expression.

"Well then, you have no right to judge and decide for him," nodded his grandfather. "Give him a chance to get to know you."

Philippe faced the picture hanging on the wall. To find and meet John Fury is not such an easy task. Luckily, he has Victoria who can help him with his new quest. She lived in the States, so it was even closer than trying to find him from here. That meant he must return to Chicago and ask Victoria for help. Plus, his sister lived in Chicago, which is even better than ever. Caroline would be happy to see him again.

He turned to Mohammed and said, "I need some time here. I'll fly to Chicago after New Year's Eve."

"That's all right, son. You know my house is always open for you." The old man smiled at him and pulled out his desk to draw a thick folder. He carefully opened it and asked Philippe to come closer and have a look at some documents.

"What's this, Grandpa?" Asked Philippe with curiosity in his voice.

"This is a money settlement for you and your sister, the insurance payment and money that both of you inherited from your parents."

Philippe looked through the papers in the folder and his eyes glowed; now his and Caroline's future could be better, and they can continue their college. He is touched so much that he couldn't handle barely visible tears of joy in his eyes.

"Thank you, Grandpa! That means a lot for us."

"Son," Mohammed touched his shoulder, "Life is a very interesting thing, but remember that money never should possess you; money is just a tool in our hands to get things."

"You're right." Nodded happy Philippe.

At very late evening, he finally went to bed feeling free, and a strange thought didn't let him go. 'Grandfather knew John in person and had even met his kids before. Why, then, did Mohammed never even mention John Fury? Why has Caroline never contacted me? Her act was pretty strange because if something happened, it was me and only me, the first who got to know about everything. She knew I could help her with anything, but not this time. Something really has changed.' Philippe was staring at the ceiling with all these questions going through his mind. And perhaps everything will go back to normal when they see each other again.

That night, Martin couldn't sleep well, all the time, he was shaken and moving from side to side. He was standing on a house's verge and observing his surroundings. In his hands was a shiny black gun. He was dressed in dark clothes and had leather gloves on. He looked at the night sky covered in glowing stars and breaths hard. All of a sudden, he noticed a running girl away from the house. She hurried deep in weeds and bushes, her golden wavy hair disheveled. Her image was so familiar. She glanced back at him, and he saw her deep green eyes. Her pale, fearful face comes closer to him, and he hears her words, 'Thank you, Monsieur, you saved my life.' He felt attraction, and his thoughts say, 'Too young to take her seriously.'

He let her go, and she went down the trail. He woke up wet and found out it was just a dream. Martin relaxed on a bed and squeezed his pillow; 'Caroline Sauvage Roux,' he whispered, 'this is the girl from Raymond's garden. The girl that Jason Parker was fighting in Morocco, the girl from my dream on the boat,' Martin was terrified. And now she is Victoria's girlfriend. He looked away to the window and felt himself awake. She was here; she was coming for them, and she was the only one who survived that night when his dad killed all the members of that family. He rose from his bed and walked to the bathroom. Martin softly balanced the temperature and carefully stepped into the shower. He sighed peacefully when the warm stream of water splashed on his face. He took some shampoo, washed his hair, and then, with a body wash, rinsed his body.

Standing on the soft rug in front of his mirror, he carefully shaved, brushed his teeth, and combed his hair. Squeezed some hair gel into his palm and fixed his forelock. Smiling at his reflection with obvious content he put some cologne on. His towel enveloped his hips. Walking carefully from the bathroom to his closet he stopped and opened the draw of his dresser.

Martin took out a wallet and checked it out, a couple hundred dollars. He shook his head. 'I forgot when the last time I had fun in the casino. It's time to go,' he slightly smiled to himself. This time, he put on his outfit from Polo Ralph Lauren, he looked amazing in this style. Softly walking through the hall, Martin opened the garage and took his favorite burgundy, Aston Martin. The engine of it trembled, and he drove his car out. His elegant watch shows five o'clock. He pushed a button and turns on his radio channel, and the music from the seventies starts playing. 'Who loves you, pretty mama?' Martin was singing together with a singer for himself.

He was in a mood to start this morning with good music. On a green light, he turned his steering wheel to the right and went in the line for a coffee at Starbucks. Feeling better after some soft sip of coffee, Martin drove to the Horseshoe Casino. He gave his car to the valet and went inside. There was almost nobody this early morning, so he pulled out a couple hundred dollars and placed it at the roulette table. He bought red chips and placed five of them on the numbers five, fifteen, twenty, thirty-two and two of them on the black spot. The dealer threw the ball and later announced number five. Martin smiled wide and made the next bet. He won four times in a row.

After that, he left and tried his luck at the blackjack table. The Chinese woman there bit him four times until the last bet of his. He squeezed five black chips in his hand and went to the cashier. At the casino restaurant Martin had his breakfast and left to work. All day long, he had appointments with clients and business meetings. At lunchtime, he deposited John's check into his account and had a juicy steak at the Grill House. In the evening, he received a call from Jason Parker.

"Hey, man! What are you doing tonight?" Jason's voice sounded fresh and alive.

"Nothing important, why?" Answered Martin.

"Let's have a couple of drinks tonight. I'm in town!" Offered Jason.

"Sounds good to me," Martin's velvet voice sounded relaxed.

"All right, I'll text you later the address."

"Perfect," answered Martin.

In an hour, Martin was sticking around at home. He went through his closet and put unwanted clothes in a big white bag. 'Church and poor people need it more' – he thought. He pulled out a nice cream jacket from the hanger and wrinkled his nose with a thought, 'Dating with Easter, oh!' Martin packed it in the bag with the rest clothes, and then he touched his black linen trousers and slightly smiled. That was exactly what he was looking for. He put them on and looked in the mirror. They still fit. 'Perfect, I'll wear them tonight,' he found some shirts and looked at the temperature outside, 'I'll wear long sleeve white shirt,' he thought. A dark grey blazer finished his look.

He rushed to the bathroom and looked at his favorite Hadrian Absolu Annick Goutal perfume. Martin held it in his hand, thinking it was time to find a new girl for his needs. This perfume he received from his sister on his birthday, without thinking too much he sprayed it twice on his neck and winked to himself. On the nightstand by his bed, his phone vibrated, letting him know the incoming message received. Martin slides the screen and reads it: 'Hey, man! I'll meet you at Crimson Lounge on 333 North Dearborn St. if you don't mind,' Martin frowned. He knows this place; it's all about the antique atmosphere, and the women there are special. If Jason invites him there it means he's going to be not alone. He quickly rushed out of his bedroom and hurried to his car. The engine started and he moved from the garage fast.

When partying with a group of friends, it can be a lot of fun to partake in the ultimate VIP clubbing experience. What better way to really live it up than with bottles of your favorite spirits to enjoy with your favorite people?

Chicago's Crimson Lounge hotspot was a great place to see and be seen while enjoying VIP seating and top-notch bottle service in a posh, upscale setting. Crimson Lounge was located on the lower level of the luxurious Sax Hotel in Chicago's River North neighborhood. The Crimson Lounge's atmosphere lent itself to its own brand of classic chic with its deep stained wood bars, antique-looking furniture, and oil paintings lining the walls. This was a great location to truly feel like you are among the elite and fabulous. The bottle service here includes VIP seating in the lounge's luxurious VIP area, express entry, and wonderful service. All of these things love Jason Parker and his friends. Chris Wren, Brian Fury, Jason Parker, Reina, and Victoria were already inside and waiting for Martin. Guys were dressed in nice suits and holding glasses of champagne. They were having a pleasant conversation with ladies Victoria and Reina. Laughs and talks surrounded the celebrating atmosphere; Brian glanced at his sister and only now noticed her stunning grace from head to toe. Curly brown hair peacefully lay on her shoulders; brown eyes were especially eloquent in a green velvet deep V-neck gown from Gucci. Her long diopside earrings emphasized her neck as well as the pretty same gemstone pendant on her chest. Her index finger was adorned long marquis yellow gold ring, and her graceful arm was decorated with a golden bracelet with the same pattern as a ring.

Brian couldn't stare at her anymore; he looked in to his goblet half full of champagne and shifted his blue eyes on Reina. She was not less beautiful than his sister. Combed on a side, dark hair made her look more girlish and flirtier, and pretty peach lips were half opened when she was listening to one of her brother's jokes. The deep blue glitz Elie Saab gown with a cut on the side made her taller than she really was. Reina had less jewelry on than Victoria; she was wearing only medium-long drop sapphire earrings and a white sapphire gold setting ring. And still, Brian admitted her restrained beauty. He slightly smiled on the side and thought about his future girlfriend; she has to be tall as well, with fair hair and blue eyes, intelligent, and first of all, a good friend.

The waiter brought them some really tasty snacks and more spirits.

"Wait, wait," Quickly said Jason, covering drinks with his hand, "Martin is coming, guys! Don't forget about our brother, from another mother," he smiled with one of his gorgeous smiles.

"WOW!!!" Exclaimed Chris, laughing, "That's him!"

Martin entered the room and looked around with a big, surprised expression on his face. He spread his arms:

"What the hell are you guys doing?"

"Martin," called him Jason, holding his sister's waist, "Join our dreamboat! Who was there with us all the time? Who won the battle?"

Martin's side smile appeared in the corner of his lip; he got the hint. They gathered here to celebrate the victory over Raymond Moulay Ali. That was really a good surprise. Hugging and smiling to his close ones he joined the company and sat between Victoria and Reina. His hands lay on their waists and smiled at them:

"The dreamboat is supposed to be surrounded by beautiful women."

"Oh..!" The guys exclaimed, "This is our Martin! Champagne for Martin!"

"No!" Protested with his index finger Martin. "Martini, please!"

Everybody looked at each other:

"And a smoke!" Added Jason.

"No!" Protested Martin, shifting his eyes away. "No, smoke!"

Brian moved his head in surprise and said:

"Did you give up smoking?"

The silence hung in the room. Everyone was staring at Martin, waiting for his response. He looked from one side of the company to another and nodded:

"Yes!" He said it out loud, "I did, no smoking!"

"Oh!" Raised his glass, Brian smiled at everyone: "We have to celebrate this too!"

"Martini! Martini! Bring a Martini for Martin!" Laughing, requested Jason to be their waiter.

A minute later rang glasses at the table and while celebrating, guys started telling scary stories to Victoria and Reina about how they were fighting on the battlefield.

Jason shook his head and looked at everyone;

"Brian and Martin were really cool, not like me; I still can't believe that a girl was fighting me! Really, man, I was training all of this time for what? To fight a girl?!"

Reina crossed her eyebrows on a bridge:

"Wait, a girl? Women are not allowed fighting there!"

"That's what I thought too," nodded Martin, "Raymond's crazy fiancé tried to kick Jason's butt!"

Victoria slightly opened her mouth when she heard those words from her brother:

"Fiancé?"

"Yes, Raymond was engaged to a French chick, didn't you know that?" Glanced at her Reina, drinking champagne.

"No," she shook her head, Victoria. Now she is really confused about this news. The French girl was engaged to Raymond and then Reina's strange meeting with Caroline, and all of these questions about her big diamond ring, if she was engaged before. Someone really makes a fool of her. "And what happened then?"

Jason pursed his lower lip:

"She ran away. That crazy girl left him and just disappeared."

"Yeah," nodded Martin and glanced out with the corner of his eye at Victoria.

He saw what he was expecting to see, confusion. She knows what he is talking about, so she interfered in this dirty business as well. Martin's curiosity was tearing him up. He planned on making Victoria drunk tonight, taking her home, and there attacking with questions. But he is not the only one who knows her secret.

Reina smiled at Victoria and offered her some more champagne:

"Oh no," she protested, "I'm done."

"Don't worry, sister," said Foxy Martin, "I'll take you home. By the way, you have to celebrate this victory very well; you were the one who took part in this battle, too."

"We have to gather like this more often," said Reina. "I love this party tonight. Hm, next time, don't forget to bring your friend, Victoria."

Martin looked at both, his eyes widened, and with a curious smile, he said to his sister:

"Friend. Why didn't you bring her with you?"

Victoria looked at Reina, and her face expressed a little anger:

"She doesn't drink, plus she didn't participate in this organization." Abruptly said Victoria.

"I thought that Caroline would love it, with a smile said Reina." Her brown eyes were glowing, and she shifted them on Martin. She knows that he's a playboy and to throw Caroline into his arms would be the best revenge over her. Reina couldn't forgive Caroline that she stole her Raymond.

"Caroline?" Said Martin with intrigue that froze on his lips.

Victoria lowered her eyes to her knees and realized that Martin would never let her go until he met her in person.

"Is she pretty?" Raised one eyebrow, curios Martin looked at Reina.

"Oh yeah!" a satisfied voice murmured in Reina's response; "She is gorgeous, out of lack of words to describe."

Victoria couldn't hold her temper anymore:

"Come on, Reina! She is just plain, nothing special about her!"

Martin looked at both girls, first at his sister and then at Reina;

"Girls," he said, "Chillax, let me judge her beauty!"

He winked at Victoria.

"No!" Protested his sister, her nostrils quivered with anger. "You would never meet her, Martin!"

He looked at her and moved a little when Victoria got up and didn't allow touching her.

"Why not?" Martin's eyes were shiny from the interest; his evil look disturbed Victoria a lot.

"I said no, my no is enough."

Reina couldn't understand Victoria's reaction; she was protecting this girl like a mother protecting her child.

"What did she do for you, Victoria? You attached to her like to your daughter." Hissed Reina.

"This is none of your business." Hissed back Victoria.

Jason didn't like his sister's tone, and he interfered in the upcoming conflict:

"Girls, girls, it's a party, not a freaking battle. We just returned from the war zone. It's not a good time to have conversations like this at the table."

Brian stopped his discussion with Chris and looked at the rest table members:

"What's going on? Are you guys drunk?" He was annoyed by the women's argument and was positive that his brother would blow the fire out of nothing.

Victoria sat back at the table closer to Jason. She glanced with such an angelic look at him that he couldn't hold it anymore. His warm palm touched her cold fingers and squeezed her hand.

"Reina," he said, "didn't you change your mind about marriage with Raymond?" Jason tried to change the subject so nobody would be hurt.

"I don't know," she answered back; "If he writes me back and asks me to marry him, maybe I'll do it."

Victoria's eyes showed interest and were no longer asked Reina back: "Really? I remember you telling us you're going to marry right after Jason."

"Weddings!" Exclaimed Martin, "I love weddings!"

"Shut up, Martin!" Victoria rolled her eyes.

Reina swallowed hard and nodded positively, glancing from the corner of her eye at Jason:

"Yes, if he asks me."

Jason stretched into a satisfied smile at the answer. In spring he's going to be married and happy with Helen. They are planning to buy a cozy house closer to Santa Monica or maybe in Santa

Monica itself. Next Year, Jason plans to sell his Jaguar and buy something more luxurious. He tries to get rid of the idea that he isn't single anymore. He also wants to try himself in design. Jason even started taking online courses in designing and he's doing pretty well. At least like, he realized later that his father's business isn't his shoe. John and Trey can play their own games but without Jason. His father likes Helen and her family and he hopes that Jason is going to be a good husband and a father.

"Guys," he said; "What are the plans for Christmas?"

Martin and Brian looked at each other and shrugged their shoulders; Victoria glanced at her brothers and said:

"Father is actually planning to invite Trey and you guys to us. Well, that's what I know, and this day is supposed to be my birthday."

"That's right", nodded Martin in response.

"So, you're welcome!" Softly said Victoria and lowered her eyes when she remembered about Caroline. How sad that she can't invite her too. Fury's nest is too dangerous for her and not a suitable place at all. Caroline is desperate about Fury's family and she is looking as hard as she can. The key moment is in fear of her discovering that Victoria is Fury and she is a direct daughter of John; Caroline might hate her forever.

The party finished late, and Martin took Victoria home. She didn't feel well at all. Jason picked up Chris and Brian. In the front seat was sitting next to his sister – Reina. She was half drunk with a silly smile. She glanced at Jason and slowly mumbled:

"Jason, I saw her…"

"Who?" Raised his eyebrows, Jason.

"Caroline," barely said Reina, "She is here in Chicago. Victoria is her best friend."

Jason smacked his lips and shook his head;

"Who are you talking about?"

"Raymond's girlfriend, Caroline."

All of a sudden, Jason realized her words and stopped at a red light. Caroline is Raymond's fiancée. She saved his life, and he saw her statue in the garden. The French girl who was forced to be engaged with Hakim. Jason's heart ached with sorrow. He glanced at his sister but she was sleeping already. He looked back at the road and squeezed the steering wheel of his car. Jason took a decision to meet Caroline and the best way to do it is to follow Victoria and see who she meets after work. Especially now, when he isn't working at Lex as often as he used to.

Victoria was speechless on her way to the mansion while Martin was driving. He tried several times to talk to her, but silence was her best friend. When they arrived, he helped her to get out of his Aston Martin; she fell into his arms, and he took her upstairs back to her bedroom. Carrying her through the house hall, Martin silently opened the door to her room and carefully placed her on the bed. He covered her with a blanket and, backing off, closed her door. He sighed deeply and walked away to his bedroom.

Martin carefully took off his jacket and put it on his bed. He came close to the window and looked at the full moon. So, Reina saw the girl. Caroline is here, and moreover, Victoria is protecting her. So, it's obvious! Victoria clearly told Jerry Smith not to mention her last name, which means she knows the story about her father's murder. Martin realized that he had to find Caroline and talk to her as soon as possible. Tomorrow at Lex he has to call his special agent and find out the whole information about Caroline Sauvage Roux.

# CHAPTER 19

*There is nothing more interesting than secret, sweeter - forbidden, bitter - useful, more expensive - lost - in short tempered and boring - the usual.*

### *Yuri Tatarkin*

This city, this smell of smoke and money, Caroline feels she gets tired of it every day. Nothing has changed since she arrived in this God's forgotten place. Yes, she has to stay and study and be stable in her desire to find Fury. This pretty apartment is nothing but a golden cage. Victoria's request not to go out and wait for her because it's dangerous outside is killing her. In Marseille, she was free; whenever she wanted to go, she went. And here you have to drive or spend money on a taxi, what a waste! Caroline finished her hair in front of the mirror and silently came closer to her closet full of clothes. She picked a pink silky blouse with buttons up to her neck and black stretchy pants. The matching belt was hanging on a hook. Caroline returned to her dresser and opened a cosmetic bag. There, she found her favorite beige eye shadows and black liner. She put careful makeup on and finished her look with ivory powder and peach lipstick. Caroline turned to a mirror again and smiled to herself. She believes in the statement if you start your morning with a smile, all day will be pleasant and easy. The girl put casual shoes on and a wallet in her purse and left the apartment. She went downstairs and outside crossed the street, so she could see some goods in the shops. Walking around here and there, she finally felt tired in her new shoes.

Caroline turned to a corner and saw a small cafeteria with fresh bakery. She walked there rapidly. When she opened the door the freshly baked bread and the coffee aroma attracted her. Caroline walked inside and asked for two fresh croissants and a cup of coffee. She was served in a minute, sitting in a little corner. Caroline noticed fresh magazines; she picked one and opened it in the middle. There was an article, 'Why is Fuego avoiding upcoming races in 2015?' Caroline read it carefully, and her face became serious. She found out that Fuego is actually Martin Fury. That guy who saved her life was Fury. Her heart squeezed, and she felt a punch under her stomach. That means that Victoria knew who Fuego was, and she never told her about it. How dare she be! She camouflaged his real name, but why? She knew that Caroline was looking for Fury all of this time, and she was so close, and Victoria didn't tell her the truth. Caroline didn't even finish her coffee as she picked up her purse and rushed outside. She found a taxi and asked to take her to Westwood. Caroline wants to see Jerry Smith and ask him about Fuego and how she can find him. On her way, Caroline felt her fast-beating pulse, and it didn't even bother her.

Since early morning Martin was on his knees at Westwood. The weather promised to be sunny, despite on frost, it was very pleasant outside. First, Martin met his jockey and discussed with him the upcoming race, and then he asked to prepare for him Ivanhoe, so he could ride him. Dressed in tight pants and a jacket, he put high boots on and pulled out leather gloves. He came outside and took Ivanhoe under its reins. The horse seemed to be in a mood every time when saw its lord. His shiny winter fur was fluffy and so soft to the touch. Martin put his foot in the stirrup and sat in the saddle, and then he rode Ivanhoe inside the corral.

The yellow cab slowly parked at the entrance to the ranch. Caroline carefully opened the door and got out of it. The taxi drove away behind her back to the road. She closed her eyes and let the fresh, cool wind to kiss her face. She breathed the air and sighed.

Caroline went inside and got into the yard. It was empty and not as crowded as usual; she noticed a guy riding Ivanhoe in the corral. She came closer to the white fence and touched it accurately, trying to see the man's face. Her lips pursed together, and she waved her head to the sides. She recognized Martin Fury. It seemed to Caroline he noticed her, Ivanhoe stopped galloping and he walked closer to her. The fellow dismounted from his horse and let him walk by himself. Caroline didn't move; her eyes were on him. He hasn't changed: the same forelock, shiny dark brown eyes, broad shoulders and slim waist, slender legs, and a charming smile. Martin is coming closer to her, taking off his riding gloves. He raised his head, and their eyes met. The moment as fast as the seagull's cry, it seemed the whole century had passed since their last meeting. He recognized her from the first gaze; a woman so bright like her is always unforgettable. She has become nicer and more attractive since the last time he saw her at the coast. He thought that she was the most beautiful woman he ever met. Martin felt his heart beating with his indescribable easiness. His lower lip opened slightly, and he smiled nicely, "You!"

Caroline moved a little, feeling nervous, inside of her were fighting two opposite feelings: sympathy and harm. She didn't know how to act. Instead, she just said, "Hey!" She lowered her eyes.

Martin approached her closer and she could feel his breathing on her. He lightly touched her chin and lifted her head in the desire to see her eyes again. Caroline's eyelashes went up, and he drowned in her green eyes. She stepped back from him like a wild gazelle, and her eyes showed. 'She is angry,' he thought.

"What are you doing here?" Martin finally broke the hanging silence between them.

Caroline's chest was rising up and down in deep breathing, full of excitement. All of this time she lived with the hope of meeting him again in her life just to say 'Thank you!', but now she didn't know if she wanted to do this. He is Fury, and that night, Fury's members who made murder, Martin was one of them. Otherwise, it can't be a coincidence.

"I came to see Jerry," she said these words so uncomfortably to herself and all of a sudden felt herself silly.

Martin's eyes narrowed, and a light smile moved a corner of his lip. He shook his head, "Jerry knows what I know. If you are interested in something particular, just ask me directly."

Caroline pursed her lips and shifted her shiny eyes; she turned to him with her back so he wouldn't see her burning cheeks. She slowly moved to the ranch entrance. Martin frowned; she was walking away without saying a word to him, just walking away. He rushed and touched her elbow, trying to face the girl. Caroline stopped and froze when she felt his hand on hers. Under her lowered eyelashes, her face turned pale, and she abruptly said, "Don't touch me!"

"Look at me," he demanded.

But she didn't obey.

"I'm sorry!" said Martin unexpectedly to himself. He looked at her pink lips and moved away his arm. She is so seductive. "Please, don't go!"

"Mr. Fury," she called him with her voice cold, "there's nothing to talk about."

Martin's eyes widened, and he looked at her right away, "You know my name?"

Caroline nodded, "I do."

"Why you didn't do anything then? What are you waiting for?" Martin got nervous and mean at the same time.

Caroline didn't answer; she stepped away and turned left, leading to the stable. She was walking, tears stuck in her eyes; she didn't want to show him her weakness. At this very moment, she hates herself for these silly tears rolling down now. Caroline felt herself in a trap. Her hands are shaking, and her heart is beating fast. How silly she is showing up here. Martin realized if he let her go now he'll never see her again. He followed her and caught her at the wall in the lobby. He pressed her to the door at the entrance to the locker room. She didn't push him away and didn't fight him either. Caroline closed her eyes and lowered her head, feeling faint. The whole world was spinning in front of her eyes. She lost consciousness and weakened. Martin picked her up. Carefully holding her in his hands, he brought her to his ranch office and placed her on a couch. He felt nervous and rubbed his knees. He placed next to her and gently touched her hand. Caroline's skin is white and so shiny compared to his golden arm. 'Oh my Lord, she is so sweet!' He thought. Martin smacked his lips and got up to look for cold water; he opened a refrigerator and pulled out one bottle. He sprinkled water on her face, and Caroline's eyelids clenched; she breathed out hard and opened her eyes. Martin is looking at her with expressive eyes.

"I have such an impression that you like me to carry your helpless body."

His words touched her to the core. She rose up in a sitting position and looked around, trying to figure out where she was. Then her eyes met with his and locked in a long gaze. She felt butterflies in her belly and a very strange, weak feeling, and she moved her head, "You don't even know how much I dislike you!" Her words came from her mouth with a stream of air. However, he only just laughed out loud. This led her into confusion.

Martin came closer to his little bar and poured some martini into his glass. He turned to her with a satisfied smile on his face and said, "You don't even know how many times I heard that from different women, and after that, in a month, they have been dying just to kiss me."

Her eyes showed like two expensive emeralds, and he noticed her anger when she raised her chin, "Braggart!"

"Hahaha!" He roared with laughter.

Caroline rose from the couch and rushed to the door, but he was quicker than her; Martin pressed it with his back facing the girl. She stepped back a little and took a pose, raising her head with pride like someone tried to whip her:

"What do you want?"

"Me?" Martin pointed at himself and shook his head. "Nothing! What do you want?" He pointed out at her. "Hm? Miss Sauvage Roux…"

Caroline looked at him with surprise, and her eyes widened when she heard her full name from his mouth. She didn't expect him to know her that well. Confusion and shock filled her mind. He took her by surprise.

"I could easily turn your beautiful neck right now, but don't dare."

"Why not?" I'm your enemy. "She kept her eyes on him," swallowing hard.

Martin sarcastically smiled and answered to her back:

"No. Not mine," my father's. I don't play his dirty games.

Caroline's lips slightly opened in another shockwave. She thought that he and John were one team.

Martin's eyes got sad, and he lowered his long eyelashes as if he was sorry for what happened. He said:

"I don't kill people."

"Maybe you rape teens?" Her voice sounded cold, when she remembered the crying Emilie under man.

Martin looked at her, and his face expressed disgust. His eyebrows went on a bridge, and he got mad:

"You lost your mind! I never raped any woman in my life!"

Caroline turned her back to him and pursed her lips. Now she saw he was telling her the truth, but who raped her sister? She came closer to the window and, placing her hands, said:

"Martin, that night in my house were four men. And one of them went upstairs and raped my twin sister. I was there under the bed, he never saw me. John Fury is the one who killed all my family."

"And you think that after I've saved you at the coast, I raped her?"

"His voice and yours sounded the same." Caroline touched her lips with sorrow. "I have to find John Fury and make a judgment upon him. It's all about justice now."

Martin came closer to Caroline and tried to look into her face. He noticed tears stuck in her eyes and burning hot cheeks. He tried to touch her on the shoulder and couldn't.

"Caroline," he called her for the first time gently and softly, "John Fury is too powerful and smart for such a brace teenager like you. He has bodyguards and always carries a gun. You are the worst and easiest enemy, and he'll kill you in a second."

Caroline swallowed and nodded to him: "You're right."

"Please, go home." He barely said these words.

"Home?" She exclaimed, and her light green eyes turned to a deep greenish wood color. "I have no home. You and your father destroyed it and left only ash. I have nobody. Do you hear? Nobody."

Caroline was mad and angry; finally, she could vent her pain on him.

Martin returned to his couch and comforted himself there. He looked at her and moved his head to the side. He sighed and smacked:

"I saw you running before the explosion; I was there on a house's verge and had a chance to shoot you, but I didn't."

She turned to him, and his face was pale from his own words: "What?"

"Yes." He nodded. "I saved you in the morning and saved you in the evening. You have to live, dear."

Caroline came closer to him and protested, "Why didn't you shoot me? I would never have this feeling of being an orphan. And would never." She couldn't talk anymore; her sorrow filled her throat.

Martin saw her pain, and he felt pity for the girl, "Somebody has to stop my father." His lips moved in a slow motion.

Caroline turned around, opened the door, and slammed it hard; she rushed outside and asked Jerry to call for a taxi. Martin left by himself in the room. Now he understands her pain, but there's nothing that he can do. He knows his father is a monster. If John finds out about her presence in Chicago, nothing will stop him from another sin. Martin thinks that he has to make sure that she leaves before he discovers her living here. The best way to act is through his stubborn sister. If she is her real friend, she'll understand his point. Martin changed his outfit, picked some pieces of paper, and placed them in his folder. He found the keys to his car and was ready to leave when he decided just to glance at Flash. It was not hard to find this beautiful reddish horse. He was eating at his stable very quietly. Martin came closer, and his professional eye gave him an excellent mark. Gorgeous stallion! There's nothing else to say. He pursed his lips and nodded to himself. Martin rushed to his car and left for Lex.

This evening is really cooler than yesterday. All of a sudden, snowflakes were coming down. One of them landed on Philippe's palm. He looked at it closer and noticed that it didn't look like the rest of them. Each one has a different look. Philippe sighed and turned his head on the road when he noticed a yellow cab coming.

"Grandpa!" He called Mohammed.

Philippe was waiting for this car to see who it was so late. Mohammed came out on the verge and narrowed his eyes, trying to look. He wasn't expecting anybody at this time, every order was done and clients left, but the taxi car really disturbed him. Philippe and Mohammed were just waiting. Finally, the taxi parked by them, and four doors opened. Mohammed recognized his Moroccan relatives: Jain Mozhardin, Moulay Ali, and Raymond. He rushed to them with his arms open; they hugged and kissed after Mohammed invited them to the house. They passed Philippe talking to each other in their Arabic and entered the house. Jain sat at the table and helped herself with tea while Moulay Ali and his son Raymond took a seat next to a fireplace on a couch. Philippe closed the door behind them and placed his hands standing in a pose.

"How did you decide to visit me so soon?" Asked Mohammed in English.

"Soon?" Exclaimed Moulay Ali, "That's not soon. We wanted to give you a surprise!"

"You did." Noticed happy Mohammed, "Moulay, let me introduce you to my grandson Philippe!"

"Oh!" Loudly sighed his relative, "I remember him a boy!" Noticed Ali and smiled. "What a stunning fellow! Raymond," he called his son, "Come here and meet Philippe Sauvage Roux!"

Raymond came to Philippe and shook his hand:

"Philippe, your sister told me about you!" Slightly smiled, Ray.

"Really?" He raised his eyebrows; "Hopefully, only nice things!"

They both laughed and moved closer to the fireplace. Jain never moved her eyes from Caroline's brother. He is good-looking and stunning, with dark brown hair shining from the firelight and straight white teeth. Finally, Philippe turned to her and frowned:

"Excuse me, and what's your name?"

She moved her head, and her heavy earrings jingled:

"My name is Jain Mozhardin. I knew your sister very well!"

Philippe smiled wide and lowered his eyes in a shy:

"Really? That well? Was she stubborn?"

"It's not the word!" Jain smiled back, raising her arms.

"I knew that!" Winked to her Philippe.

Moulay Ali and Mohammed, together with Jain, laid a table and surrounded some courses for a late dinner. They placed carefully in a Turkish way, and Ali started his speech:

"I'm really sorry that Caroline disappeared. We tried to take care of her, but see," he silenced and then continued: "She left without any notice."

Philippe glanced at Raymond and noticed his sadness; of course, she was his bride. He didn't want to show anybody his real feelings, but when old Ali stopped talking, Philippe added:

"I know where she is."

Raymond instantly glanced at Philippe and his face became pale first and then started changing into color.

"What?" Questioned Hakim. Everyone looked at Philippe. Jain's eyes widened, and her face brightened; she was the one who broke the hanging silence:

"Where is she? Caroline, where?"

Philippe made a pause on purpose so they would question him. His eyes showed with obvious excitement, and he said:

"Thanks to modern technology, we can get emails through the Internet. We received a letter from her a couple of days ago; she says that we shouldn't worry; she is fine and peacefully lives in The US."

Raymond went nervous and mad:

"That's impossible!" He exclaimed, and his voice sounded like a lion's roar. "She couldn't go to The US without her documents and money. I know how much this trip costs. It's nonsense!"

Mohammed raised his bushy grey eyebrows and smiled to his guests:

"Are you trying to say that she's lying?"

Raymond became very serious with his eyebrows crossed on a bridge:

"Caroline never lied to me, but how could she leave Morocco without papers? It's logical… Unless the Americans picked her up!" He couldn't believe his words, but that was just a theory.

"What else did she say?" Jain's curiosity was biting her.

"She says that she has a wonderful friend helping her around, and soon, she's going to study hard to get a degree."

Raymond's temper went down; he rose up and walked back and forth. All of this time she just used him for her ambitions, and she has never wanted to marry him like all of them thought. Caroline has been studying from his best teachers everything she needs in college, and now she has a wonderful friend helping her there.

"What an absurd!" He exclaimed, realizing how fool he was.

"Hakim!" Preached Jain.

"At least she's fine," said softly Moulay Ali. He didn't want to admit her stubbornness in Morocco, but thanks God she and Raymond didn't unite their friendship into marriage. It would be the biggest shame ever for them. Her behavior in Morocco would kill Raymond and her reputation forever.

People in Rabat would stop trusting their hakim, and he would face a conflict; she would be punished.

"What is done can't be undone, Ali!" Mohammed said these words with any regret in his voice.

Philippe received a great pleasure to see Raymond in anger. Secretly he wanted somehow to punch him for being with Caroline. She is his favorite, and Philippe's heart was much more hurt when he received information about her engagement with Hakim. He never wanted her to know any other man around, especially an Arab. Philippe disliked Arabs with all of his human beings: their theory, morality, and just poor world. He played this evening a nice guy for his grandpa because these people dare Mohammed but never Philippe.

Raymond was so mad about Caroline; he discussed her all evening. First, he said he wanted to see her for giving her a good punishment. The second time, Raymond said he wanted to see her because he missed her so much, and it was hard for him to be without her. And the third time, he said that he never wanted to hear her name again. Philippe watched Jain all evening, and he noticed that this silence covered a great eloquence. She obeys any word that Hakim says but nobody cares what she thinks and what she knows. She might be a great source for the scout. Philippe sat next to her and placed his arms on a table, glancing at her from time to time, trying to give her a hint that he was open to having a conversation with her. But he forgot one main thing – women in the Far East never talk to a man first. Jain reminded him of a sheep in the herd. That is an annoying thing!

"I wonder," finally said Philippe to Jain so she could only hear. "If Hakim knew where Caroline was, what would he do?"

"I'm sure he would go for her." Softly and quietly answered Jain.

"Hm. to do what?"

"To bring her home and marry her."

Raymond turned to Mohammed and, with his eyes sad, looked at him; Philippe read a hope in his look:

"Did she say anything about her physical location?"

Mohammed opened his mouth in response, but Philippe cut him off:

"No, she didn't. Caroline just informed us in her letter that she is in The US and nothing else. We wrote to her twice and didn't receive any response back, so she might be busy." Philipp's eyes glowed when he was obviously lying that knew his grandfather since the fellow was little.

Mohammed wrinkled his nose, trying to get Philipp's idea of hiding Caroline. And it must be his feelings for her, he jealousies sister to Raymond. This is the only reason that he covered her real presence in Chicago; if he told the truth to Hakim, he would no longer send his people to Chicago and find Caroline. They will bring her to Rabat and punish them. On the other side, they have no right to do this because she doesn't belong to Islam, and they are not her parents. Next year Caroline will be twenty.

"We don't know where she is in The US," twice Philippe said, making his face pretty serious and sad.

Mohammed caught his game and took a decision to participate in Philipp's plan: "When we find something, we will tell you right away," promised Mohammed, looking at Moulay Ali and the rest members of this family.

Philippe glanced at his grandfather and lowered his head, smiling. So, Mohammed agrees with his idea to hide Caroline from hakim.

"Well," said Mohammed to his guests, "you must be tired after this long trip. You can feel at home here, and rooms upstairs are waiting for you, guys!"

Ali nodded his head and smiled:

"You're as always kind, Mohammed. Thank you!"

Raymond was not ready to go to bed yet. He stayed downstairs, and Philippe was sitting opposite him in a tall armchair that left from his mother's first house. Both of them were enjoying the fire noise in the fireplace. In his right hand, Raymond was holding a tall glass filled with red wine. Philippe drank almost half of it. For Hakim, it was pretty unusual to stay at someone's house and, especially far from home. He was observing Philippe and, slightly moving his knees, finally said:

"Caroline loves you, Philippe."

"Yea? Is this what she said?

"No, she didn't," sighed Raymond, "She always talked about you with some kind of tenderness and respect."

"Hmm," nodded Philippe, obviously enjoying it.

"She is an amazing woman, but unfortunately not mine," admitted Raymond.

Philippe looked at Hakim with his eyes narrowed and pursed his lips:

"I thought you subdued her, did you?"

"You're kidding me." Whispered Raymond. "She subdued a wild colt and me. Nobody over there could even touch her."

Philippe lowered his eyelids, and a slight smile moved a corner of his lip. 'Yes, that's her! My stubborn sister, Caroline! Ray is right. She can tame anyone.

Being in her bed Caroline was staring at the ceiling, curling her hair on a finger. 'Martin is completely right about John Fury; he's a hundred times stronger than me, and it won't be hard for him to finish with the last member of the Sauvage Roux family. I need a plan and a strategy for my actions. Victoria is good, but she hid Fuego from me, and there is supposed to be a reason. If I ask her directly, she will invent a new excuse for me.' Caroline rolled on another side of her bed and looked at her nightstand; she touched the surface of it and bit her lip: 'Ivanhoe's owner is such an attractive fellow, why? His velvet voice, golden skin, his tiny waist, and brought shoulders!' Caroline never realized that she was absolutely calm about skinny guys with no body; she had never given a slight thought about a man's body. Martin's stunning grace was the best that she had ever seen; Raymond was handsome but not that much, so she would stop thinking; the guy from the battlefield was good-looking but not impressive to her. Martin. Martin is different!' Her cheeks blushed from the slight idea of what he does to women. She shook her head when she remembered his words. 'You don't even know how many times I heard that from different women, and after that, in a month, they have been dying just to kiss me.' Caroline remembered Jain's words about men's boasting: 'If a man tells you that he's good in bed, that means that he's worst.' Then she closed her eyes slowly and spread on a bed, putting the blanket up to her neck. How much wisdom things she learn from Morocco? It's hard to count! Caroline pulled her arm out of the blanket and, looked at the diamond ring on the left hand and sighed, 'How silly all of these people are! They think I'm engaged!' Different rainbow colors glittered in the gemstone, attracting with its magnetic charm. She smiled to herself, closed her eyes, relaxed, and fell asleep. In her dream, Caroline brushed her hair with a wide golden brush in front of her mirror and, in reflection, saw Victoria coming into her room and holding a sparkling diadem in her hands. She turned to face her with a wide smile and put jewelry on her head, saying that Caroline was going to be the most beautiful bride ever. Caroline walked slowly to her wedding dress on a layman figure and asked Victoria,

"Why do I have red ribbons on a wedding dress? It's ugly, and I don't need them! Take them away!!!"

"I thought you would love it – a special gift from me!" Protested Victoria.

"No, I don't! Take them away now!" Almost screaming, said Caroline, and felt indescribable anger. "I want my dress just to be white without any decorations, especially of this color!"

Victoria, without saying a word, turned her back and disappeared through the opened door. Caroline left by herself in the room and, being mad, took a seat next to her wedding dress. A man's voice behind her back softly whispered in her ear: 'Don't worry, babe! I'll take you as you are.

Caroline shivered and opened her eyes wide; she looked around and hugged the pillow closer. 'It was just a dream,' she thought. 'Victoria hides something, and this secret I won't like definitely.' Caroline noticed since her arrival in Chicago, she started more often seeing a man in her dreams. First, he touched her behind, and then she met him in the open field, and now, this wedding. Probably, a different climate hit her head. She got up from her bed and came barefoot to her wide French windows that were closed with heavy curtains. She touched them gently and spread them wide, allowing light to brighten her room. Caroline's eyes widened when she saw a city covered with white snow. Even some snowflakes stuck in the corners of her window. A wide smile spread her corner lips. Snow everywhere: on the street, on the roof, and on the balconies. Her cell phone rang, and she rushed for it. The incoming call was from her girlfriend:

"Victoria! Did you see snow? Oh my God, it's everywhere!"

"I know, ha? It's awesome!" Exclaimed Victoria.

"Let's meet! I want to see you, Vicky!" Said Caroline with her voice breaking off.

"Sure. I'm downstairs, Caroline! Hurry up!" Victoria hangs the phone and puts it in her purse. She was almost there by Caroline's apartment, still driving the car because of the bad traffic. Victoria was so busy with her working schedule that she almost forgot about spending time with Caroline properly. She felt guilty about that and was thinking of buying some nice Christmas presents for her darling friend.

Silver Cadillac SRX was following Victoria all the way from her house. She didn't notice a tail behind her because she didn't pay much attention, thinking only about Caroline. Victoria parked on the street and hurried to the building entrance. Cadillac stopped not far from her. Men's hands in brown leather gloves were squeezing the car's steering wheel and turning the music on. He sighed and took a cup of coffee next to him in the cup holder. He brought it closer to his lips and made a sip, than put it back. He glanced to the left and saw Victoria, together with a fair-haired girl, coming outside and opening a blue Bentley. A light smile appeared in the corner of his lip. He grabbed his phone and took a picture of them several times, then he glanced at the building and took a photo of its address. He glanced at the phone to make sure that he did everything right. The scout started the engine and drove his car back to the street from which he followed Victoria.

The noise at the Lex building sounded like a buzz, people hanging on the phone, rushing from one department to another taking signatures and talking to each other. "It's the end of the month. We must hurry," somebody yelled from the corner of the office. "Give me the report now, and John will cut my salary off if you don't do it now," - a man with a nervous voice talked on the phone from his working desk.

With a foxy smile, Martin walks along the corridor and hears different demands from co-workers. He is holding his briefcase and shakes hands greeting employers from his floor department. His eyes are looking for his friend Henry Douglas, the curly head was moving from one white screen to another. Martin came closer and put a hand on his shoulder;

"Henry, can I have you on one minute, please?"

"Hold on," answered Henry. When he finished, he turned to Martin and said: "What's up, man?"

"I need you to find a special agent for me," looking around, said Martin and raised on his tiptoes.

"Agent?" Narrowed his eyes, Henry. "What for, Martin?"

"Mm...m, you know, to find information about one person, it's pretty confidential."

In his relaxed walking manner, Jason is walking to Martin and Henry, taking off brown leather gloves. His face expressed confidence and a mysterious smile at the same time. Martin noticed his friend's shiny eyes and rapidly said to Henry:

"Wait, I'll be back."

Jason stopped by Henry's desk and looked at Martin while that one was coming closer to him.

"Hey, what's up?"

Jason handled his phone to Martin and looked into his face directly:

"Have a look and tell me what you think."

Martin swiped the screen and his eyes were glued to the picture of his sister together with a fair-haired girl. He recognized Caroline, that girl which he saw yesterday and had a conversation with. He didn't show Jason his acquaintance with her; instead, he expressed a surprised look;

"Is this a person that Reina mentioned at the party?"

"Ehm" he nodded. "She is!"

Martin smiled on a side and said:

"Good job, man!"

Jason grabbed Martin on his elbow and turned on a side so only he could hear:

"This morning, I followed Victoria and now I know where Raymond's fiancé lives."

Martin glanced at Jason with a serious, concerned look:

"Fiancé? She has nothing to do with him!"

"Yes, she does. A statue in his yard, do you remember? He was mad when he lost her. Reina was telling me about her. This girl attacked me in the desert," pointing his finger at a picture, said Jason. "Well, I have to admit that she saved me too."

Martin shook his head:

"What's your point?"

"She might be his spy." Jason proposed the idea to Martin, biting his lower lip.

Martin looked into Jason's eyes and made his statement:

"I'll take this picture, I have her full name, and I want to find out about her, everything since her childhood till the present day, and get a spy for her."

Jason was rubbing his chin:

"Do you want to say that she's dangerous?"

"We don't know." Martin smacked his lips. "But I want to find out."

Walking wide, Martin returned to his friend Henry and asked him to send him the agent to the office. Jason put his gloves back and turned to the exit.

In half an hour, a knock on Martin's door disturbed him from work. He looked at the entrance and said loudly: "Yes?"

The door opened, and a pretty brown hair woman dressed in black appeared in front of Martin's eyes. His lips opened, and he got annoyed a little bit: "What?"

She slowly walked in and closed the door behind her. Her grey eyes were fixed on him:

"Were you looking for me, sir?"

Martin rose up from his chair and put his hands in the pocket. He walked out from his working table and slightly laid on it:

"Who sent you?"

"Henry Douglas," she said.

"Hm," he nodded, observing her from head to toe. Black tiny suit fitted her perfectly, grey eyes Martin never liked. He touched the tip of his nose and said: "So, you are an agent?"

"Sir," she moved her head.

"Ok, what's your name?" Martin raised his head proudly.

"Melanie Stewart, sir." She slightly smiled at him when she admitted his good-looking features. The woman perfectly knew a lot about Martin Fury, but she had never seen him before until this present time.

"Ok, Melanie," he nodded to her; "I need you to get me the information about Caroline Sauvage Roux, here is her photo."

Martin handled the paper to the agent and swallowed; "Find as much as possible."

Melanie Stewart looked at the photo and pursed her lips. She glanced back at Martin, and he felt goosebumps from her cold look;

"By the end of the day, is ok?"

He nodded positively in response, and when she left, he sighed hard. Martin didn't like her at all. First of all, she had this energy that made him uncomfortable. Secondly, Martin didn't like the way she observed him, it was too unprofessional. He took his blazer off, having a weird feeling as if he was raped.

He came back to his working place and started typing his unfinished document.

Meanwhile, Victoria and Caroline are having breakfast together. Both girls were dressed this morning in warm cashmere. The intrigue and silence were hanging between them so much that Victoria couldn't handle it anymore and was the first to break the silence:

"What have you been doing these days?"

Caroline, chewing her omelet, glanced at Victoria furtively, thinking to tell her the truth or a sweet lie:

"Nothing much. Just was busy with my Internet."

"Caroline," called her Victoria, "Christmas is in a day. What would you like to receive from Santa?"

Caroline's fork in her hand didn't move, she looked at her girlfriend sitting opposite and didn't know what to say, she was really surprised by this nice gesture:

"Oh," she sighed, "Maybe a good fun on ice!" Caroline smiled at Victoria, and her eyes were shiny like a fresh morning forest. She almost forgot when she had good times wearing ice skates.

In winter, the sun goes down fast, and at five, it's already dark outside. This is a perfect time for rest and a cup of tea. Lex's company clock on the wall showed four-thirty. Some employers finished their all-day report and were preparing to leave home. Martin planned to stay at his office till six. A knock at the door disturbed him from work, and he said out loud:

"Come in!"

"Sir," appeared his agent.

"Ah, Melanie! Do you have any good news?"

The woman entered his office room holding one thick folder with papers. She came closer to his table and placed it right in front of him. Her face expressed satisfaction when Martin glanced at her with a corner of his eye.

"I found the information about Caroline Sauvage Roux like you requested, sir."

"All right," he said with a pleasant smile. He took the folder and opened it. On the first page he saw her picture in the right corner and the story of her life: birth date, college experience, even the document from her personal doctor and school marks.

"That's it, isn't it?" She asked him with a cold facial expression.

"What do you think about her, Melanie?" Martin lay on his armchair back and looked into the woman's open face.

"I think she's just an ordinary girl, nothing impressive!" Melanie shook her head and sighed.

"Ok," nodded Martin, "that's it for today. Yeah, goodbye!"

"Bye! Have a good day!" She opened the door and left.

Martin glanced at the paperback and read once more. He noticed that despite her beauty, she had excellent grades at school, and she was athletic. Caroline has almost never been sick with anything, and her physical condition was good. Then he smiled when he read that she had terrible behavior at primary and elementary school. Then Martin turned a page and read a questionnaire about her likes. He sighed. She likes 'Martin Eden' by Jack London and her favorite colors are red and yellow. He shook his head and smiled to himself. 'She likes what I like.' He closed the folder and placed it in his table's drawer under the key. Martin pulled out a phone and texted a message to his sister 'Tonight I have to talk to you. It's important! PS: Don't forget a good bottle of wine. Victoria pursed her lips together after this message and scratched her head, trying to figure out her brother's emergency. She glanced at Caroline and slightly smiled at her:

"We need to go to the store…"

"What for?" Caroline widened her eyes.

"Hm," I have to buy some presents for my relatives on Christmas Day.

"Oh," sighed Caroline and took off her skates.

Victoria with her girlfriend spent their time at the skating club. Both of them were pretty good at this kind of fun. At least it raises your mood and gives you good memories. They took pictures together on Caroline's phone and ate at the cafeteria downstairs.

"So, tomorrow is a pre-holiday day. Do you have any plans?" Smiling, Caroline glanced at her friend.

"I don't have to go to work, so we can go to Westwood." Proposed the idea, Victoria.

Caroline narrowed her eyes and looked away, she wasn't sure that wants to go there again. What if Martin Fury would be there? She doesn't want to see him again, never in her life. Her face changed from a smile into madness.

"What is it?" Looked at Victoria, and her worried look disturbed Caroline.

"Nothing," the girl shook her head, "I just don't want to go to Westwood tomorrow."

"Why? I thought you missed Flash..." Victoria looked into Caroline's face, trying to read anything from her features.

"No... It's too cold for riding a horse," found an excuse Caroline and nervously smiled back at Victoria.

"Ok, if not Westwood, then what do you want to visit?" Victoria changed her skates into regular high shoes and zipped them on her ankle.

Caroline bit her lower lip and relaxed a little, looking around at the skating couples who were holding hands. She lowered her head and looked at her manicured hands. No anger or madness in her voice. It sounded softly:

"How about bowling?"

"Bowling? But guys usually play this game." Victoria was surprised by this idea.

"Not at all. Girls also can show their strengths and be even better than guys." Caroline smiled at it, and Victoria noticed her warmness. Sometimes, Caroline is happy, and sometimes, she's absolutely hopeless about making life brighter.

"All right," answered back Victoria, "you won."

"What?" Caroline smiled; "It wasn't an argument at all!"

Her look became softer and tender. She put her coat back and wrapped her neck with a scarf.

"You know red looks good on you." Winked Victoria.

"This is one of my favorite colors," Caroline winked her back. "Ok, let's go to the store!"

The girls left the club, and as soon as they came out on the street, they sighed with relief. The snow, together with a strong wind blow, circled around the passerby. It is a real winter! Victoria rushed to the car, and they got inside fast. The car was already warm with a blowing heater and music on. Technology! Just push a button on your key and get in. Everything is ready for you. Victoria put a seat belt on and started her car; they slowly moved onto a street and went on a line. The traffic was awful!

"I have a feeling we'll arrive at the store tomorrow." Squeezed her steering wheel, Victoria.

Several emergency cars and police rushed by them.

"Probably it might be an accident," she left her comment to Victoria. "Idiots like to slow down and rubberneck as if they can help."

"That's because they don't watch TV."

"And what is on TV?" Victoria didn't catch Caroline's idea.

"Violence!"

"That's true." Nodded Victoria.

They parked at the nearest grocery store and took a cart. Surprisingly to Caroline, her friend didn't buy too much but she noticed Victoria grabbed two bottles of wine. The price was impressive, too. Caroline raised her eyebrows but didn't say a word. She didn't expect Victoria to drink that much, probably, it happened after her French boyfriend left. Victoria was in a rush and didn't talk too much. She organized her time carefully. First, she spent her morning with Caroline at the ice skating, and now she's rushing home with wine. 'Poor Victoria,' thought Caroline, 'Love makes people crazy. It is better never to fall in love.'

In the Fury's mansion was nobody except Martin. Victoria's older brother was busy with his briefcase and folders from work. He was sitting at his father's library and doing paperwork. John and Adeline Fury left to go to the opera with their friends; Brian is practicing tennis with Chris Wren. His sister appeared at the door entrance with a handbag. She was standing quietly and simply watching her brother. Sometimes, he reminded her father, John, but sometimes he is so like mother: gentle, accurate, and aristocratic. Victoria softly made a noise. Martin looked up and noticed her standing in the half-dark corner.

"Vicky, come in! I'm glad you are here."

"What's wrong, brother?" She came up closer and put a bottle of wine on the table in front of Martin's eyes.

"Oh," he smiled, "take two glasses and pour some."

Victoria opened a cupboard and took out two tall crystal glasses. She poured red wine into each of them and, holding them, came to Martin and gave it to him:

"So, what's the story?" She asked, trying to guess her brother's mood. At such moments, he is really unpredictable, like John.

"Well," he started, "I brought you some documents to read from work, and I want you to have a look at them now."

"That sounds interesting!" She crossed her legs, sitting in the armchair.

Martin brought a glass of wine closer to his lips and made a sip. He was watching his sister when she carefully opened his folder, and her eyes widened. He noticed surprise mixed with fear in her eyes.

"So, what do you think about Caroline Sauvage Roux?" His eyes were shown, and he slightly smiled to the side.

"You... Where did you get this?" Victoria barely pronounced the question. She got nervous and her hands start shaken from fear for her little secret.

"Well, sister, I don't know what game you play, but Caroline Sauvage Roux is our dad's enemy. If he discovers your friendship with her, you're done." Martin rose from his chair and walked closer to the window with his hands in his pocket.

Victoria made another sip of wine, trying to prevent her rising fear. She realized that Martin knew everything and probably John's murder, too.

"How did you find out?"

"It was easy. Her name was on a dashboard in Westwood," and he turned to her, and their eyes met.

"Shit!" She slammed the table's surface with her hand.

"So, what is it, Victoria? Tell me about you and her? What unites you with Caroline?" Martin returned to the table, took a chair, and slowly rolled it closer to his sister. He sat on it and looked into Victoria's eyes, piercing like Excalibur sward.

She was breathing hard and tried to figure out how to start. Victoria didn't see any other decision but to tell him the truth and find out the truth about her dad's hate:

"I met her in Morocco; we fired from the ship and finished Bloody Desert Killers, and I saved her by picking her up and her horse on board. We crossed the ocean and arrived in New York, where her documents were ready for border control..." - Victoria paused and hardly swallowed, keeping her head lowered.

"Go on." Martin rubbed his chin and paid attention to every word she said.

"Caroline told me that she is an orphan and is looking for the Fury family. She needs to see John Fury, who killed all of her family; she wants to take revenge. This girl made me promise her to provide help, and I didn't deny it."

With his hands placed on a chest, Martin nodded to his sister and shook his head:

"So, you want to help her to kill our dad, right?"

"No, I just want her to get a good degree, like compensation for her missing parents." Tears rolled down Victoria's face, and she covered her mouth with her palm. "I feel sorry for her and want to help her, that's it."

"Victoria," Martin moved to her closer, "John hated her dad because in the past he put him into jail and stole his love; after that, John was looking for a Sauvage Roux man for twenty-three years when he finally found him our dad destroyed Mr. Sauvage Roux. This is not our war, but we have to be careful," Martin touched Victoria's hand and placed it in his palms. "Caroline is a child but a growing woman too. If she wants to find and kill our dad, we have to prevent this with all of our strength."

Victoria widened her eyes and moved her head, trying to gather all of his said words, and said:

"Is it true? Did Dad kill that family?"

Martin lowered his eyes and slowly nodded to her. It is hard to believe in it, but hiding and covering the reality is impossible. He understood that every secret finally comes out, it's impossible to hide anything.

"I'm really sorry for what happened to her, but we are Fury and must be ready for any attack. I advise you to end up with her." Martin pursed his lips, got up from his seat, and turned to a window, slowly walking with a glass of wine in his hand.

Victoria shook her head and wiped her tears off from the reddened face. She can't do this, she can't leave Caroline alone in America, and she gave her a promise.

"You're asking me the impossible, Martin." A cold voice broke the silence between them. "I gave her a promise to take care of her and help. I feel guilty, brother, and I want her to give that life that John took from her."

The heavy curtains were making the room dark; the tall and wide window through which Martin was looking made him really tall. She noticed him quiet and serious, as if he was thinking about it and trying to make the right decisions. Martin tried to put himself in Victoria's position which was absolutely not easy.

"Victoria," he finally said, "I have seen Caroline before."

These words crushed her. How many secrets he has for her? What else?

"No, that's impossible. Where did you see her?" Her patience started betraying her.

Martin turned to her and smiled slightly as if he were hiding candy from her. He came closer and said into her eyes:

"In Raymond's garden, I saw a statue of her. She's his bride."

Victoria's face got pale. She felt absolutely broken. Caroline lied to her about that ring in the club when they met Reina. In the car, she denied that she was engaged, and then Reina at their party said that Raymond was engaged. And now Martin tells a story about her statue.

"Wait, Martin!" Victoria raised her hand, trying to stop his story. "Don't tell me this! She will tell me everything when I make her to tell." Victoria's eyes were glowing from anger and offense.

She believed in a lie. Caroline wasn't honest with her from the beginning.

"No," said Martin, and his jaw muscles didn't move; "You won't do this! Leave her to me…"

Victoria looked at him with a flashy look and nervously moved a corner of her lip:

"How?"

Martin came closer to her and looked into her eyes so close that their noses almost touched. He could hypnotize, "Trust me."

# CHAPTER 20

*Men leave quickly but often return. Women think long before they leave, but if so, it's forever.*

The only thing that Raymond Moulay Ali couldn't figure out was Caroline's unique talent. He was holding her in his hands, and like sand, she went through his fingers. Disorganized and too wild creatures made everyone forget about their main abilities. His mistake was his heart's weakness. He allowed her to do whatever she wanted, she spent his money on silly things, and he never said a word to her. The woman that he loved most of all in his life was gone. Raymond put his hands together and then spread them. Feeling broken and helpless, he was ready to cry on the whole world so everyone could hear his pain. Philippe is standing by him and, like Raymond thinks he understands his feelings. He sees Philippe, his friend, and an ally. Caroline's brother is an absolutely trustworthy man; you can tell him all your pain and thoughts, and he will carry them to the grave. Maybe that was the reason Caroline loved Philippe that much. This holiday night, Ali's family stayed long, as if they were waiting for Santa through the fireplace.

"I like you, Philippe," finally said Raymond, slightly smiling at the guy. "Come with us to Morocco."

The unexpected invitation surprised Philippe, but he was too busy and had plans already after New Year's Eve.

"Thank you, Hakim! I'm afraid can't join you on your trip back home to Rabat." Politely refused his invitation, Philippe.

"Why?" Raymond got confused; "What are you going to do here with old Mohammed?"

"My girlfriend is waiting for me in the States," slightly smiled Philippe, and his chocolate eyes were shown as two bright stars in the night sky.

"Girlfriend?" Raymond was surprised.

Mohammed looked at Hakim and, smoking his shish, said, "I know, boy, it's hard to understand, but West has strange habits; they date a woman before they get married."

Raymond's eyes got round from unhearing strangeness, "What nonsense! No engagement and meeting with parents?"

Mohammed glanced at Philippe smiling and explained to Hakim clearly, "Son, they have an engagement, but before they date, if they like a girl, they decide to engage and marry her so they could build a family."

Raymond shook his head and looked back at Philippe, "I've never dated your sister!"

"Did you?" Philippe smiled and touched his nose.

"When I saw her for the first time, I knew she was going to be mine. My father agreed to arrange a wedding day."

Philippe didn't say anything in response; he shifted his eyes away from Mohammed, who was busy with his meatballs. In a relaxed atmosphere, Mohammed and Philippe shared their celebrating food with guests. Jain seemed to be very silent as never. Like a seer, she didn't even say a word. Her hazel eyes were slowly moving from one speaker to another talker. She never interfered in their conversation until she was asked. Philippe feels a little bit sorry for her. He clearly understood the rules for women in the Far East. 'Thank God Caroline ran away from those beasts!' Philippe shook his head and lowered his eyes onto his plate full of rice and a piece of chicken.

Snowflakes beautifully made a picture on Caroline's apartment windows. The night came closer, and Victoria didn't show up. She promised to go with her to the bowling club but it never happened, no message or email from her either. Caroline looked around and got sad. Christmas night she's going to spend by herself. She combed her hair very well and put it on top of her head, fixing it with a clip. Caroline took off her clothes and stepped into the hot water bath.

Relaxing and enjoying her time, she frequently remembered her wonderful bathing at Raymond's palace. How wonderful it was when they put oil on your body and massage it all that time while you're relaxing. Caroline moved into her bath and polished it well with a body scrub after she rinsed her legs and chest with a cool water shower. Caroline finished that pleasant procedure and put a little fragrance on with a smell of citrus. She glanced at the mirror and noticed an unusual charm on her face. Lightly walking, she moved to her bedroom and put on a light green chiffon nightgown.

Her neck was wide open, and a nice white low crusher decorated her collar that smoothly came into the forearms. She put on her matching color light gown and wore the silky green slippers on the little platform that was decorated with swans down. Caroline walked in a relaxed way to her dining room and placed on her table several courses that she cooked for the Christmas party expecting Victoria to come. She carefully lit two tall candles and glanced at her fir tree decorated with different glass toy balls and nice lights around. Caroline sat at the table center and crossed her fingers in a praying manner. She lowered her head and finished the prayer.

All of a sudden the doorbell rang and Caroline jumped from being happy that Victoria finally appeared and didn't forget about her. She rushed to the door with a wide smile and opened it. Her smile slowly went down.

The most unexpected thing to her happened right now.

"Merry Christmas!" Martin Fury was standing with a single red fresh rose in his hand holding it between them. He handled it to her and walked in to her place like to his house.

Caroline had a feeling that somebody had hit her with a hammer; she couldn't move, staring at just received rose. Her eyes blinked, and she was confused by this gesture. Nobody ever presented her with a rose; she touched its red petals and brought it closer to her nose. Martin looked around, and his eyes stopped on her: so graceful and vulnerable. He noticed her night charm and came closer; she was standing with her back to him.

Martin sighed and said, "So, is this your cave where you hide?"

To Caroline, it sounded like irony and laughter in his voice. She turned to him, and their eyes met.

"What do you want?" Caroline didn't express anger or fury. Her eyes didn't shift from his face. She controlled his every move.

No doubt he's attractive and magnetic; the way he moved reminded a hunting lynx. Care and gentleness were his main assets. He came closer to her so she could feel his breath on her skin; Martin lowered his eyes and noticed her excited nipples through the chiffon gown. He swallowed in a desire to kiss her as hard as he could. She seemed to notice his feelings and stepped back, now Caroline was nervous. But he moved away to the table and took a seat opposite of her chair. She crossed her eyebrows on the bridge and ran to him, "What are you doing? Nobody invited you to my Christmas table…"

He smiled back at her in response, and her aggressiveness went down, "I can't allow this beautiful angel to be alone on such a big holiday." He nodded to her with a head to take a seat at the table.

Caroline's eyes widened, and her lower lip opened in a speechless shock. She stepped to her place and carefully sat on her chair opposite her unwelcomed guest. She gracefully took a fork and started her salad, keeping an eye on Martin.

"Hmm… So delicious!" He sighed. "Did you cook this?"

Caroline moved her head, "No. The food is from the restaurant," she lied to him looking into his eyes. She noticed every time when their eyes meet she has a strange feeling in her stomach, as if it tickles. Caroline was afraid that he could notice this unusual thing in her.

His lips stretched in a smile, "Liar… You cooked it. None of Chicago's restaurants can cook something like this."

She swallowed hard and lowered her eyes; 'Dang! How did he find out? Probably, there's nothing that I can hide from Fuego. He always looks at me with his shiny dark brown eyes so that he knows every detail about me.' Caroline finished her salad and some fresh mesh potato together with juicy chicken. She took a napkin and slightly cleaned her lips; she glanced at him and met his eyes again.

Their gaze on each other locked. Martin finished his meal before her and was just observing her. She felt uncomfortable and slightly moved in her chair.

"What?" She asked him impatiently with a nervous voice.

He smacked his lips and offered her, "Dance with me."

Caroline slightly opened her lips in a desire to accept his offer but decided to lie instead, "I...am, I don't dance," her voice is shaken so obvious to both of them. "And we have no music, so we won't dance."

Martin's lip corner moved in a slight smile, and eyes glimmed. She is predictable from head to toe, "Liar... Very bad girl!" He shook his head.

Caroline didn't know what to say about this, Americans are strange – you never know when they're serious. At first, she thought it was offensive but lately realized that it sounded like a compliment to her. Martin was adamant. He put slow music on his phone, slowly rose from his chair, and came closer to Caroline, staring into her eyes. He gave her a hand and nodded, "Come with me. Give me a dance, please." In a slow motion, Martin moved his lips on which she was staring and couldn't resist.

Her hand lay in his palm, and he helped her to get up. They came to the center of the living room and he was the first who started to lead. Caroline shifted her eyes from his face onto their hands and noticed how graceful they looked together. In a slow twist with him, she felt his sent and hot breath. His palm was burning her hand; she looked into his pink lips and felt a great desire to taste them. Martin is moving slowly, holding her tiny waist with his right hand while in his left hand. His lips touched her golden hair, and he closed his eyes. The pleasant citrus scent was his favorite. She is so soft and slender. He moved her down, holding hard with one hand, and their eyes met, her widened green eyes glowing from unexpected motion. And her breasts went up and down from being nervous. He noticed her shiny skin from being perspired and slowly moving her up. His eyes stopped on her half-opened lips. She closed her eyes without protesting her wish. Martin gently pressed his lips against hers, closing his eyes, too. Caroline felt a sweet taste and moved her lips in response to his. It was so gentle and tender, an accurate touch as if a bumble bee spreads the flower's petals. No passion or harshness, warmth, and sweetness. And then her knees got weak and she saw a hundred stars and fireworks above, and an amazing feeling caught her and whirled. Inside, something twinkled and made her tremble. Caroline gently touched his golden cheek with the fingertips and opened her eyes. He let his hands down, watching her. She didn't say a word either, but something united them at this very moment. Silence hung between them so that both couldn't handle it anymore.

"It was just a dance." Martin broke that intimacy right away.

"Yes," she nodded in response, staring at him still. The first man in her life who presented her with a flower and gave her first dance and a first kiss with such feeling that she had never known before. Her heart didn't want to say what her mind demanded, "You have to leave."

Martin came closer to her, and she didn't move. Keeping an eye on him, he took her hand gently and moved it closer to his face, opened and kissed her palm, "Caroline," he pronounced her name so sweet that she closed her eyes and then opened and looked into his eyes. "There's no future for you here. You have to go."

His words hurt her, but she didn't show him her pain. Instead, she proudly raised her head and let him finish his speech.

"I know you are stubborn, and you would never do what people tell you to do. This is just my advice, to use it or waste it, it's up to you. Go and get a degree and build a new life far from here. Live and let others live." He placed a piece of paper in her palm and squeezed it with her hand.

She opened her mouth, trying to say, but faced his index finger in front of her nose and gently landed on top of her lips.

"Think nine times before to do some stupidity and only once act!"

Martin grabbed his jacket on her couch and, without looking into her face, went through the door and closed it. She was standing in the middle of the room with her hands down. Inside were too many feelings ripping her off: confusion, disappointment, frustration, joy and... It is hard to describe. She moved, trying to realize what had just happened, and opened her palm. Caroline unfolded a piece of paper and froze when saw a number on his check – six hundred thousand dollars.

Victoria stayed in her bed up till the afternoon. Christmas and her birthday party went pretty cool, all of her friends and relatives had a good surprise for her, and presented many presents so her whole bedroom was full of flowers. After drinking too much, she sat in her bed for half an hour because she couldn't hear. Her mouth was dry, too, but it absolutely didn't bother her. She rose from her bed and rushed to the shower.

In the living room, Adeline is drinking tea with her sons. Brian didn't drink that much last night, that's why he looked better than Martin. Adeline glanced at her older son and smiled, "Martin, are you okay?"

He nodded in response and looked at Brian. That one just frowned in response, "Last night, Martin drank two bottles of martini and didn't even leave me a single olive."

Adeline shook her head and said, "Oh, Martin! You're hopeless!"

Martin's pain was undescriptive. Last night, he realized that, for the first time in his life got trapped. Until now, he went through beautiful women, and none of them bothered him that much like a French angel. Her green eyes were always in front of his. The smell of her hair didn't let him sleep. He let her go with his own hands. But this entire nothing compared to the thought she is the enemy. Even the martini didn't work. He looked at his mother and asked, "Mom, if something really bothers you, what do you usually do?"

"Martin, if it happens, I let it go, and with time wounds don't hurt anymore. Switch your interest onto something valuable."

Brian tried to understand Martin's hint, but he wasn't open to anybody.

"Ok, mom. Valuable things, like what?" Martin insisted.

"My dear," she sighed, "you have a great imagination like no one in this family; I know you'll figure out something."

"Hm..m," he moved his knees and looked at the ceiling.

Brian finished reading his fifth book about technological construction and put it away. He rubbed his chin and proudly said, "Well, I'm almost ready for my final exam at the University."

Adeline glanced at him and slightly smiled, "Oh, that sounds great to me. Dad would be very glad for you, too."

Clicking with her high-hill winter shoes, Victoria appeared in the living room, "Good morning, everybody!" She smiled and moved a little on the side.

Brian pursed his lips together and smiled, too, "It's already afternoon, Vicky! The party was good, hah?"

"Ha?" She answered back. Her face got red from embarrassment, and she couldn't hear the words that well. "I'm in a hurry. I'll see you later!"

Victoria rushed through the massive doors to her Maserati and placed there comfortably. She needs to see Caroline as soon as possible and explain everything if she can. The promised bowling club, the holiday evening all of these simple things went out of her mind yesterday when friends organized her day and evening party. She glanced several times in the car mirror, practicing her sorrowful look and none of them worked. Victoria sighed hard and pulled out a gum from her purse and placed it in her mouth. She turned the heater higher and relaxed, holding her car wheel. As usual she parked in the indoor garage in Caroline's apartment building and went to the elevator.

Chewing gum, she came out from the elevator and knocked on Caroline's door, but nobody answered. Then she smacked and rang the doorbell, waiting for a response, but nothing happened. Victoria got nervous, so she went downstairs, showed her identification card, and got the keys to the apartment. She returned back and unlocked the door. Everything was super clean around; even Caroline's Christmas tree was gone. Victoria walked rapidly to her bedroom, but the girl was not there; she opened her closet, and her eyes widened; the hangers were empty, and shoes were gone together with purses. Victoria sat on the bed and tried to realize what had happened. Caroline left; she didn't even leave her a notice on the kitchen table. But how it happened, she doesn't have enough money? Victoria swallowed hard and pulled out her cell phone. With her shaking hands, she dialed Jerry Smith's number.

"Hello!" He answered.

"Jerry," Said Victoria.

"Miss Fury, how can I help you?"

"Did you see Miss Caroline recently?"

"Well, I've got a notice from her this early morning," said Jerry with a confident voice.

"What did she say?" Victoria was almost crying.

"I haven't seen her, but we sent her horse out like requested to France."

Victoria's eyes widened, and tears rolled down one after another. She hangs up the cell phone and swallows hard in a feeling that everyone always leaves her broken, that's unfair! 'How? How the hell did it happen?' She screamed out loud. Caroline doesn't know how to drive; she can't go so far because Victoria didn't provide her financially enough. Victoria rushed downstairs and checked what time her girlfriend left.

"Miss, she left at five in the morning," said a lady at the reception; "She gave us a key and put a signature for checking out and left."

Victoria nodded to her in response and walked away to the garage. She opened her car and sat there with disappointment; 'French are so rude, so ungrateful,' Victoria thought. 'You treat them, and they spit on you.' She drove back home.

Winter days got colder in Chicago; the temperature went to twenty-five. All the roads were covered with snow, and people tried to stay home while kids had fun outside playing with snowballs and making snowmen. Westwood was empty all day; Jerry even turned the heater on for the horses at their stables. Martin sighed hard and placed on his couch in his bedroom holding a cell phone. He dialed Jerry's number and was waiting for an answer.

"Yeah?" Replied Jerry Smith.

"This's Martin Fury," said Martin, lowering his voice. "How's Ivanhoe? Did you call for a vet like I asked you?"

"Sure, sir. He has just a cold, but like the doctor said he's going to be fine if she continues to give him a proper treatment."

"Yeah, sounds good to me. Well, anything else?" Asked Martin sadly.

"Yeah, This morning Flash left our stables, Ms. Sauvage Roux requested his transporting." The young fellow twisted rapidly.

Martin smiled to himself and turned off the phone. 'So, she accepted my advice and left. Good for her' – he thought and took the photo of her profile on the document that Melanie brought to him the other day. He glanced at it and slightly smiled, expressing satisfaction and joy from the work that he had done. 'At least she is going to have a good life,' - murmured Martin, 'She won't be killed by John.' He shifted his eyes on the door to his room when, without a knock, Victoria opened it fast and saw him. Her face was pale, and her eyes were red, probably after tears.

"Martin," she said with a weak voice, "She left."

"Who?" He played a fool.

"My girlfriend, you know." Victoria entered his room and closed the door behind her.

"Really?" Martin raised his eyebrows and moved in his armchair.

Victoria walked deeper and took a seat on his other armchair, which was located next to his bed. She lowered her head, and at this moment, she looked absolutely broken and helpless:

"I don't know how did it happen," she started her explanation, "First of all, she doesn't have enough money to go somewhere. I don't even say about moving her horse to France."

Martin listened to her with great attention; Victoria was talking and talking, moving her hands around. Her tears rolled down her face, and her hands were shaken, too.

"Sister, you have to let it go," Martin finally interrupted her, "please, I know it's hard for you, but you have to. Keep yourself in your hands."

"She is my best one." She looked at Martin, his sister, and shook her head, "You don't know her. I spent time with Caroline.

"Tsh…" Martin put an index finger closer to his lips, "Don't speak loud."

Victoria lowered her voice almost to a whisper, "Everyone just likes to leave me without any explanation."

Right now, Victoria reminded him of a little sister from their childhood. She always was like that when her favorite toy disappeared or got broken. He remembered himself as a calm boy, and everything didn't matter that much. Father would get him a better thing. When Martin turned eighteen, John Fury stopped treating him like a child. He immediately changed his attitude and sent Martin to Academy, which Martin no longer is going to finish.

"Listen," said Martin to his sister, "relax and find another object of your admiration."

Her chocolate brown eyes looked at him with confusion and surprise, "What?"

"Mom says if you let it go and with time, wounds don't hurt anymore. Switch your interest onto something valuable."

"Is this what she said?" Victoria pursed her lips.

"Yes," nodded Martin.

Victoria took off from his armchair and, with speed, flew through his door, leaving it open. Martin glanced at the flower in the pot above on the wall and thought, 'At least this one survived.

Nothing can be so sweeter than freedom. Everything doesn't matter after slavery: rules, manners, and laws. One step is behind, up ahead is only the future. Right now, just present, and nothing can be sweeter than a day spent the way you want. Cities and states are passing one by one in front of Caroline's eyes. She traveled to the west and to the south, and finally, she finished the east. From the International Airport in Orlando, Florida, Caroline purchased her plane ticket to Paris. Her new year is going to start in Paris; she missed her Motherland, its food, and her way of life. Caroline sighed looking at her plane boarding pass that she was holding in her hands. This Christmas changed everything in her life. She looked outside through the wide airport window and slightly smiled to herself. That catastrophe in her life a year ago left her behind. Raymond Ali and Moroccan adventures in the past, Victoria and her prisoner in the apartment is a week ago, a time that doesn't make sense to her anymore. Martin. Caroline sighed again, and this time heavily and deeply. Thanks to his nice Christmas present, she was far from Fury.

On the radio announced her plane's number to a boarding pass. She picked up her handbag and placed it on her shoulder. In a line to a plane, she showed her document to the officers and walked inside. Caroline found her place on the plane and was glad that it was near the illuminator. She took a seat and followed the directions of the students. Caroline pulled out the book from her handbag and opened it. The first line said, 'Everything starts from your thoughts." She touched her lips with a finger and smoothly rubbed them.

Then she turned a page and read: "There is no such thing as a hopeless situation. Every single circumstance of your life can change! " Caroline sighed freely and moved her head, turning another page. "A lot of people feel like they're victims in life, and they'll often point to past events, perhaps growing up with an abusive parent or in a dysfunctional family. Most psychologists believe that about 85 percent of families are dysfunctional, so all of a sudden, you're not so unique. My parents were alcoholics. My dad abused me. My mother divorced him when I was six...I mean, that's almost everybody's story in some form or not. The real question is, what are you going to do now? What do you choose now?

Because you can either keep focusing on that or you can focus on what you want. And when people start focusing on what they want, what they don't want falls away, and what they want expands, and the other part disappears. (Jack Canfield)" Caroline pursed her lips together, closed the book, and looked at the cover to see what she had just bought: "The Secret" by Rhonda Byrne. Caroline frowned and didn't even notice her plane in the air. The book she is reading is really exciting; there were a lot of things that Caroline discovered herself, too much wisdom. It sounded differently, not like Raymond and his teachers used to teach her. That entire she realized later she was too silly and young. Fuego was right, and she would never be equal to John's Fury if she stayed and found him and tried to kill him. This would never happen until she had a lack of knowledge and theory. On board they served some food and all the time offered drinks.

After a good meal, Caroline fell asleep, and when she woke up they announced thirty minutes left to reach Paris. Nine hours in the plane flew to Caroline fast when she had been busy with a book and then with lunch. She looked through the round little window in the plane and noticed sunny weather. On the screen in front of her, they showed the current weather forecast. 'It is colder than in Chicago' – she thought. Caroline turned to pick up her bag and pulled out winter gloves and scarf, she prepared her winter coat, too. The passenger plane is landing, and everyone tries to stay calm, waiting for the ground. For the first time, Caroline discovered that she loved to be on the board, especially when they took off. This pleasant feeling is always tickling in her belly and makes her giggle. They landed hard, and she felt the rolling tires under her feet. She glanced outside, and the unexplained feeling of being made her cry a little bit. She tried to prevent her tears and couldn't. They slowly rolled down on her face, and she didn't even notice like somebody asked her if she was all right. Caroline pleasantly nodded and went on a line to get out of the airplane.

In the large hall inside the airport, she found her luggage and picked it up. Caroline wiped off her happy tears and finally heard the mother language. She walked outside and got a yellow cab immediately.

Sunshine, great food, pastis and pétanque… These are a few of the charms of France's second-biggest city, warm-hearted and lively Marseille. Even cold winter days and wind blowing can't stop you from visiting the fish market at the Old Port and then heading across the street for an exquisite bouillabaisse (fish soup) in one of the many wonderful restaurants facing the port. Later, stroll along the Cannebière for some shopping and people-watching. In the evenings, let yourself be tempted by a night out at the 18th-century opera house, or for the ultimate Marseille experience, check out the Marseille Olympics and do their magnificent thing at the soccer arena. No matter which activity you choose, you will be experiencing the South of France in all its glory. Hop on a cruise ship in Marseille and see more of Europe. With a wide variety of cruises, you can opt for a relaxing vacation at sea, or you can immerse yourself in local culture and history… It's a tough life!

"It's a tough life!" Raymond's eyes were shiny when he was standing together at the airport with his relatives.

"I love it!" Shook his head, Philippe "That's the life of my childhood with sisters and my parents." They say, "Never anything is going to be the same."

Raymond helped his father and Jain with their luggage, and they checked for the tickets in their hands and discussed some details about the trip. Raymond's blue eyes were on Philippe; he smacked his lips and shook the guy's hand with words:

"If you change your mind about coming to the States, know my doors are always open for you. We'll be glad to see you in Rabat. I also have many nice places to take you with me."

Philippe politely smiled at Raymond and nodded in answer, "Thank you, Ray! It was a pleasure meeting you!"

Jain covered her face from cool air, but through her scarf, Philippe noticed her soft look and friendship. If Hakim invited him to his tent, that means he's her friend too. "What strange rules and habits?" thought Philippe. From this meeting, he made One conclusion – he would never go to Morocco for any gold coins. Arabs and their strangeness were not for him.

The guest's plane took off. Mohammed left together with Philippe at the airport to wait for Philippe's plain to Chicago. They were sitting in the waiting hall and staring at each other. Mohammed rubbed his head and sadly glanced at his grandson, "Are you sure about leaving for Chicago?"

"Positive," answered back Philippe. "I have to go. I must talk to Victoria so she can help me in my search. I have a feeling that my main target is close."

Mohammed didn't answer it, and he was just sad that he had not spent enough time with his only grandson. No one knows what expects him in that foreign country especially with those people in power. Philippe was very decisive about finding his biological father. Something tells him that he's going to do it very fast, and Victoria will be the one who leaves a deep mark on his heart. He loves two women in his life: Caroline and Victoria. But both of them are so different and he has feelings to them as strong as a stone.

They announced Philippe's plane, and it was ready for departure. Mohammed hugged Philippe hard and whispered in his ear, "Good luck, son! Take care, and don't forget your grandpa!"

Philippe nodded to him, and a slight smile touched his lips while Mohammed was in his tears. The guy picked up his duffle bag and hurried to the check exit. In the plane were business people, just some travelers. Philippe quickly found his seat in the middle row and placed in it comfortably.

Mohammed walked to his green Peugeot and drove back to his ranch. He widened his eyes when he saw a couple of people who brought a horse's trailer and were walking around his property. He stopped by them and asked, "What's going on, guys? I didn't make any orders."

"Messier, this is from the US, Chicago, Illinois."

"That must be a mistake," objected Mohammed, "I didn't receive any orders from the US."

"That was paid and requested to be delivered to this address from Miss Caroline Sauvage Roux."

"Oh," Mohammed sighed and placed his hand on his forehead, "OK. Then it is the right address. "

Mohammed helped the deliverymen to take the horse out. Flash was nervous and looked around for his owner. He became more anxious when he didn't find her. Flash tried to kick, but Mohammed made him calm down. The horse grunted and danced while they were holding him under his lead rope. Mohammed looked at him from head to toe and decided to put in the stables for new arrivals. He has only two, so Flash is going to be number three. Mohammed turned the conditioning on for them and placed some hay for them to eat. The truck with a trailer left, and Mohammed finally relaxed in his house, checking some emails on the computer; one of them was from Caroline:

*"Dear grandfather,*

*I apologize for the unexpected inconvenience that you might have with my horse, but to me, it is really important. Flash Magnifico is Raymond's present to me on my birthday and I'm not planning to stay in the US anymore because there are some complications that are hard to explain, so it doesn't make sense to keep him there. I moved to France back and right now I'm in Paris applying to the University at Law. I think I to follow my father's steps. I feel that I am going to be pretty good at it, so don't worry about me. I'm going to be fine. Today my college documents arrived from Marseille College, and I'm at a medical examination tomorrow. Promise you to write as regularly as possible.*

***"Love you, Caroline."***

Mohammed closed her letter on the corner page with his computer mouse and sighed. He felt proud of her, but there was another question that bothered him: "How is she going to study without money? Nowadays, you can't do anything without a solid amount of money in the bank account."

He opened his email and wrote back asking about money. "She thinks that everything is possible to do without payment. Nonsense!" He thought and walked to the kitchen for his meal in the fridge.

# CHAPTER 21

*Things have never been the same whether you try or leave it; the*
*result is going to be different.*

A severe winter came and Chicago trudged proudly on as if
nothing has changed. On a recent Saturday morning, as the city sat
beneath a foot of fresh snow, people strolled in Millennium Park,
the city's front yard along Lake Michigan, even as three snow plows
scraped circles around them. Still, without violating the city's code
of stoicism, one can find the ideal winter day here by alternating all
that outdoor grit with a smattering of permitted hideaways. Brian
started his morning renting skates at Millennium Park
and cruised the ice to cheery tunes booming from loudspeakers.
Victoria took her professional camera with her and was standing by,
taking pictures. When Brian finished his skating, they moved to the
Northside to capture a few more photos of beautiful Chicago. It was
a nice sunny 17 degrees outside with some pretty cold winds coming

in from the lakefront. She and Brian ended up in Uptown and Montrose Harbor. Montrose Harbor is located on the northern edge of Lincoln Park, a short walk from Montrose Beach. With a great neighborhood feel, Montrose offers outstanding northern views of the skyline, a strong dinghy fleet, and friendly boaters that call the harbor home.

Easy access to parks and beaches, along with its location that straddles Lincoln Park, Lakeview, and Wrigley Ville, make it a favorite amongst families. Home to the Corinthian Yacht Club, the harbor has 711 slips, mooring cans, and star docks that can accommodate boats from 25'-50' in length. Victoria took some more picturesque photos and posted them online on her Facebook page. Her friends immediately liked and left comments. Brian took her camera out of her hands and took some selfie pictures with her hugging. Their toes grew numb, and they were led to the nearest pub, where they got some whisky and warmed up. A navy blue Bentley was ready outside for them to go. Brian and Victoria returned to their car and left for the city center. She helped her brother with a shopping at the great mall downtown. He wanted to refresh his closet at home, so Victoria picked nice trousers and shirts for Brian while he was trying some new suites from Cole Haan. His sister has the best taste in men's outfits, and nobody could deny it. Even Martin always took her out with him so she would find something outstanding. But Martin is the best at dressing women; everything is always elegant and rich. Victoria lost her honey-sweet boyfriend and it made her switch on to her brothers.

Brian and Victoria were planning to take Martin with them to go and have some fun together, but he disappeared somewhere this morning, and nobody has seen him at home.

Sun went down, and the beautiful day turned into evening. Brian arrived together with Victoria to their mansion. Inside were two men Trey Parker and John Fury. They have been discussing their new marketing and recent sales. Their conversation interrupted John's children. Victoria is laughing, holding Brian under his hand while they are walking inside.

"Victoria," looked at her Trey Parker.

She turned to him, and their eyes met.

"Oh, Mr. Parker! What a wonderful surprise!"

His eyes had a special glow when she said that, and he glanced at his friend John and then shifted his look back to her, "You look so like your father! Look at you! Same smile, same eyes, and even laugh!"

"Of course!" She smiled; "My dad is the most handsome man!"

John lowered his eyes and his cheeks got blushing, "Victoria, come on! You make me shy in front of my friend!"

She came closer to him and hugged his shoulders, left a kiss on his cheek and that gesture killed him. He got embarrassed, and white teeth appeared after his wide smile. John remembered her little to do this thing in front of his friends. He never liked to show his true feelings. Trey Parker didn't say anything about this; he knows how it is to grow a daughter.

John glanced at Trey, and his right eyebrow rose, "How is Jason doing?"

"Oh, he is all busy with wedding preparations and Helen is all over him."

"Yeah? So, when the party is coming?"

"In April, like they wanted."

John moved in his couch, letting Victoria go, and asked Trey, "I heard Jason is quitting his job at Lex."

Trey Parker pursed his lips and answered back to John, "I think so. He's going to move to Santa Monica and wants to start his marriage life there."

"Nice choice!" Nodded John. "I always liked sunny California."

"Yea, that's not a cold area like Chicago."

"So," John's voice went rougher, "We have to hire somebody on to his place, ha?"

Trey shook his shoulders and said, "I think so, but right now, I don't see a suitable applicant, maybe with some time in the future. Jason is still working, and he's really good even at being in the distance."

John Fury came closer to his little bar and poured some whiskey for his friend and himself. He gave one glass to Trey and, without shifting his eyes, said, "All right, I'll try tomorrow to see if there's someone in my department who matches. If yes, I will start a training of an employer."

"It sounds good to me," Trey smiled, being unsurprised by John's gumption.

The next day, Victoria started with a cup of coffee in her car and smelled the freshness of it with a delightful taste. 'Oh my Lord!' - She thought, 'I might be in heaven after all these crazy events in my life. Someone says that richness makes you happy. Fool! Money can't make you happy. They only help you to get things that you like. Some people like nice things but really don't want to work for them. I usually call this laziness and frustration.' With these thoughts, she entered the Lex building and got a fresh post. When Victoria opened her office, she saw a huge bucket of red roses on her table. She came to it closer and looked for a note, but there were nothing, just a pretty ribbon. Victoria put her coat on a couch and placed her bag on a table; she took the phone receiver and dialed Alice downstairs. A male's index finger pushed a button on it so she wouldn't make a call. Victoria got mad and frequently glanced at the man standing next to her.

"I don't think you have to bother Alice," He said this with a velvet voice on purpose so she would have goose-bumps.

"You!" Victoria widened her eyes when she saw her boyfriend in the office. It happened so unexpectedly that she couldn't talk. Her eyes were on him, and she didn't move.

"I know you don't wait for me. You think it's over between us, but it's just confusing." He came closer to her so she could see his eyes and feel his warmness. His hand lay on her hand and slowly went up to her shoulder. Victoria relaxed under his gentle touch, and her cheek touched his hand. She turned to him, and their lips merged into a single sweet kiss. It seemed that the whole world could wait while they enjoyed each other. He kissed her deep and slowly, squeezing in his arms. Victoria opened her eyes, and their gaze locked.

"So, did you discover your past?" She asked him with her facial features relaxed.

"I did," he nodded in response, "and my real name is Philippe."

"Philippe," she pronounced his name so that her heart started beating faster.

"Don't worry, I'm single." He sighed to her with an intrigue smile.

Victoria smiled back and hugged him around his neck. He responded to her kiss and, closing his eyes, enjoyed the taste of her lips with coffee sweetness. Victoria's hands went down, and she stepped a little bit back from Philippe.

"What's wrong?" He narrowed his eyes.

She shook her head and rubbed her hand with another:

"I gave our apartment away. I couldn't stay there anymore because everything reminded me of you: walls, furniture, and even glasses."

He slightly smiled at her back and softly said, "It doesn't matter. I'm not going to live with you until you ask me. I want to marry you."

Victoria quickly looked at him, and her eyes showed. She bit her lower lip and asked, "So?"

"So, I can't do that until I find my real father." Philippe lowered his head in embarrassment and pursed his lips.

"What?" She narrowed her eyes. "Father? But what did happen to your present father?"

Philippe took a seat on her armchair in the office while she was standing opposite him with her hands placed.

"My parents died last year, and when I talked to my grandfather, my memory started coming back to me, and I remembered mom telling me a secret of hers. She said that I don't look like Rafael just because I'm the product of her first love."

Victoria was staring at him with her mouth open, and eyebrows crossed on a bridge. She couldn't believe his words; it sounded so terrible to her imagination.

"No." She said. "You must be kidding me, Philippe! I'm so sorry for your parents, it's awful!!!"

"I know, but there's nothing I can do. She married my imaginary dad when she was already pregnant when I was born; he said that I'm too big and heavy for the premature child." Philippe closed his face with his arms to cover his weakness.

Victoria walked closer to him and rubbed his brown hair with her tiny fingers, trying to make him comfortable, "Oh dear," she said softly, "how sad is that. I can't even imagine her terrible act. How dare she was! What a lie!"

She stepped back to her working desk and smelled the roses that he brought for her. She looked at the wall picture that was hanging on the wall above her couch and let the air go with her breath, "So, what are you going to do now?"

He looked at her, but she was standing with her back to him, and he couldn't see her eyes. At this moment, Victoria was as tense as a violin string.

"All I know is it's my father's name. He's American, and I want you to help me to find him." Philippe made a fist and tapped it on his palm.

"Yea?" Victoria answered back. She turned around and her lips pursed, "I can do that. What is his name?"

Philippe glanced at her and, with his moody facial expression, said, "John Fury."

The words that he had just said were like hundreds of knives that cut Victoria's heart deep. That shock that hit her with an unexpected wave made her absolutely speechless. 'What's going on? Her dad is evil: he destroys someone's family, kills people, and now this bastard son! Moreover, he's my brother now! Oh my Gosh!!! What we had done?'

Deep pain and disgust distorted her face. Anger flashed with fury in her eyes. She hissed through clenched teeth, clenching her fists to keep from falling, "Your father, I know where your father is!"

Like an arrow from a bow, hard and sharp, she flew out of the room without knocking on the door to her father, Victoria burst into his office.

John stood up from her unceremonious unexpected behavior and strictly looked at his daughter, "What's the matter?"

Victoria was burning with anger, "What's the matter? You're asking me what the matter is. What have you done? You..." - Victoria lowered her head and closed her face with her hands.

John's hair perspired with excitement and he was trying to understand the cause of her frustration, "What? What do you mean?"

"How can you explain me this person? He says that you are his father."

Philippe accurately entered his office, trying to hug Victoria's shoulders, and met eyes to eyes with John Fury. Victoria stepped back closer to her dad and looked at him with her eyes red, begging for an answer.

John shifted his eyes from Philippe onto his daughter and then back at the young man in front of him. Philippe is standing speechless. He finally saw his biological father, and both of them had the same hair color and eyes, their lips outline, and even their nose. Philippe didn't expect Victoria to know John Fury that close. He pursed his lips and had no force to glance at his loving woman again.

"Dad," she said with tears in her eyes, "Please, tell me that this man is lying! Please say something!"

It was hard to tell to powerful John a lie when he had just seen the reality with his own eyes. Young fellow and John are look-alike as two drops of water. Despite, John knew his sin before he made Adeline marry him. He lowered his eyes, embarrassed, and without looking into her eyes, invited Philippe to take a seat, "What's your name, fellow?"

"Philippe, sir." He slowly occupied a place next to John's table and didn't even look at Victoria, who was trembling in terror.

She widened her eyes when John invited her ex-boyfriend to have a seat for a talk.

"Victoria," John looked at her and, with a cold face expression said to her, "Please, leave us!"

Philippe slowly closed his eyes; his cheekbones went pale when she was passing by him. That horrible sin that they did was disgusting to both of them. He feels her heavy look and can't even move. Philippe swallowed hard when she closed the door, and he left face to face with John Fury.

That one kept his eye on him and finely broke the heavy silence, "My son," - said John with extreme caution. "What's your mother's name?"

Philippe proudly raised his head and looked into John's eyes as if somebody had hit him:

"Francine, sir."

John grinned. He moved his one leg to another, and his chair rolled closer to the table between them, "I know her pretty well. She was twenty-one when I met your mother. Pretty, white skin French lady with high manners, no doubt she was sweet…"

"Sir," Philippe tried to interrupt him, but John didn't let him.

"As the result of all of this mess, we have you!" John's eyes showed with marvel, and he grinned wide in nervousness or something. He scrutinized Philippe up and down and noticed so many features of his when he was young. John nodded positively to him as if he couldn't resist some of his statement, "Why are you looking for me, Philippe?"

"I want to know you and tell you that Mom has passed away." Philippe sniffed with his nose, and his voice trembled with sadness.

"Really?" John's eyebrows went up to his forehead, and his face changed into surprise. He lowered his eyes, rolling a pen in his hands. "I'm so sorry, she was an amazing woman!"

Philippe didn't say anything to this. He looked up at his biological father, and his chin trembled.

"How did it happen?" John's eyebrows went on a bridge, and he glanced at Philippe, trying to remember if he had seen him that night when he killed all the members of the Sauvage Roux family.

"Well, I lost my memory from the car accident and wasn't at home for almost a year, but then started remembering my life step by step, and when I came back home, my grandfather told me that all of them died from the explosion in the house. Like gas leaking something like that." Philippe glanced at John, whose face expressed sorrow and understanding.

"That's so sad," shook his head, John, 'Car accident, Philippe said,' – thought John, nodding his head, 'So, this is my son, and I tried to kill him with my assassins, thinking that this fellow is Raphael's offspring.' John rose from his chair and came closer to Philippe, "What do you want? How can I help you?"

Philippe rose from the chair too and noticed that he was as tall as John; he looked into his face and said:

"I want you to recognize me as your son in front of everyone. You must put an end to this long separation between us. Face the truth and introduce me to my brothers and sisters, if any." Coolness and determination took over Philip. For the first time in his life, he spoke like a real Fury, feeling no fear. John listened to him attentively and nodded in reply to his son's statement.

## An Open Letter to Dear People and to My Readers, Who Guided Me to Where I Am Today

**JAN. 19, 2014**
By <u>**DIANA ROJAS**</u>

At this point in my life, I'm considered an adult. Yes, maybe sometimes I don't completely act like it, but that's part of life, right? As I was growing up, I realized just how much my parents did for me. And, for that, I need to truly thank you – something I don't think I've appropriately done today.

Dad, thank you for telling me what I'm capable of. Thank you for spending countless hours after you got home from work each night to teach me math that I wasn't going to learn in school for a few years later. It kept me challenged and ahead of the class and gave me the support that I needed to build a dream to chase after and, especially for believing that I have the talent to reach my goals.

Mom, thank you for making me realize that I'm worth everything in this world. That I must be treated like a queen, and that I should never settle for less than what I deserve. Thank you for getting to know my friends – all of them – to make sure that I was choosing them wisely, that I was continually surrounding myself with respectable and responsible people through each and every phase of my life.

My special regards to my husband. You are my supporter and a strong shoulder to lean on. You made my life richer, fuller, more interesting, and so full of compassion. When we decided to join our lives together I had dreams of flowers and romance and making each other happy. And there have been days like that. Thank you for your support and true belief in me, and thank you for joying me in this great adventure – Marriage!

I am so grateful to all of you who make up the loyal community of readers to whom I am connected.

To the ones who write encouraging emails or speak to me in person on the road ... your feedback means the world to me. I am so grateful for the writers whose works have helped me, and to think I've been of some help to others is humbling and deeply gratifying. Thank you!

To the ones who pass on books they have enjoyed to friends, relatives, and neighbors, you are multiplying the impact of each book. Thank you!

# DEDICATION

*"Family Secrets" is dedicated to my muse and morning star: without you, this book wouldn't come to life. You are the reason behind my pen, the brushstroke on my canvas. When I write, I imagine your eyes scanning each syllable, a celestial connection. Your spirit is the North Star that guides me through creative storms. In this pixelated universe, we share secrets. You – the silent reader; I – the cosmic storyteller. Together, we unravel mysteries, paint sunsets, and chase moonbeams. When inspiration wanes, your messages arrive as a meteor shower of encouragement. "Write on," you whisper, and so I do, fueled by your cosmic cheer. For you are not just my muse; you are a celestial companion. May our orbits intersect our pixels entwine. Let us continue this cosmic dance a waltz of words, a tango of tales. For in this vast expanse, you are my favorite constellation. Love you to the Moon and back.*

*"Family Secrets" holds strong belief for a better future yet to come. Dedicated to the young travelers and ambassadors holding*

*their wild secrets at heart. To those who have courage and are thoughtful, to those who can forgive and plant love instead of hate. To those who seek truth within a lie and to family-oriented minds.*

### *"Let love lead in whatever you do."*

*~ Diana Rojas*

# PERSONAL OPINION ABOUT NOVEL

### *By DIANA ROJAS*

"Family Secrets" is a romance novel that was created ten years ago. The characters are all fictional and events have no relation to the present and the past. The novel developed during the last college life and continued to develop in 2005. After severe working years the narration was slowly growing with its hard inspiration. Hollywood celebrities have been my inspirations all these years (Margot Robbie, Chris Evans, Jessica Alba, Tom Cruise, Giovanna Antonelli, Paul Walker, and Puerto Rican singer Ricky Martin). Characters were developing and growing by themselves in my imagination; all of a sudden, I decided to make them alive and finally made myself take a pen and finish the unfinished. My friends and relatives kept asking me about my book all the time, and then I said to myself: 'Diana, wait, you can do this! Let everyone see your creation and enjoy their comments and feedback. Make your close ones proud of you. The whole year 2012, I spent in translating my novel from my native language into my second speaking language, English. It was incredibly hard because Russian is quite more descriptive than English. Some words I couldn't convert because of the meaning, and finally, when it was done, it sounded to me different. I'm a linguist by degree and have to master the word. In 2013, I spent my days finishing the story, and luckily, after New Year's Eve my story of the first book came to an end. So, I think I did a great job!

In "Family Secrets," which is the first part called 'Love and Hate.' I made in the beginning Caroline Sauvage Roux like a main character. Through her eyes, I described the action of her life in the story. I think that she is a complicated character in the whole narration. Caroline, despite her beauty is very fragile outside but pretty strong inside. She has to fight with herself all the time. On one hand, she decides to take revenge for her family, and then she slowly steps back. Like a nineteen-year-old girl, she makes the right decisions and uses opportunities. Well, I personally enjoyed her throughout the whole story.

There are a lot of guys who adore her and admire her, so Caroline has a great choice to connect her love story. I'm pretty positive that readers adore Martin Fury as well as Jason Parker; both are funny and great in their lives. They are different and yet they have something in common.

I think it is their charm and jokes, those two things that women can't resist, and it makes them hear catchers. According to Victoria, I may say that she's a rich, spoiled American daughter by her father. She has been treated like everything in this life. Thus, John Fury regrets later because what he has done can't be undone. This is like an appeal to society not to pamper their children because they can ruin their lives. I have never been to Morocco and in my story, I wrote it like I visualize it after movies and literature that I've read and went through. My special appreciation to O Clone/El Clon songs (Mactub III, Kheops, Alto la, Mirage II ) and to my favorite pop group Roxette. So, the Morocco episode and its food are taken from the college books during my philosophy classes. Back then, I was fascinated and admired by the ancient culture that this country offers. Since teenhood, my dream has always been to visit Chicago, IL, and I have studied lots of books and maps and watched documentaries about it. My dream came true, and I finally visited all those places described in my book through the chapters.

I had never owned horses till 2014 when my first Arabian horse was presented to me by my husband on my birthday in July. He was a 4-year-old stallion, bay and untamed, just like Flash Magnifico, though my horse was named Krusader I. We had ranch and stables and did breedings, shows, and training. That was another dream come true.

The end of the story that finishes with the conversation between Philipp and John Fury has its own magnetism because after we are left confused and start questioning ourselves like, 'Is that the end?

Why?' Well, this first part has ended like that, so readers will look forward to the second part of the story, which is going to be named "Family Secrets. The Way to Peace" We're going to enjoy Caroline's adventures and her new way of life. New characters will appear with their own grace and glory. Finally, Caroline will make her last only choice and the war between families will come to an end.

# ABOUT THE AUTHOR

### *DIANA ROJAS*

DIANA ROJAS is the author of the #1 book Family Secrets: Love and Hate

She graduated from Cherkasy National University in Ukraine with a degree in English literature and English as a second language, and she currently lives with her family in the United States in the Lone Star State

You can follow her on her personal social platform or write her a letter with feedback

www.facebook.com/Diana.S.Khomenko

dianadiva2012@mail.com